Introduction

Cables are classic elements found in many knitwear designs. They add beauty, fluidity and a touch of class to a simple design. Knitting cables on a knitting loom requires the manipulation of stitches, which is easily done by using a cable needle. Work the cables on a background of reverse stockinette stitches to make your cables pop even more!

The designs included in this booklet will introduce you to a few cabling techniques. Master the cabling techniques at the front of the book, and you can design your own projects too!

Cables work best when worked with yarns that have some inherent elasticity; for this reason, yarns with wool content are a good choice. The yarns used in this booklet were selected because of their elasticity/bounce. When selecting your yarns, stretch them out and test their bounce.

Have fun knitting these classic designs!

Design Directory

General Directions
Page 2

General Directions

Begin with the following materials to get started knitting cables on circle looms.

Materials
- Knifty Knitter™ circle- and long-loom series from Provo Craft*
- Knitting tool included with loom
- Cable needle
- Crochet hook (for casting on)
- 2 size 5 (3.75mm) double-pointed knitting needles (for holding stitches)
- Yarn needle
- Split-ring stitch markers
- Scissors
- Measuring tape/gauge checker
- Blocking wires (optional)

Samples were knit on Provo Craft Knifty Knitter series looms; however, patterns can be knit on other knitting looms. Be sure to check for gauge and peg count when substituting knitting looms.

Pattern Note
All of the patterns are worked in a clockwise direction around the knitting loom (where the first row starts from right to left).

Basic Techniques
Chain Cast On
To cast on, move your loom from left to right. Working yarn should end up on the right side to begin the first row (in order to have the first row start from right to left).
Make a slip knot and place it on the peg. Take the working yarn towards the inside of the loom.

Photo A: Cast-on chain placed on next empty peg to right

Step 1: Insert crochet hook through the slip knot. Hook working yarn, forming a chain.
Step 2: Place chain on next empty peg to the right.
Step 3: Insert crochet hook through chain just made. Hook working yarn forming a chain.
Step 4: Place chain on next empty peg to the right (Photo A).
Step 5: Repeat Steps 3 and 4 until desired number of stitches have been cast on. Each peg will have 1 loop.

Knit Stitch (k)
The knit stitch is a smooth V-shaped stitch; it is identical to the knit stitch created with knitting needles.

Step 1: Place working yarn in front of the peg and above the loop on the peg.
Step 2: Insert knitting tool from bottom up and catch the working yarn with the tool, thus forming a loop.
Step 3: Hold the newly formed loop (from Step 2) with the knitting tool (Photo B).
Step 4: Pull up on the loop on the tool to take the loop that was originally on the peg, off the peg.
Step 5: Place the loop you are holding (from Step 3) on the peg. Pull on the working yarn to tighten the stitch.

 American School of Needlework • Berne, Indiana 46711 • DRGnetwork.com

Photo B: Knitting tool holding loop made by working yarn

Step 2: Insert knitting tool from the top down and hook the working yarn with the tool (Photo D).

Step 3: Pull the loop caught with the tool, up through the stitch.

Step 4: Continue to pull up on loop to remove the original loop from the peg.

Step 5: Place the loop you are holding (from Step 3) on the peg. Gently tug on the working yarn to tighten the stitch.

Stockinette Stitch

The stockinette stitch is created by knitting every row.

Garter Stitch

The garter stitch is formed by 2 rows.

Row 1: Knit.

Row 2: Purl.

The combination of these 2 rows creates 1 garter-stitch row and 1 garter-stitch ridge.

Twisted Knit Stitch (also known as single stitch)

In needle knitting, this stitch is known as the twisted knit stitch or a stitch knit through the back loop.

Step 1: Take the working yarn (yarn coming from the ball of yarn) to the inside of the knitting loom.

Step 2: Moving in a clockwise direction around the knitting loom, encircle the peg counter clockwise with the yarn to form e-wrap (Photo C).

Step 3: Continue to e-wrap all the pegs. Each peg should have 2 loops on it.

Step 4: Using your knitting tool, lift the bottommost loop off the peg, let it fall towards the inside of the knitting loom.

Purl Stitch (p)

The purl stitch is the opposite of the knit stitch. Instead of a smooth V, you will see bumpy fabric.

Step 1: Place working yarn in front of peg and below the loop on the peg.

Photo C: Encircle peg with yarn to make e-wrap

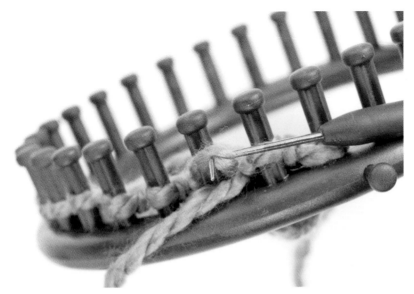

Photo D: Knitting tool ready to pick up working yarn for purl stitch

Adding Another Skein

To attach a new skein of yarn at beginning of the next row, join the 2 ends of yarn with a slip knot. Knit the first 3 stitches of the row with both yarns together. Drop the old strand and continue knitting with the new strand.

Basic Bind Off (also called flat removal method)

Step 1: Knit the item until you have only 1 loop on each peg. The working yarn is coming from the last peg. Knit the first 2 loops. Move the loop from the 2nd peg over to the first peg. Lift the bottom loop over the top loop and off the peg to bind off first stitch (Photo E). Move the loop from the first peg over to the vacated 2nd peg.

Step 2: Knit the next loop. Move this loop over to the previous peg. Lift bottom loop over and off the peg (2nd stitch bound off).

Step 3: Repeat Step 2 until all stitches have been bound off.

Step 4: When you reach the last peg, cut the working yarn leaving a 5-inch tail. Knit the loop. Remove the stitch from the peg. Pull the yarn tail end through the loop.

Shaping Techniques
Decreases

There are 2 decrease techniques used in this book, the terms used are the same as used in needle knitting.

These decreases take place on 2 pegs. Peg 1 is on the right and Peg 2 is on the left.

K2tog (knit 2 together—slants to the right)

Step 1: Take the loop from Peg 1 and place it on Peg 2.

Step 2: Knit all the pegs as you normally would. When you reach the peg with 2 loops, treat the 2 loops as 1 and knit them together.

Ssk (slip, slip, knit—slants to the left)

Step 1: Take the loop off Peg 1 and hold it. Take loop off Peg 2 and hold it. Place the loop from Peg 1 on Peg 2. Place the loop that was on Peg 2 back on Peg 2. Peg 1 is empty, Peg 2 has 2 loops.

Step 2: Knit all the pegs as you normally would. When you reach the peg with 2 loops, treat the 2 loops as 1 and knit them together.

Increases
M1 (Make 1)

Step 1: Create an empty peg where you need to increase a stitch by moving the loops to the outer pegs.

Step 2: With knitting tool, reach for the ladder that runs from 1 peg to the next, pick it up, twist it and place it on the empty peg.

Step 3: Knit on the knitting loom as usual, when you reach this peg, treat it just as any other peg and work it as per directions in pattern.

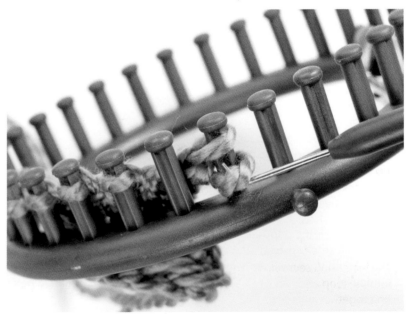

Photo E: Knitting tool lifting bottom loop over and off peg

American School of Needlework • Berne, Indiana 46711 • DRGnetwork.com

Yo (yarn over)

The yo increase is used in conjunction with the k2tog and the ssk decrease techniques.

Step 1: To create a yo, take the yarn towards the inside of the knitting loom.

Step 2: Go around the peg in a counterclockwise direction (e-wrap the peg).

Wrap & Turn Short Rows

When working a sock, the heel is created in 2 parts—a decreasing part and an increasing part.

The decreasing section requires the knowledge of a technique known as **Wrap and Turn (W&T)**. The increasing section requires the knitter to knit over the wrap and the loop together.

Decreasing section

Short row: The term "short row" means that a row is not knit to the end; instead, knit to a certain point and stop. Then turn and knit back in the opposite direction. To avoid creating a hole, use W&T.

To work W&T short row

Step 1: Knit to the designated turning point. Take the next loop off the peg.

Step 2: Take the working yarn towards the inside of the knitting loom and wrap around the peg, bring the yarn towards the front of the loom.

Step 3: Place loop back on the peg. The peg now has 1 wrap and the knit stitch.

Step 4: Pick up working yarn and knit back in the other direction.

Be sure to leave the peg with the wrap untouched.

Increasing section

In the increasing section, the wrap and the loop are treated as 1 and knit together.

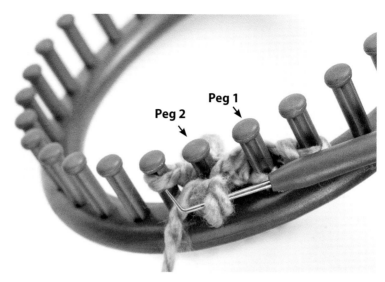

Photo F: For Left Twist, skip Peg 1 and knit Peg 2

Cable Techniques
Cables over 2 stitches

LT (Left Twist)

Step 1: Skip Peg 1, knit Peg 2 (Photo F).

Step 2: Place loop from Peg 2 on cable needle.

Step 3: Move loop from Peg 1 to Peg 2.

Step 4: Place loop from cable needle on Peg 1.

Step 5: Knit loop on Peg 2.

RT (Right Twist)

Step 1: Place loop from Peg 1 on cable needle and hold to the center of the knitting loom (Photo G).

Step 2: Knit loop on Peg 2 and move to Peg 1.

Step 3: Place loop from cable needle on Peg 2.

Step 4: Knit loop on Peg 2.

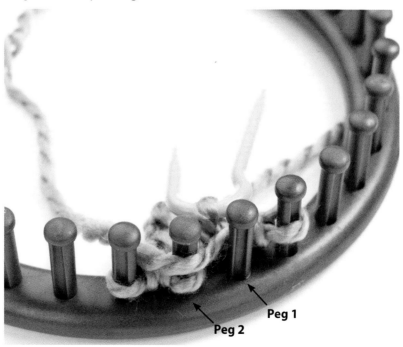

Photo G: Loop from Peg 1 on cable needle ready to knit loop on Peg 2

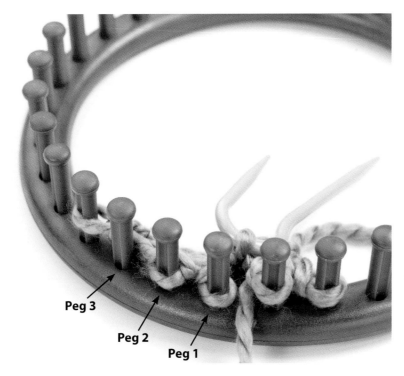

Photo H: Loops moved to Peg 1 and Peg 2

Step 4: Knit loop on Peg 1 and Peg 2. Purl loop on Peg 3.

LPC (Left Purl Cross)
Step 1: Skip Peg 1 and Peg 2. Purl Peg 3.
Step 2: Place loop from Peg 3 on cable needle.
Step 3: Knit skipped pegs. Move loop from Peg 2 to Peg 3 and loop from Peg 1 to Peg 2.
Step 4: Place loop from cable needle on Peg 1.

Cables over 4 stitches
4-st LC (4-stitch Left Cross— work over 4 stitches, on Pegs 1–4)
Step 1: Skip Peg 1 and Peg 2 (Photo J).
Step 2: Knit stitches on Peg 3 and Peg 4, place these loops on cable needle and hold to the center of knitting loom.
Step 3: Knit skipped loops on Peg 1 and Peg 2. Place loop from Peg 1 on Peg 3 and loop from Peg 2 on Peg 4.
Step 4: Place loops from the cable needle and on Peg 1 and Peg 2.
Step 5: Gently pull loop on Peg 3 and then the loop on Peg 4 to tighten the stitches.

Cables over 3 stitches
RC (Right Cross)
Step 1: Place loop from Peg 1 on cable needle and hold to center of knitting loom.
Step 2: Move loops from Peg 2 and Peg 3 to Peg 1 and Peg 2 (Photo H).
Step 3: Place loop from cable needle on Peg 3.
Step 4: Knit loop on Peg 3.

LC (Left Cross)
Step 1: Skip Peg 1 and Peg 2. Knit Peg 3 (Photo I).
Step 2: Place loop from Peg 3 on cable needle.
Step 3: Knit Peg 1 and Peg 2. Move loop from Peg 2 to Peg 3 and loop from Peg 1 to Peg 2.
Step 4: Place loop from cable needle on Peg 1.

Note: The following 3-stitch cables are worked in the same manner as the Right Cross and Left Cross except the crossing stitch is purled rather than knitted.

RPC (Right Purl Cross)
Step 1: Place loop from Peg 1 on cable needle and hold to center of the knitting loom.
Step 2: Knit Peg 2 and Peg 3. Move loop from Peg 2 to Peg 1 and loop from Peg 3 to Peg 2.
Step 3: Take loop from cable needle and place it on Peg 3.

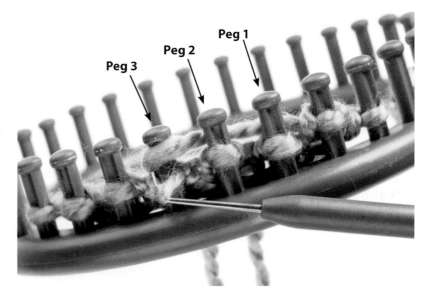

Photo I: Skip Peg 1 and Peg 2, knit Peg 3

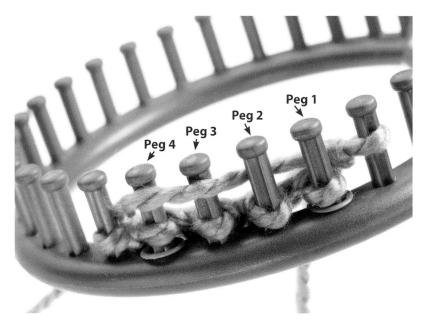

Photo J: Skip Peg 1 and Peg 2, ready to knit Peg 3 and Peg 4

Step 4: Place loops from the cable needle on Peg 1, Peg 2 and Peg 3.

Step 5: Gently pull loop on Peg 4, loop on Peg 5, then Peg 6 to tighten the stitches.

6-st RC (6-stitch Right Cross—work over 6 stitches, on Pegs 1–6)

Step 1: Place loops from Peg 1, Peg 2 and Peg 3 on cable needle.

Step 2: Knit Peg 4 and place it on Peg 1.

Step 3: Knit Peg 5 and place it on Peg 2.

Step 4: Knit Peg 6 and place it on Peg 3.

Step 5: Take Loop 1 from cable needle and place it on Peg 4. Knit it.

Step 6: Take Loop 2 from cable needle and place it on Peg 5. Knit it.

Step 7: Take Loop 3 from cable needle and place it on Peg 6. Knit it.

4-st RC (4-stitch Right Cross—work over 4 stitches, on Pegs 1–4)

Step 1: Place loops from Peg 1 and Peg 2 on cable needle (Photo K).

Step 2: Knit Peg 3. Place it on Peg 1.

Step 3: Knit Peg 4. Place it on Peg 2.

Step 4: Take Loop 1 from cable needle and place it on Peg 3. Knit it.

Step 5: Take Loop 2 from cable needle and place it on Peg 4. Knit it.

Step 3: Knit skipped loops. Place loop from Peg 1 on Peg 4, loop from Peg 2 on Peg 5 and loop from Peg 3 on Peg 6.

Cables over 6 stitches

Note: Work in same manner as 4-stitch cables, except cross 3 stitches instead of 2.

6-st LC (6-stitch Left Cross—work over 6 stitches, on Pegs 1–6)

Step 1: Skip Peg 1, Peg 2 and Peg 3.

Step 2: Knit loops on Peg 4, Peg 5 and Peg 6, place these 3 stitches on cable needle and hold to center of knitting loom.

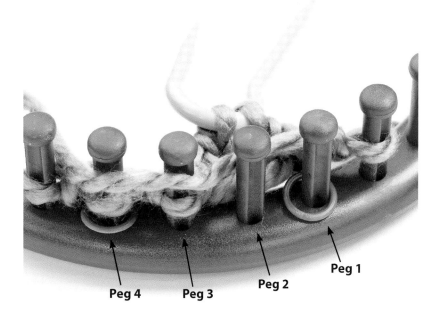

Photo K: Loops from Peg 1 and Peg 2 on cable needle ready to knit loops on Peg 3 and Peg 4

Finishing Techniques
Mattress Stitch
Lay the pieces side by side, with right sides facing up.

Start the seam at the bottom edge. First join the cast-on rows, inserting the yarn needle between the first and 2nd stitch in from the edge, underneath 1 of the "bars" of yarn that run between the stitches. Then, working with the other piece, do the same.

Pull gently on the yarn to close the stitches.

Grafting/Kitchener Stitch
Place stitches onto knitting needles as indicated in pattern, making sure that the stitches are set up on the needles correctly.

Insert the yarn needle into the first stitch on the needle closest from right to left, pull needle through, leaving stitch on the needle. Insert the needle into the first stitch on the back needle from the left, leave the stitch on the needle. Pull the yarn through.

Needles are set for grafting, following the next 4 steps:

Step 1: Insert the tapestry needle into the first stitch on the front needle from the left. Slip stitch off the needle.

Step 2: Insert the needle into the next stitch on the front needle from the right. Leave stitch on the needle. Gently pull on the working yarn to tighten stitch. Do not pull too much.

Step 3: Insert the needle into the first stitch on the back needle as if to right, and slip it off the needle.

Step 4: Insert the needle into the next stitch on the back needle as if to left. Leave this stitch on the needle. Snug up the yarn by pulling gently on the working yarn.

Repeat Steps 1–4. At the end, the needles will have 2 stitches remaining. Repeat Step 1 and then repeat Step 3.

Photo L: Carrying yarn behind pegs

Weave in the ends to the wrong side of piece.

I-cord
I-cords are used in this book as drawstrings.

3-stitch I-cord
Step 1: Cast on 3 stitches.

Step 2: Knit to end of row.

Step 3: Take working yarn to the back of the pegs and run the yarn behind the pegs to the front of Peg 1 (Photo L).

Step 4: Knit to the end of row.

Repeat Steps 3 and 4 until I-cord reaches desired length.

Bind off.

Pull on the I-cord to set the stitches.

2-stitch I-cord
Step 1: Cast on 2 stitches.

Step 2: Form a figure 8 with yarn on both pegs (Photo M).

Step 3: Lift the bottommost loop off the peg.

Photo M: Form figure-8 with yarn on pegs

Repeat Steps 2 and 3 until I-cord reaches desired length.

Bind off.

Pompom
Cut 2 doughnut-shape pieces out of cardboard, about 1 inch bigger than the desired size of pompom.

Cut a small square out 1 of the sides to create a small opening.

Sandwich a piece of yarn in between the 2 cardboards, tie a temporary knot.

Grab working yarn and wrap it around the 2 pieces of cardboard. Start at the left and move towards the right.

When the cardboard is completely full, find the temporary knot and hold on to it. With scissors slip in between the 2 pieces of cardboards and begin cutting around the circle. When you are finished cutting, tighten the knot securely.

Trim pompom to desired size.

American School of Needlework • Berne, Indiana 46711 • DRGnetwork.com

Felting Instructions

Set the washer to the smallest setting, regular cycle and hot water. Add 1 tablespoon of Eucalan Woolwash or shampoo.

Designer Note: Eucalan Woolwash saves rinsing the item by hand and makes the wet wool smell better.

Place the item to be felted in a zippered pillowcase; put it in the washer. Add 2 pairs of jeans to aid in agitation. It is not recommended to use towels, as these may leave fuzz in felted items. Start the washer.

Check the felted items frequently. Stop the machine completely before placing your hand inside. If additional felting is required, reset the washer and continue the felting process. Check the progress closely and shape item as the felting process continues by pulling at the corners. Item is felted when it feels firm, and the stitches are indistinguishable. Keep felting the bag until you are completely satisfied. It may take a few cycles. Do not let the machine go into the rinse-and-spin cycle, as this will create creases that are very difficult to remove.

When the item reaches the desired look, remove it from the zippered pillowcase, place it between towels and squeeze out as much water as possible. Shape again by stretching damp item over a suitable-sized form. If nothing that resembles the shape is available, use plastic bags inside to give it its form. The felted item should fit over the fitted form snuggly. Shape all the corners. Make sure that everything looks the way you want it to look. Feel free to pull at it. Do not let it dry until you are completely satisfied with the way it looks. Once it looks the way you desire, let it dry completely, away from sunlight and from any heating vents. It may take up to 2 full days to dry completely. Keep shaping it during the drying process, if you so desire. ●

Classic Cables Scarf

Skill Level

 INTERMEDIATE

Finished Size

4½ x 70 inches

Note: Instructions are given for an adult-length scarf. A shorter scarf can be made by working fewer cable repeats.

Materials

- Lion Brand Jiffy bulky weight yarn (3 oz/135 yds/85g per skein): 2 skeins camel #124
- Blue Knifty Knitter round loom (24 pegs)
- Knitting tool
- Tapestry needle
- Cable needle

5 BULKY

Gauge

16 stitches and 14 rows = 4 inches/10cm

Special Abbreviations

4-st RC (4-stitch Right Cross): Place loops from Peg 1 and Peg 2 on cable needle. Knit Peg 3 and place loop on Peg 1. Knit Peg 4 and place loop on Peg 2. Place Loop 1 from cable needle on Peg 3 and knit it. Place Loop 2 from cable needle on Peg 4 and knit it.

4-st LC (4-stitch Left Cross): Skip Peg 1 and Peg 2. Knit loops on Peg 3 and Peg 4, place these stitches on cable needle and hold to center of knitting loom. Knit skipped loops on Peg 1 and Peg 2. Place loop from Peg 1 on Peg 3 and loop from Peg 2 on Peg 4. Place stitches from cable needle on Peg 1 and Peg 2. Gently pull on the loop on Peg 3 and then on the loop on Peg 4 to tighten the stitches.

Pattern Note

Wrap the row before cable crossing loosely.

Instructions

Cast on 18 stitches.

Border

Rows 1, 3 and 5: K2, p2, k4, p2, k4, p2, k2.
Rows 2, 4 and 6: P2, p2, k4, p2, k4, p2, p2.

Body

Row 1: K2, p2, 4-st RC, p2, 4-st LC, p2, k2.
Row 2: P2, p2, k4, p2, k4, p2, p2.
Row 3: K2, p2, k4, p2, k4, p2, k2.
Row 4: P2, p2, k4, p2, k4, p2, p2.
Repeat Rows 1–4 until piece measures about 2 inches less than desired length.

Border

Rows 1, 3 and 5: K2, p2, k4, p2, k4, p2, k2.
Rows 2, 4 and 6: P2, p2, k4, p2, k4, p2, p2.
Bind off and weave in ends.
Block to measurements. ●

Fairamay Shawl

Skill Level

 INTERMEDIATE

Finished Size

18 x 65 inches

Materials

- Lion Brand Lion Cashmere Blend medium weight yarn (1.5 oz/84 yds/40g per skein): 8 skeins silver #150
- Long Blue Knifty Knitter Long loom series (62 pegs)
- Knitting tool
- Cable needle
- Tapestry needle

Gauge

13 stitches and 18 rows = 4 inches/10cm

Special Abbreviations

Yo, sl 1, k1, psso (yarn over, slip 1, knit 1, pass slipped stitch over): Take loop off Peg 1 and place on cable needle. E-wrap Peg 1. Knit Peg 2. Take loop off Peg 2 and hold it with knitting tool or fingers. Place loop from cable needle on Peg 2. Replace loop from Peg 2 on top of loop. Lift over the bottommost loop, leaving only 1 loop on the peg.

K2tog, yo (knit 2 together, yarn over): Move loop from Peg 1 to Peg 2. Knit both loops together. Move remaining loop from Peg 2 to Peg 1 to leave Peg 2 empty for the yo. E-wrap (see page 3) Peg 2 to create a yo.

4-st LC (4-stitch Left Cross): Skip Peg 1 and Peg 2. Knit loops on Peg 3 and Peg 4, place these stitches on cable needle and hold to center of knitting loom. Knit skipped loops on Peg 1 and Peg 2. Place loop from Peg 1 on Peg 3 and loop from Peg 2 on Peg 4. Place stitches from cable needle on Peg 1 and Peg 2. Gently pull on the loop on Peg 3 and then on the loop on Peg 4 to tighten the stitches.

Pattern Note

Work your stitches with a loose tension making it easier to move the stitches.

Instructions

Cast on 62 stitches.
Row 1: Knit.
Row 2: Purl.
Row 3: Knit.
Row 4: Purl.
Row 5: *P2, k2tog, yo, p2, k4; repeat from * to last 2 stitches, p2.
Row 6: P2, *k4, p2, k2, p2; repeat from * to end of row.
Row 7: *P2, yo, sl 1, k1, psso, p2, 4-st LC; repeat from * to last 2 stitches, p2.
Row 8: P2, *k4, p2, k2, p2; repeat from * to end of row.
Row 9: *P2, k2tog, yo, p2, k4; repeat from * to last 2 stitches, p2.
Row 10: P2, *k4, p2, k2, p2; repeat from * to end of row.
Row 11: *P2, yo, sl 1, k1, psso, p2, k4; repeat from * to last 2 stitches, p2.
Row 12: P2, *k4, p2, k2, p2; repeat from * to end of row.
Repeat Rows 5–12 until piece measures 64 inches.
Repeat Rows 5–9.
Next row: Purl.
Next row: Knit.
Next row: Purl.
Bind off.

Finishing

Wet block as follows by immersing shawl in warm, soapy water for about 20 minutes. Squeeze out as much water by using a towel, do not wring. Block to dimensions given. Designer recommends blocking wires to block shawl. ●

Jamie's Mitts

Skill Level
◼◼◼◻ INTERMEDIATE

Size
Adult

Materials
- Lion Brand Wool-Ease Thick & Quick super bulky weight yarn (6 oz/106 yds/170g per skein): 1 skein grass #131
- Blue Knifty Knitter round loom (24 pegs)
- Knitting tool
- Cable needle
- Stitch marker
- Tapestry needle

Gauge
11 stitches and 19 rows = 4 inches/10cm

Special Abbreviations
4-st LC (4-stitch Left Cross):
Skip Peg 1 and Peg 2. Knit loops on Peg 3 and Peg 4, place these stitches on cable needle and hold to center of knitting loom. Knit skipped loops on Peg 1 and Peg 2. Place loop from Peg 1 on Peg 3 and loop from Peg 2 on Peg 4. Place stitches from cable needle on Peg 1 and Peg 2. Gently pull loop on Peg 3 and then on loop on Peg 4 to tighten the stitches.

4-st RC (4-stitch Right Cross):
Place loops from Peg 1 and Peg 2 on cable needle. Knit Peg 3 and place loop on Peg 1. Knit Peg 4 and place loop on Peg 2. Place Loop 1 from cable needle on Peg 3 and knit it. Place Loop 2 from cable needle on Peg 4 and knit it.

Pattern Stitch
Rib Stitch
Round 1: *K2, p2; repeat from * to the end of round.
Repeat Round 1 for pattern.

Instructions

Left Hand
Cuff
Cast on 21 stitches.
Rows 1, 3 and 5: *K2, p2; repeat from * to last stitch, k1.
Rows 2, 4 and 6: K1, *p2, k2; repeat from * to end of row.

Body
Row 1: K3, p2, k4, p2, k10.
Row 2: K10, p2, k4, p2, k3.
Row 3: K3, p2, 4-st LC, p2, k10.
Row 4: K10, p2, k4, p2, k3.
[Repeat Rows 1–4] 5 times.

Shape thumb
Place stitch marker on Peg 14.
Move stitches outwards to leave an empty peg at Peg 14.
Note: See page 4 for instructions on M1 increase.

Next row: K3, p2, k4, p2, k to marker, m1, k to end.
Next row: K11, p2, k4, p2, k3.
Move stitches outwards to leave an empty peg at Peg 14.
Next row: K3, p2, 4-st LC, p2, k to marker, m1, k to end.
Next row: K12, p2, k4, p2, k3.
Move stitches outwards to leave an empty peg at Peg 14.
Next row: K3, p2, k4, p2, k to marker, m1, k to end.
Join to work in the round.
Work 3 rounds in Rib Stitch pattern.

Bind off and weave in ends.
Block lightly.
Seam below thumb opening.

Right Hand
Cuff
Cast on 21 stitches.
Rows 1, 3 and 5: K1, *p2, k2; repeat from * to end of row.
Rows 2, 4 and 6: *K2, p2; repeat from * to the last stitch, k1.

Body
Row 1: K10, p2, k4, p2, k3.
Row 2: K3, p2, k4, p2, k10.
Row 3: K10, p2, 4-st RC, p2, k3.
Row 4: K3, p2, k4, p2, k10.
[Repeat Rows 1–4] 5 times.

Shape thumb
Place stitch marker on Peg 8.
Move stitches outwards to leave an empty peg at Peg 8.
Note: See page 4 for instructions on M1 increase.

Next row: K8, M1, k2, p2, k4, p2, k3.
Next row: K3, p2, k4, p2, k11.
Move stitches outwards to leave an empty peg at Peg 8.
Next row: K9, M1, k2, p2, 4-st RC, p2, k3.
Next row: K3, p2, k4, p2, k12.
Move stitches outwards to leave an empty peg at Peg 8.
Next row: K10, M1, k2, p2, k4, p2, k3.
Join to work in the round.
Work 3 rounds in Rib Stitch pattern.
Bind off and weave in ends.
Block lightly.
Seam below thumb opening. ●

Adestan Slipper Socks

Skill Level
■■■□ INTERMEDIATE

Size
Adult

Materials
- Patons Shetland Chunky Tweeds bulky weight yarn (3 oz/123 yds/85g per skein): 4 skeins biscuit tweeds #67024
- Blue Knifty Knitter round loom (24 pegs)
- Knitting tool
- Cable needle
- Stitch markers
- Tapestry needle
- 2 size 8 double-pointed needles (for holding stitches to graft the toe area)

Gauge
13 sts and 18 rows = 4 inches/10cm

Special Abbreviations
LT (Left Twist): Skip Peg 1, knit Peg 2. Place loop from Peg 2 on cable needle. Move loop from Peg 1 to Peg 2. Place loop from cable needle on Peg 1. Knit loop on Peg 2.

W&T (Wrap and Turn): Knit to turning point. Take next loop off peg. Take working yarn to the inside of loom and wrap the peg, bringing yarn toward front of loom. Place loop back on peg. Pick up working yarn and knit back in other direction. Leave peg with wrap untouched.

Pattern Stitch
Rib Stitch
Round 1: *K2, p2; repeat from * to the end of round.
Repeat Round 1 for pattern.

Pattern Note
For more information on creating a heel and toe using short-row shaping see page 5.

Instructions

Leg
Cast on all pegs in the round.
Work 4 rounds of Rib Stitch pattern.
Round 5: P1, k8, p1, k2, p1, k8, p1, k2.
Round 6: P1, k8, p1, k2, p1, k8, p1, k2.
Round 7: P1, k8, p1, LT, p1, k8, LT.
Repeat Rounds 5–7 until leg measures 7½ inches or desired length.

Heel
Place stitch marker at Peg 24; from this point on, this peg will be Peg 1. Count 11 pegs to the left, place a stitch marker on the 11th peg; there should be a stitch marker on Peg 1 and Peg 12. The heel is worked as a flat panel on these 12 pegs. The cup for the heel is formed by knitting short rows. Remember to wrap each of the turning pegs.

Row 1: K11 (from Pegs 1–11), W&T Peg 12.
Row 2: K10 (from Pegs 11–2), W&T Peg 1.
Row 3: K9 (from Pegs 2–10), W&T Peg 11.
Row 4: K8 (from Pegs 10–3), W&T Peg 2.
Row 5: K7 (from Pegs 3–9), W&T Peg 10.
Row 6: K6 (from Pegs 9–4), W&T Peg 3.
Row 7: K5 (from Pegs 4–8), W&T Peg 9.
Row 8: K4 (from Pegs 8–5), W&T Peg 4.
Row 9: K5 (from Pegs 5–9). Make sure to knit 2 over 1 on Peg 9.
Row 10: K6 (from Pegs 9–4). Make sure to knit 2 over 1 on Peg 4.
Row 11: K7 (from Pegs 4–10). Make sure to knit 2 over 1 on Peg 10.
Row 12: K8 (from Pegs 10–3). Make sure to knit 2 over 1 on Peg 3.
Row 13: K9 (from Pegs 3–11). Make sure to knit 2 over 1 on Peg 11.
Row 14: K10 (from Pegs 11–2). Make sure to knit 2 over 1 on Peg 2.
Row 15: K11 (from Pegs 2–12). Make sure to knit 2 over 1 on Peg 12.
Row 16: K12 (from Pegs 12–1). Make sure to knit 2 over 1 on Peg 1.

Foot

Note: The foot is worked in the round.

Round 1: K8, p1, k2, p1, k8, p1, k2, p1.

Round 2: K8, p1, k2, p1, k8, p1, k2, p1.

Round 3: K8, p1, LT, p1, k8, p1, LT, p1.

Next rounds: Repeat Rounds 1–3 until foot measures 2 inches less than desired length.

Shape toe

Next 2 rounds: Knit.

Note: The toe is worked as a flat panel using the same instructions from the heel.

Work Rows 1–16 of Heel instructions.

Finishing

In preparation for closing the toe, take the stitches off the knitting loom and place them on the size 8 knitting needles.

Take stitches from Pegs 24–11 and place them on 1 knitting needle. Take stitches from Pegs 12–23 and place them on the 2nd knitting needle.

Graft front and back stitches together using the Kitchener stitch (page 8).

Weave in all ends.

Block lightly. ●

Felted Backpack

Skill Level

 INTERMEDIATE

Size

Pre-felted: 14 inches tall x 12½ inches wide x 5 inches deep

Finished Measurements

Felted: 11 inches tall x 10 inches wide x 4 inches deep

Materials

- Lion Brand Lion Wool medium weight yarn (3 oz/158 yds/85g per skein): 6 skeins goldenrod #187 **[4 MEDIUM]**
- Yellow Knifty Knitter Loom (40 pegs)
- Knitting tool
- Tapestry needle
- Cable needle
- ¾-inch magnetic snap closure (optional)

Gauge

11 stitches and 14½ rows = 4 inches/10cm with 2 strands of yarn

Special Abbreviations

Yo (yarn over): Take yarn towards the inside of knitting loom and go around the peg in a counterclockwise direction.

4-st LC (4-stitch Left Cross): Skip Peg 1 and Peg 2. Knit loops on Peg 3 and Peg 4, place these stitches on cable needle and hold to center of knitting loom. Knit skipped loops on Peg 1 and Peg 2. Place loop from Peg 1 on Peg 3 and loop from Peg 2 on Peg 4. Place stitches from cable needle on Peg 1 and Peg 2. Gently pull loop on Peg 3 and then loop on Peg 4 to tighten the stitches.

K2tog (knit 2 stitches together): Place loop from Peg 1 on Peg 2. Treat the 2 loops as 1 and knit them together.

Pattern Stitch

Garter Stitch

Row 1: Knit.

Row 2: Purl.

Rows 1 and 2 make 1 garter-stitch ridge.

Pattern Note

Use 2 strands of yarn held together throughout.

Instructions

Front Top Band

Cast on 40 stitches.

Work 12 rows in Garter Stitch pattern. (6 garter-stitch ridges)

     American School of Needlework • Berne, Indiana 46711 • DRGnetwork.com

Next row (eyelet row): *K4, bind off 2 stitches; repeat from * to last 4 stitches, k4.

Next row: *K4, [yo] twice; repeat from * to last 4 stitches, k4.

Body

Rows 1 and 2: K5, p2, k4, p2, k1, p12, k1, p2, k4, p2, k5.

Row 3: K5, p2, 4-st LC, p2, k14, p2, 4-st LC, p2, k5.

Row 4: K5, p2, k4, p2, k14, p2, k4, p2, k5.

Repeat Rows 1–4 until body measures 14 inches.

Bottom

Work 20 rows Garter Stitch pattern. (10 garter-stitch ridges)

Back

Work in stockinette stitch for 10 inches.

Next row (eyelet row): *K4, bind off 2 stitches; repeat from * to last 4 stitches, k4.

Next row: *K4, [yo] twice; repeat from * to last 4 stitches, k4.

Work 12 rows in Garter Stitch pattern. (6 garter-stitch ridges)

Flap

Rows 1 and 2: K5, p2, k4, p2, k1, p12, k1, p2, k4, p2, k5.

Row 3: K5, p2, 4-st LC, p2, k14, p2, 4-st LC, p2, k5.

Row 4: K5, p2, k4, p2, k14, p2, k4, p2, k5.

[Repeat Rows 1–4] 7 times.

Next row: K2tog, k3, p2, k4, p2, k1, p12, k1, p2, k4, p2, k3, k2tog. (38 stitches)

Next row: K2tog, k2, p2, k4, p2, k1, p12, k1, p2, k4, p2, k2, k2tog. (36 stitches)

Next row: K2tog, k1, p2, 4-st LC, p2, k14, p2, 4-st LC, p2, k1, k2tog. (34 stitches)

Next row: K2tog, p2, k4, p2, k14, p2, k4, p2, k2tog. (32 stitches)

Next row: K2tog, p1, k4, p2, k1, p12, k1, p2, k4, p1, k2tog. (30 stitches)

Next row: K2tog, k4, p2, k1, p12, k1, p2, k4, k2tog. (28 stitches)

Bind off all stitches.

Sides

Make 2 alike

Cast on 12 stitches.

Work in Garter Stitch pattern until piece measures 10 inches from cast-on edge.

Next row: K2, bind off 2 stitches, k4, bind off 2 stitches, k2.

Next row: K2, [yo] twice, k4, [yo] twice, k2.

Work in Garter Stitch pattern until piece measures 14 inches from cast-on edge.

Bind off.

Sew sides to body of bag.

Straps

Cast on 6 stitches.

Work in Garter Stitch pattern until piece measures 25 inches.

Bind off.

I-cord

Cast on 3 stitches.

Following instructions for 3-stitch I-cord on page 8, work a 40-inch length of I-cord.

Bind off.

Finishing

Felt as per felting instructions on page 9.

Referring to photo for placement, sew straps securely to back of bag.

Thread the I-cord through the eyelets.

If desired, attach magnetic snap closure to hold flap in place. ●

Aran Throw

Skill Level

Finished Size

51 x 56 inches

Materials

- Lion Brand Wool-Ease Thick & Quick super bulky weight yarn (6 oz/106 yds/170g per skein): 12 skeins fisherman #099
- Yellow Knifty Knitter Loom (40 pegs)
- Knitting tool
- Cable needle
- Tapestry needle

Gauge

9½ stitches and 14 rows = 4 inches/10cm

Special Abbreviations

3-st RC (3-stitch Right Cross): Place loop from Peg 1 on cable needle and hold to center of knitting loom, knit Peg 2 and Peg 3 and move loops to Peg 1 and Peg 2. Place loop from cable needle on Peg 3. Knit loop on Peg 3.

3-st LC (3-stitch Left Cross): Skip Peg 1 and Peg 2. Knit Peg 3. Place loop from Peg 3 on cable needle. Knit Peg 1 and Peg 2. Move loop from Peg 2 to Peg 3, and loop from Peg 1 to Peg 2. Place loop from cable needle on Peg 1.

3-st RPC (3-stitch Right Purl Cross): Place loop from Peg 1 on cable needle and hold to center of knitting loom. Knit Peg 2 and Peg 3. Move loop from Peg 2 to Peg 1 and loop from Peg 3 to Peg 2. Take loop from cable needle and place it on Peg 3. Purl loop on Peg 3.

3-st LPC (3-stitch Left Purl Cross): Skip Peg 1 and Peg 2. Purl Peg 3 and place loop on cable needle. Knit skipped pegs. Move loop from Peg 2 to Peg 3 and loop from Peg 1 to Peg 2. Place loop from cable needle on Peg 1.

4-st LC (4-stitch Left Cross): Skip Peg 1 and Peg 2. Knit loops on Peg 3 and Peg 4, place these loops on cable needle and hold to center of knitting loom. Knit skipped loops on Peg 1 and Peg 2. Place loop from Peg 1 on Peg 3 and loop from Peg 2 on Peg 4. Place loops from cable needle on Peg 1 and Peg 2. Gently pull on the loop on Peg 3 and then the loop on Peg 4 to tighten the stitches.

Pattern Stitches

A. Garter Stitch

Row 1: Knit.

Row 2: Purl.

Rows 1 and 2 make 1 garter-stitch ridge.

B. Medallion Stitch

Row 1: P2, k10, p6, k4, p6, k10, p2.

Row 2: P2, k2, p6, k2, p6, k4, p6, k2, p6, k2, p2.

Row 3: P2, k10, p6, 4-st LC, p6, k10, p2.

Row 4: P2, k2, p6, k2, p6, k4, p6, k2, p6, k2, p2.

Row 5: P2, k10, p5, 3-st RC, 3-st LC, p5, k10, p2.

Row 6: P2, k2, p6, k2, p5, k2, p2, k2, p5, k2, p6, k2, p2.

Row 7: P2, k10, p4, 3-st RC, k2, 3-st LC, p4, k10, p2.

Row 8: P2, k2, p6, k2, p4, k2, p4, k2, p4, k2, p6, k2, p2.

Row 9: P2, k10, p3, 3-st RC, k4, 3-st LC, p3, k10, p2.

Row 10: P2, k2, p6, k2, p3, k2, p6, k2, p3, k2, p6, k2, p2.

Row 11: P2, k10, p3, k10, p3, k10, p2.

Row 12: P2, k2, p6, k2, p3, k2, p6, k2, p3, k2, p6, k2, p2.

Row 13: P2, 3-st LPC, k4, 3-st RPC, p3, k10, 3-st LPC, k4, 3-st RPC, p2.

Row 14: P3, k2, p4, k2, p4, k2, p6, k2, p4, k2, p4, k2, p3.

Row 15: P3, 3-st LPC, k2, 3-st RPC, p4, k10, p4, 3-st LPC, k2, 3-st RPC, p3.

Row 16: P4, k2, p2, k2, p5, k2, p6, k2, p5, k2, p2, k2, p4.

Row 17: P4, 3-st LPC, 3-st RPC, p5, k10, p5, 3-st LPC, 3-st RPC, p4.

Row 18: P5, k4, p6, k2, p6, k2, p6, k4, p5.

Row 19: P5, 4-st LC, p6, k10, p6, 4-st LC, p5.

Row 20: P5, k4, p6, k2, p6, k2, p6, k4, p5.

Row 21: P5, k4, p6, k10, p6, k4, p5.

Row 22: P5, k4, p6, k2, p6, k2, p6, k4, p5.

Row 23: P5, 4-st LC, p6, k10, p6, 4-st LC, p5.

Row 24: P5, k4, p6, k2, p6, k2, p6, k4, p5.

Row 25: P4, 3-st RC, 3-st LC, p5, k10, p5, 3-st RC, 3-st LC, p4.

Row 26: P4, k2, p2, k2, p5, k2, p6, k2, p5, k2, p2, k2, p4.

Row 27: P3, 3-st RC, k2, 3-st LC, p4, k10, p4, 3-st RC, k2, 3-st LC, p3.

Row 28: P3, k2, p4, k2, p4, k2, p6, k2, p4, k2, p4, k2, p3.

Row 29: P2, 3-st RC, k4, 3-st LC, p3, k10, p3, 3-st RC, k4, 3-st LC, p2.

Row 30: P2, k2, p6, k2, p3, k2, p6, k2, p3, k2, p6, k2, p2.

Row 31: P2, k10, p3, k10, p3, k10, p2.

Row 32: P2, k2, p6, k2, p3, k2, p6, k2, p3, k2, p6, k2, p2.

Row 33: P2, k10, p3, 3-st LPC, k4, 3-st RPC, p3, k10, p2.

Row 34: P2, k2, p6, k2, p4, k2, p4, k2, p4, k2, p6, k2, p2.

Row 35: P2, k10, p4, 3-st LPC, k2, 3-st RPC, p4, k10, p2.

Row 36: P2, k2, p6, k2, p5, k2, p2, k2, p5, k2, p6, k2, p2.

Row 37: P2, k10, p5, 3-st LPC, 3-st RPC, p5, k10, p2.

Row 38: P2, k2, p6, k2, p6, k4, p6, k2, p6, k2, p2.

Row 39: P2, k10, p6, 4-st LC, p6, k10, p2.

Row 40: P2, k2, p6, k2, p6, k4, p6, k2, p6, k2, p2.

Instructions

Panel 1

Cast on 40 stitches.
Work 208 rows in Garter Stitch
    pattern (total of 104 garter-stitch
    ridges), or until panel measures
    56 inches from cast-on edge.
Bind off.

Panel 2
Make 2
Cast on 40 stitches.

Lower Border
Work 4 rows in Garter Stitch
    pattern. (2 garter-stitch ridges)

Body
Work [Rows 1–40 of Medallion
    Stitch pattern] 5 times. (200 rows)

Upper Border
Work 4 rows in Garter Stitch
    pattern. (2 garter-stitch ridges)
Bind off.

Assembly

Place a Panel 2 on each side of
    Panel 1. Sew seams.
Block to size. ●

Cables Purse

Skill Level

 ■■■□ INTERMEDIATE

Finished Size

7½ x 9 inches, not
including handles

Materials

- Caron Simply Soft Quick
super bulky weight yarn
(3 oz/50 yds/85g per
skein): 2 skeins bone #0003
- Yellow Knifty Knitter round loom
(41 pegs)
- Knitting tool
- Cable needle
- Tapestry needle
- 2 purse handles with 5-inch-wide
opening

Gauge

12 stitches and 15 rows = 4
inches/10cm

Special Abbreviations

6-st LC (6-stitch Left Cross): Skip
Peg 1, Peg 2 and Peg 3. Knit loop
on Peg 4, Peg 5 and Peg 6, place
these 3 stitches on cable needle
and hold to center of knitting
loom. Knit loops on Peg 1, Peg 2
and Peg 3. Place loop from Peg 1
on Peg 4, loop from Peg 2 on Peg
5 and loop from Peg 4 on Peg 6.
Place stitches from cable needle
on Peg 1, Peg 2 and Peg 3. Gently
pull loop on Peg 4, then loop on
Peg 5 and then loop on Peg 6 to
tighten the stitches.

6-st RC (6-stitch Right Cross):
Place loops from Peg 1, Peg 2 and
Peg 3 on cable needle. Knit Peg
4 and place loop on Peg 1. Knit
Peg 5 and place loop on Peg 2.
Knit Peg 6 and place loop on Peg
3. Take Loop 1 from cable needle
and place it on Peg 4. Take Loop
2 from cable needle and place it
on Peg 5. Take Loop 3 from cable
needle and place it on Peg 6.

Pattern Notes

Leave a long tail at cast-on edge
and bind-off edge to be used for
seaming the handles in place.
Wrap the row before crossing for
cables loosely .

Instructions

Handle casing

Cast on 20 stitches.
Rows 1–14: Knit.
Cast on 4 sts at beginning of next 2
rows. (28 stitches)

Body

Rows 1–4: P3, k6, p3, k4, p3, k6, p3.
Row 5: P3, 6-st LC, p3, k4, p3, 6-st
RC, p3.
Rows 6–10: P3, k6, p3, k4, p3,
k6, p3.
Row 11: P3, 6-st LC, p3, k4, p3, 6-st
RC, p3.
Rows 12–16: P3, k6, p3, k4, p3,
k6, p3.
Row 17: P3, 6-st LC, p3, k4, p3, 6-st
RC, p3.

Rows 18–30: P3, k6, p3, k4, p3,
k6, p3.
Row 31: P3, 6-st LC, p3, k4, p3, 6-st
RC, p3.
Rows 32–36: P3, k6, p3, k4, p3,
k6, p3.
Row 37: P3, 6-st LC, p3, k4, p3, 6-st
RC, p3.
Rows 38–42: P3, k6, p3, k4, p3,
k6, p3.
Row 43: P3, 6-st LC, p3, k4, p3, 6-st
RC, p3.
Bind off 4 stitches at beginning of
next 2 rows. (20 stitches)

Handle casing

Rows 1–14: Knit.
Bind off using the basic bind off on
page 4 and weave in all ends.

Finishing

Block lightly. If necessary, adjust
the stitches on the cable-
crossing rows.
Place piece right side down on a
table. *Place 1 of the handles
on either the cast-on or bound-
off edge. Pass the stockinette
portion of the bag through the
handle, fold over the stockinette
fabric so it covers the entire
lower portion of the handle.
Sew the edge (on the wrong side of
the fabric) to secure the handle
in place.
Repeat from * with the
other handle.
Sew sides of the bag with mattress
stitch (page 7). ●

Cion Earflap Hat

Skill Level

■ ■ ■ ▢ INTERMEDIATE

Sizes

Child (adult) Instructions are given for smaller size, with larger size in parentheses. When only 1 number is given, it applies to both sizes.

Finished Measurement

Circumference: 22 (25) inches, slightly stretched

Materials

- Lion Brand Wool-Ease Thick & Quick super bulky weight yarn (6 oz/106 yds/170g per skein): 1 skein sky blue #106 or raspberry #112
- Red Knifty Knitter round loom (31 pegs)
- Knitting tool
- Tapestry needle, cable needle, 2 stitch (peg) markers
- Cable needle

Gauge

9½ stitches and 17½ rows = 4 inches/10cm

Special Abbreviations

4-st RC (4-stitch Right Cross): Place loops from Peg 1 and Peg 2 on cable needle. Knit Peg 3 and place loop on Peg 1. Knit Peg 4 and place loop on Peg 2. Place Loop 1 from cable needle on Peg 3 and knit it. Place Loop 2 from cable needle on Peg 4 and knit it.

4-st LC (4-stitch Left Cross): Skip Peg 1 and Peg 2. Knit loops on Peg 3 and Peg 4, place stitches on cable needle and hold to center of knitting loom. Knit skipped loops on Peg 1 and Peg 2. Place loop from Peg 1 on Peg 3 and loop from Peg 2 on Peg 4. Place stitches from cable needle on Peg 1 and Peg 2. Gently pull on the loop on Peg 3 and then loop on Peg 4 to tighten the stitches.

Instructions

Front/Back Panel
Make 2 alike
Note: See page 4 for instructions on ssk and k2tog decreases.

Cast on 14 (16) stitches.
Row 1: Purl.
Row 2: Knit.
Row 3: Purl.
Row 4: Knit.
Rows 5–24: Knit.
Row 25: Ssk, knit to last 2 stitches, k2tog. (12, 14 stitches)
Row 26: Knit.
Rows 27–36 (38): Repeat rows 25 and 26. (2 stitches remain)
Place remaining stitches on waste yarn.
Block lightly and weave in ends.

Side panel
Make 2 alike
I-cord tie
Cast on 2 stitches.
Work 2-st I-cord (see page 8) for 12 (18) inches.

Cable earflap
Note: See page 4 for instructions on M1 increase.

Row 1: K1, M1, k1, M1. (4 stitches)
Row 2: Knit.
Row 3: K1, M1, k2, M1, k1. (6 stitches)
Row 4: Knit.
Row 5: K1, M1, k4, M1, k1. (8 stitches)
Row 6: Knit.
Row 7: K1, M1, k2, 4-st RC, M1, k1. (10 stitches)
Row 8: K1, p1, k6, p1, k1.
Row 9: K1, M1, p1, 4-st LC, k2, p1, M1, k1. (12 stitches)
Row 10: K2, p1, k6, p1, k2.
Row 11: K1, M1, k1, p1, k2, 4-st RC, p1, k1, M1, k1. (14 stitches)
Row 12: K3, p1, k6, p1, k3.
Continue with body below.
For large size only
Row 13: K1, M1, k2, p1, 4-st LC, k2, p1, k2, M1, k1. (16 stitches)
Row 14: K4, p1, k6, p1, k4.
Continue with body below.

Body
For small size only
Row 1: K3, p1, 4-st LC, k2, p1, k3.
Row 2: K3, p1, k6, p1, k3.
Row 3: K3, p1, k2, 4-st RC, p1, k3.
Row 4: K3, p1, k6, p1, k3.
Repeat [Rows 1–4] 6 times.
For large size only
Row 1: K4, p1, k2, 4-st RC, p1, k4.
Row 2: K4, p1, k6, p1, k4.
Row 3: K4, p1, 4-st LC, k2, p1, k4.
Row 4: K4, p1, k6, p1, k4.
Repeat [Rows 1–4] 6 times.

Crown

For both sizes

Continue in pattern as established, decreasing 1 stitch at each end by using ssk on the right side, and k2tog on the left side, every other row until 8 stitches remain.

Work in stockinette stitch and continue decreasing as before until 2 stitches remain.

Place 2 stitches on waste yarn.

Finishing

Weave in ends.
Block lightly.
Sew all pieces together.
Thread yarn end through tapestry and weave through 8 stitches at top to close.

Pompom

Following instructions on page 8, make 2 pompoms. Referring to photo for placement, attach 1 pompom to each end of the I-cord. ●

Baby Sweater

Skill Level

 INTERMEDIATE

Sizes

12 (18, 24) months Instructions are given for smallest size, with larger sizes in parentheses. When only 1 number is given, it applies to all sizes.

Finished Measurement

Chest: 21¾ (23¼, 24¾) inches
Fits snuggly.

Materials

• Caron Simply Soft Quick super bulky weight yarn (3 oz/50 yds/85g per skein): 4 (4, 5) skeins berry blue #0015

6 SUPER BULKY

• Yellow Knifty knitter (40 pegs)
• Knitting tool
• Cable needle
• Tapestry needle

Gauge

11 stitches and 15 rows = 4 inches/10cm

Special Abbreviations

4-st RC (4-stitch Right Cross):
Place loops from Peg 1 and Peg 2 on cable needle. Knit Peg 3 and place loop on Peg 1. Knit Peg 4 and place loop on Peg 2. Place Loop 1 from cable needle on Peg 3 and knit it. Place Loop 2 from cable needle on Peg 4 and knit it.

4-st LC (4-stitch Left Cross):
Skip Peg 1 and Peg 2. Knit loops on Peg 3 and Peg 4, place these stitches on cable needle and hold to center of knitting loom. Knit skipped loops on Peg 1 and Peg 2. Place loop from Peg 1 on Peg 3 and loop from Peg 2 on Peg 4. Place loops from cable needle on Peg 1 and Peg 2. Gently pull loop on Peg 3 and then loop on Peg 4 to tighten the stitches.

Pattern Stitches

A. Garter Stitch
Row 1: Knit.
Row 2: Purl.

Rows 1 and 2 make 1 garter-stitch ridge.

B. Braid Cable
(worked over 10 stitches)
Row 1: P2, 4-st RC, k2, p2.
Row 2: P2, k6, p2.
Row 3: P2, k2, 4-st LC, p2.
Row 4: P2, k6, p2.

Instructions

Back

Cast on 30 (32, 34) stitches.
Work 4 rows in Garter Stitch pattern. (2 garter-stitch ridges)
Work in stockinette stitch until piece measures 7½ (8, 9) inches from cast-on edge, or desired length to underarm.

Shape raglan
Bind off 2 (2, 3) sts at beginning of next 2 rows.
Decrease 1 stitch at each end [every other row] 8 (9, 9) times.
Bind off rem 10 stitches.

Front

Cast on 30 (32, 34) stitches.

Work 4 rows in Garter Stitch pattern. (2 garter-stitch ridges)

Next row: K10 (11, 12) stitches, work Row 1 of Braid Cable pattern over next 10 stitches, knit rem sts.

Continue to work in patterns as established, working center 10 stitches in Braid Cable pattern and remaining stitches in stockinette stitch until piece measures 7½ (8, 9) inches from cast-on edge, or desired length to underarm. Discontinue Braid Cable pattern.

Divide the stitches on loom into 2 groups of 15 (16, 17) stitches each.

Join a skein of yarn at Peg 16 (17, 18). From this point on, you will work each side with a different ball of yarn.

Shape neck & raglan

Next row: Bind off 2 (2, 3) stitches, knit to center 3 stitches, p3; for 2nd half, with other skein, p3, knit remaining stitches.

Next row: Bind off 2 (2, 3) stitches, knit across both sides.

Continue in pattern following Raglan Shaping decreases as for Back at the outside edges and 3-stitch Garter Stitch edging on V-neck opening until piece measures same as Back.

Bind off remaining 5 stitches from each side.

Sleeves

Cast on 14 stitches.

Work 4 rows of Garter Stitch pattern. (2 garter-stitch ridges)

Work in stockinette stitch, increasing 1 stitch at each end [every 5th row] 5 (5, 6) times. (24, 24, 26 stitches)

Work even until piece measures 8 (9, 10) inches from cast-on edge or desired sleeve length.

Shape raglan

Bind off 2 (2, 3) stitches at beginning of next 2 rows.

Decrease 1 stitch at each end [every other row] 6 (7, 7) times, then [every 3rd row] once.

Bind off remaining 6 (4, 4) stitches.

Finishing

Block all pieces.

Sew sleeves to front and back along raglan edges. Sew side and underarm seams. ●

General Information

Skill Levels

BEGINNER
Beginner projects for first-time knitters using basic stitches. Minimal shaping.

EASY
Easy projects using basic stitches, repetitive stitch patterns, simple color changes and simple shaping and finishing.

INTERMEDIATE
Intermediate projects with a variety of stitches, mid-level shaping and finishing.

EXPERIENCED
Experienced projects using advanced techniques and stitches, detailed shaping and refined finishing.

Standard Yarn Weight System

Categories of yarn, gauge ranges, and recommended needle sizes

Yarn Weight Symbol & Category Names	1 SUPER FINE	2 FINE	3 LIGHT	4 MEDIUM	5 BULKY	6 SUPER BULKY
Type of Yarns in Category	Sock, Fingering, Baby	Sport, Baby	DK, Light Worsted	Worsted, Afghan, Aran	Chunky, Craft, Rug	Bulky, Roving
Knit Gauge Range* in Stockinette Stitch to 4 inches	27–32 sts	23–26 sts	21–24 sts	16–20 sts	12–15 sts	6–11 sts
Recommended Needle in Metric Size Range	2.25–3.25mm	3.25–3.75mm	3.75–4.5mm	4.5–5.5mm	5.5–8mm	8mm and larger
Recommended Needle U.S. Size Range	1 to 3	3 to 5	5 to 7	7 to 9	9 to 11	11 and larger

* GUIDELINES ONLY: The above reflect the most commonly used gauges and needle sizes for specific yarn categories.

Knit Abbreviations & Symbols

approx · · · · · · approximately
beg · · · · · · begin/beginning
CC · · · · · · · contrasting color
ch · · · · · · · · ·chain stitch
cm · · · · · · · · centimeter(s)
cn · · · · · · · · · cable needle
dec · · · · decrease/decreases/decreasing
dpn(s) · ·double-pointed needle(s)
g · · · · · · · · · · · gram
inc· · increase/increases/increasing
k · · · · · · · · · · · · ·knit
k2tog · · knit 2 stitches together
LH · · · · · · · · · · ·left hand
lp(s) · · · · · · · · · loop(s)
m · · · · · · · · · · ·meter(s)
M1 · · · · · · · · make one stitch
MC · · · · · · · · · main color
mm · · · · · · · · millimeter(s)
oz · · · · · · · · · · ounce(s)
p · · · · · · · · · · · ·purl

pat(s) · · · · · · · · ·pattern(s)
p2tog · · purl 2 stitches together
psso · · · pass slipped stitch over
p2sso · · pass 2 slipped stitches over
rem · · · · · · remain/remaining
rep · · · · · · · · · · repeat(s)
rev St st · · reverse stockinette stitch
RH · · · · · · · · · · right hand
rnd(s) · · · · · · · · · rounds
RS · · · · · · · · · · · right side
skp · · · slip, knit, pass stitch over— one stitch decreased
sk2p · · · · slip 1, knit 2 together, pass slip stitch over, then knit 2 together—2 stitches have been decreased
sl · · · · · · · · · · · ·slip
sl 1k · · · · · · · slip 1 knitwise
sl 1p · · · · · · · slip 1 purlwise
sl st · · · · · · · slip stitch(es)
ssk · · slip, slip, knit these 2 stitches together—a decrease

st(s) · · · · · · · · · stitch(es)
St st · · · · · stockinette stitch/ stocking stitch
tbl· · · · · ·through back loop(s)
tog · · · · · · · · · ·together
WS · · · · · · · · · wrong side
wyib · · · · · · with yarn in back
wyif · · · · · · with yarn in front
yd(s) · · · · · · · · · yard(s)
yfwd · · · · · · yarn forward
yo(s) · · · · · · · yarn over(s)

[ ] work instructions within brack-ets as many times as directed
( ) work instructions within paren-theses in the place directed
** repeat instructions following the asterisks as directed
* repeat instructions following the single asterisk as directed
" inch(es)

Inches Into Millimeters & Centimeters

All measurements are rounded off slightly.

inches	mm	cm	inches	cm	inches	cm	inches	cm
⅛	3	0.3	5	12.5	21	53.5	38	96.5
¼	6	0.6	5½	14	22	56.0	39	99.0
⅜	10	1.0	6	15.0	23	58.5	40	101.5
½	13	1.3	7	18.0	24	61.0	41	104.0
⅝	15	1.5	8	20.5	25	63.5	42	106.5
¾	20	2.0	9	23.0	26	66.0	43	109.0
⅞	22	2.2	10	25.5	27	68.5	44	112.0
1	25	2.5	11	28.0	28	71.0	45	114.5
1¼	32	3.8	12	30.5	29	73.5	46	117.0
1½	38	3.8	13	33.0	30	76.0	47	119.5
1¾	45	4.5	14	35.5	31	79.0	48	122.0
2	50	5.0	15	38.0	32	81.5	49	124.5
2½	65	6.5	16	40.5	33	84.0	50	127.0
3	75	7.5	17	43.0	34	86.5		
3½	90	9.0	18	46.0	35	89.0		
4	100	10.0	19	48.5	36	91.5		
4½	115	11.5	20	51.0	37	94.0		

Knitting Needle Conversion Chart

U.S.	1	2	3	4	5	6	7	8	9	10	10½	11	13	15	17	19	35	50
Continental-mm	2.25	2.75	3.25	3.5	3.75	4	4.5	5	5.5	6	6.5	8	9	10	12.75	15	19	25

We wish to thank ProvoCraft for providing the Kniffty Knitter looms used in this book.

American School of Needlework®
excellence in instruction

TOLL-FREE ORDER LINE or to request a free catalog (800) 582-6643
Customer Service (800) 282-6643, **Fax** (800) 882-6643

Visit DRGnetwork.com.

We have made every effort to ensure the accuracy and completeness of these instructions.
We cannot, however, be responsible for human error, typographical mistakes or variations in individual work.

ISBN: 978-1-59012-218-1   All rights reserved.   Printed in USA   2 3 4 5 6 7 8 9

SPLATTER® MOVIES

Breaking the Last Taboo of the Screen

JOHN McCARTY

St. Martin's Press New York

FOR MY DAD,
whose influence shines
through this book

Splatter Movies® is a registered trademark of FantaCo Enterprises, Inc. and is used with their
permission.

Library of Congress Cataloging in Publication Data
McCarty, John, 1944-
    Splatter movies.

    Bibliography: p.
    Includes index.
    1. Horror films—History and criticism. I. Title.
PN1995.9.H6M33   1984   791.43'09'0916   83-19134
ISBN 0-312-75257-1

First Edition
10 9 8 7 6 5 4 3 2 1

Contents

Acknowledgments

I wish to extend my special thanks and appreciation to Eric Caidin of Hollywood Book & Poster and Barry Kaufman of *Demonique* magazine for their help in securing much of the hard-to-find visual material included in this book; you guys really saved me when the chips were down.

Others who gave generously of their time in providing me with stills, advice, leads, and other kinds of support are, in alphabetical order: American-International Pictures; Analysis Film Releasing Corp; Dominick Abel; Charles Band; Carlos Clarens and Mary Corliss (Museum of Modern Art); Roger Corman; David Cronenberg; Embassy Pictures; David Everitt; Filmways Pictures; Bill George; The Jerry Gross Organization; William M. Gaines; Mick Garris; Richard C. Hassanein; Laurette Hayden (New World Pictures); John Hendricks; Daniel Krogh; Irv Letofsky; Karen Locke (Vanguard Releasing, Inc.); Tim Lucas; Lisa Mann; Robin Massey (French Cultural Services); MCA/Universal; MGM; Bob Miller; Ed Neal; Orion Pictures; Samuel K. Rubin; Paramount Pictures Corp; Richard Rubinstein; Tom Savini; Tom Schwartz (New Line Cinema); Twentieth Century-Fox; Roy Skeggs (Hammer Films); Tom Skulan; Warner Bros. Pictures.

SPLATTER MOVIES®

CHAPTER 1

What Is a Splatter Movie?

Opposite page: Heroine Adrienne King screams at the sight of the arrow-riddled body of Harry Crosby (Bing's son) in *Friday the 13th*, Sean Cunningham's low-budget splatter bonanza of the summer of '80. (© *1980 Georgetown Productions, Inc.*)

Below: A typical moment of on-stage mayhem from a live performance at the *Théâtre du Grand Guignol* in Paris—the place where splatter was born. (*French Cultural Services*)

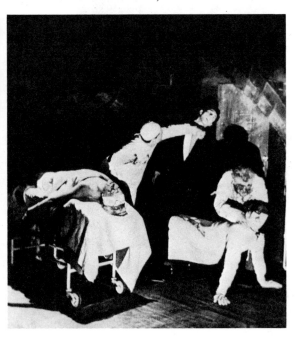

Toward the close of Sean Cunningham's highly successful 1980 movie about a knife-wielding psycho who's got it in for the entire staff and management of a New Jersey summer camp, *Friday the 13th*, the heroine (Adrienne King) finds herself locked in a prolonged struggle for her life with this selfsame psycho. During the fight, the killer's knife (actually more of a machete) gets dropped. Our heroine scoops it up and, as the psycho charges her in a final burst of murderous rage, she swings the blade wildly and in one clean stroke lops off the baddie's head.

Now ordinarily, such a scene would be just another example of that tired old cinematic standby, Gratuitous Violence. But what lifts it out of the ordinary and moves it onto an increasingly more vital plane of cinematic endeavor is the gleeful realism with which this beheading is staged: in delicious close-up (and slow motion besides), so that we are able to see every minute, bloodspurting, bony, sinewy, muscle-exposing detail. *Friday the 13th,* you see, is a *splatter movie.*

Splatter movies, offshoots of the horror film genre, aim not to scare their audiences, necessarily, nor to drive them to the edges of their seats in suspense, but to *mortify* them with scenes of explicit gore. In splatter movies, mutilation is indeed the message—many times the only one.

Splatter movies have their source in *Grand Guignol,* French theater created in the late 1800s for the benefit of those with jaded tastes. As it evolved it gravitated toward a more unsophisticated audience, the French theater-going masses, who came to marvel at grotesquely realistic eye-gougings, beheadings, and throat slittings. Plots were openly derivative or non-existent, but nobody cared: in *Grand Guignol,* gore, not drama, was the thing. It was like a ghoulish magic show. The "ooohhing" and "ahhhing" audience went only to wonder how all those gruesome tricks were accomplished right before its eyes.

Splatter movies have a lot of the same appeal. They steal plots from anywhere; after all, a plot is only a method of getting from one gory episode to the next. *Friday the 13th* brazenly swipes from John Carpenter's equally derivative *Halloween* (1979), Brian De Palma's Hitchcockian *Carrie* (1976), and a host of others. Even *Friday's* score, by Harry Menfredini, is lifted from Bernard Herrmann's score for *Psycho* (1960), but without half the orchestra. (Director Cunningham's previous splatter movie, *Last House on the Left* [1971], which was written by Cunningham but directed by another splatter movie mogul, Wes Craven, borrowed its plot from Ingmar Bergman's 1960 classic, *The Virgin Spring.*)

In their pursuit of perfect gore, splatter movies also dispense with any kind of plausibility, and minor details in particular are seldom even considered. In *Halloween,* for example, which is supposed to be set in Illinois, a number of cars sport California license plates. But again, splatter movies are not concerned with logic or consistency. Their aim, primarily, is to astonish us with the perfection of their effects. The pace of these films is almost always pell-mell, high-energy filmmaking at its

1

most furious. And the best of them can be quite amusing indeed if one experiences them on their own terms.

As a pure splatter movie, *Friday the 13th* is neither one of the best nor one of the worst. Characteristically illogical and completely empty-headed, it only wants to terrify us with its grisly special effects (created by Tom Savini). Yet even in that aim it is only marginally successful. The truly skillful splatter movie seldom uses close-ups during its shock sequences. Effects are usually held in medium shot (and without editing) so as to make the audience wonder, á la *Grand Guignol,* how in hell the scene was accomplished without killing off the actor or actors involved.

But *Friday the 13th* does cheat. It uses close-ups (as in the previously described beheading scene) and cuts away at specific moments of impact, returning moments later to reveal the grisly aftermath. Cunningham obviously chickened out. Still, his film is low-budget, it is totally lighthearted in its approach to its gore, and it doesn't have a dull moment in it—all of which qualify it as a full-fledged splatter movie, and the first of its type to have been picked up for distribution by a major studio (Paramount). It would appear that this trend is here to stay.

"Nothing in the annals of horror quite like it!" the ads for *Blood Feast* (1963) proclaimed. And in this case, they were right. (*Courtesy Hollywood Book & Poster*)

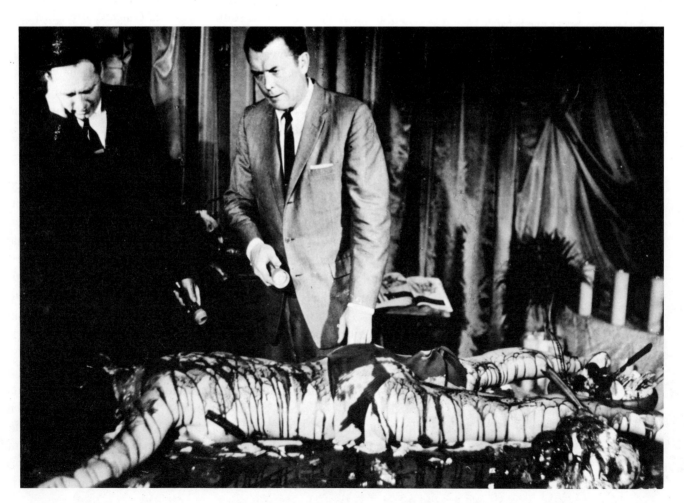

2

The dead begin to rise in George A. Romero's watershed *Night of the Living Dead* (1968), the film that introduced his EC-horror-comics approach to splatter. (© *Laurel Entertainment*)

The godfather of the genre is Chicago-based filmmaker Herschell Gordon Lewis, who began turning out his first stomach-churning little quickies (*A Taste of Blood, Blood Feast, 2000 Maniacs*) back in the early sixties at about the same time that another influence on the genre, England's Hammer Film Productions, was coming into its own.

Lewis discovered that his first love, the skin flick, was being absorbed by mainstream moviemakers. As Hollywood started exposing more flesh in its own films, Lewis realized that if he were going to stay in business, he had better carve out some new territory. The puritanical intent of the Motion Picture Production Code, established in the early thirties, had been whittled down over the years to allow just about everything to be shown on the screen. Only one taboo remained to be shattered: scenes of explicit gore. Pointedly calling his product "gore films," Lewis started his cameras rolling. Stakes were driven through human heads, tongues were ripped out of girls' mouths—all in medium shot and without editing—to keep his audiences agape. Unfortunately (for him anyway), those audiences consisted mainly of the drive-in crowd, concentrated mostly in the South, and so Lewis's reputation did not spread the way he'd hoped. Most of his work has not been seen by the vast majority of filmgoers in this country.

The first official splatter movie to gain a real reputation was George A. Romero's *Night of the Living Dead*. Made near Pittsburgh in 1968 for a paltry sum, it has since grossed millions of dollars, mostly because of frequent late-night showings at second-run houses all across the country. Romero's film, about flesh-eating zombies, paved the way for Cun-

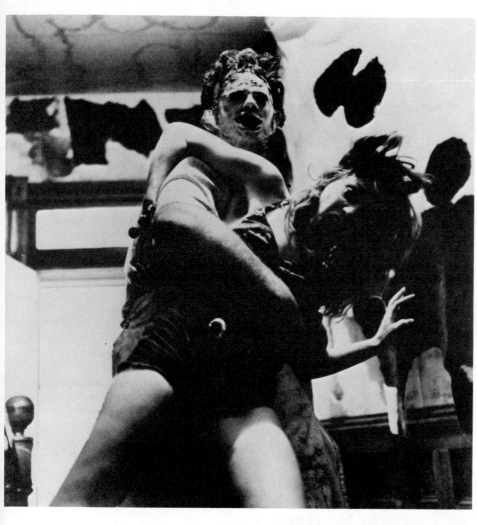

Left: Leatherface (Gunnar Hansen), the junior member of a family of four cannibal-killers, goes on the rampage in *The Texas Chainsaw Massacre* (1975). (© *New Line Cinema*)

Opposite page: The hills are alive with a family of crazed killers in Wes Craven's second splatter movie, *The Hills Have Eyes* (1977). (© *The Blood Relations Company/Courtesy Bill George*)

Below: A very flimsy door is the only barrier between a terrified Candy (Cindy Hinds) and *The Brood* in David Cronenberg's 1979 *Guignol* shocker. (© *New World Pictures*)

4

ningham and Craven's *Last House on the Left,* Craven's *The Hills Have Eyes,* the very *Guignol* films of Canada's David Cronenberg *(They Came from Within, Rabid, The Brood, Scanners),* and dozens of others, including Romero's recent *Dawn of the Dead,* a sequel to *Night of the Living Dead.* For *Dawn,* Romero himself coined the term "splatter cinema"; it is probably the most fantastically grisly film ever made. It boasts some astonishing effects (created by Tom Savini): a beheading by helicopter blade, for example, and a screwdriver being driven through a zombie's head, each of which is filmed in a continuous take to make us gasp all the more.

Romero's films, however, have an underlying layer of social satire that the films of most of his peers lack. In *Dawn of the Dead,* zombies, returning to life, head for a modern shopping center, and in one amusing sequence stumble up and down escalators, amble through stores, and sit quietly on benches to the the accompaniment of canned music, their faces a total blank. They look very much like typical Saturday afternoon shoppers at your average suburban shopping mall.

Because of the commercial success of so many of these low-budget, independently made efforts, Hollywood couldn't, of course, ignore the splatter movie phenomenon for long. And so, in 1974, it released its own. Despite its pretensions to being about the "mysteries of faith,"

This zombie apparently has his own ideas about gun control. From Romero's *Dawn of the Dead* (1979). (© *Dawn Associates, 1978/ K. Kolbert)*

5

The Shape (Nick Castle) attacks virginal teenager Jamie Lee Curtis in John Carpenter's empty-headed but enjoyable low-budget thrillshow, *Halloween* (1979). (© *Compass International Pictures*)

William Friedkin's *The Exorcist* was little more than a very posh splatter movie, utilizing every trick in the book to pulverize audiences into a single gagging mass. "How did they *do* that?" we all asked as we peeked between our fingers. *The Exorcist* went on to become one of the top-grossing films in the history of motion pictures, paving the way for other major budget splatter epics (*The Omen,* and many more).

The pages that follow offer the first comprehensive look ever taken at this wildly demented sub-genre of the horror film—its roots and rewards, its artists and its exploiters, its successes and its failures, its impact on film censorship, and its possible meaning in relation to an age filled with almost as many gross absurdities as the products of the genre itself.

For good or ill, splatter movies are having an inalterable effect on contemporary cinema. By breaking the last taboo of the screen, they are changing the definition of realism in the movies forever. For that reason alone, perhaps we should pay them heed.

:k in 1959, I read an article in *Time* magazine about an unusual theater
Paris that catered to audiences with some very specific tastes. It was
led the *Theatre du Grand Guignol,* and it had been established in 1899
a French impresario named Max Maurey.

I'd never heard of either Maurey or his *Theatre,* though the term
and Guignol was quite familiar to me, as it was usually applied in a
ogatory sense to any kind of fiction I had a special fondness for at the
e, from Mary Shelley's *Frankenstein* to Gaston Leroux's *Phantom of
Opera.*

The offerings of the *Theatre du Grand Guignol* were not a great deal
ferent in subject matter from works of horror like *Frankenstein,* but in
ms of their treatment of that subject matter they were vastly different,
d this is what caught my interest. *Grand Guignol* did not deal in horror
se, though horror was very often a by-product; it dealt instead in
onishment.

Grand Guignol's audiences in the fifties consisted mainly of working-
ss types, the less well educated ("groundlings" as they were called in
akespeare's time), who attended, according to the article, not for any
ltural upliftment, but to marvel at the ultra-realistic effects performed
right before their eyes by the actors on stage. The fact that these effects
were always tied to scenes of explicit gore—that they were gruesome or
sickening—did not seem to matter as much as the fact that they were
mind-boggling in their execution. The kick to be gotten was not from the
deed portrayed, but from the overpowering effect of the trick itself. Here
the medium alone was the message; the illusion was all.

The *Theatre du Grand Guignol* flourished for over sixty years. It
closed its doors only recently when it found that its audiences had
gradually been usurped by the movies. Today, splatter movies have
completely taken the place *Grand Guignol* once held as *the* source of
bloodily amazing illusions for those in search of a quick astonishment fix.

The term *Guignol* was derived from the name of a marionette
created by French puppet master Laurent Mourquette (1744–1844).
What distinguished this puppet from his more celebrated city cousins,
Punch and Judy, were his rough facial features and his earthy, peasant
humor. Punch and Judy's routine appealed more to urban tastes.

All puppet shows at the time, however, had one thing in common:
they were brutal, their skits laced equally with knockabout farce,
violence, and an overall heartlessness of tone. Revenge was a particularly
common theme.

When cabarets offering live-action versions of the more horrific
elements of the Punch and Judy/*Guignol* shows began to crop up in Paris,
the name apparently carried over. Max Maurey later centralized all of
these cabaret routines under one roof, calling his the theater of *Grand
Guignol.*

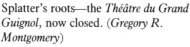

Splatter's roots—the *Théâtre du Grand
Guignol,* now closed. (*Gregory R.
Montgomery*)

Maurey's *Theatre* specialized in short plays of violence, murder, rape, the supernatural, and suicide. Many of them were adaptations of the stories of Edgar Allan Poe, written by a now forgotten dramatist named Oscar Metenier. Poe's *Murders in the Rue Morgue* and *The Tell-Tale Heart* were particular favorites, as were originals like *L'Experiment Horrible*, the title of which probably explains all.

Subtlety, psychology, love interest, all were sacrificed in these short dramas to the shock effect and the prevailing themes of pain and terror. While at first Maurey's plays drew an audience composed of people with overly sophisticated and decadent tastes, their appeal later shifted to the common folk, visitors to the big city who were out for a break in the hum-drum pattern of their lives. The genre's appeal, today in the form of splatter movies, has stayed with this group pretty much exclusively ever since.

In a more subdued, less grisly form, *Grand Guignol* crossed the Channel in 1908 to make its first appearance in England, where it quickly became a staple of the English-speaking stage. British *Grand Guignol* never reached the intensity of the French presentations, however. For one thing, censorship of the arts was stronger in Britain. And so British *Grand Guignol* emphasized instead the Gothic elements implicit in the genre, characterized by adaptations of *Dr. Jekyll and Mr. Hyde* and *Dracula*.

Later efforts such as *Angel Street* (subsequently filmed as *Gaslight* in 1944 with Charles Boyer and Ingrid Bergman) and Mary Hayley Bell's

Christopher Lee's hapless creature in *The Curse of Frankenstein* (1957) was a direct descendant of the brutal as well as brutalized French puppet *Guignol*, whose name and exploits eventually gave rise to French *Grand Guignol* theatre in the late 1800s. Half a century later, Hammer Films introduced this bloody theatrical tradition to the screen. (© *Hammer Films*)

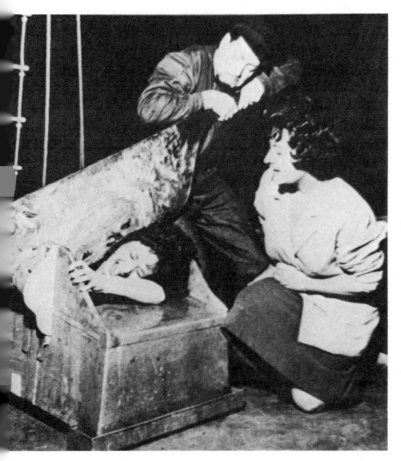
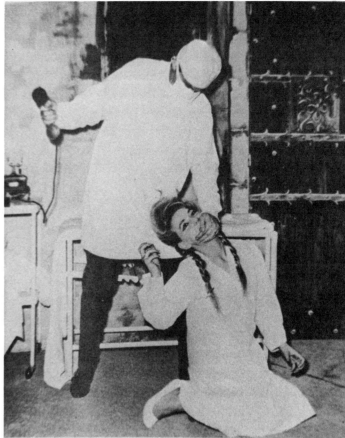

Grand Guignol's prevailing themes of pain and terror are very much in evidence in these two scenes from typical horror plays of the *Théâtre du Grand Guignol. (French Cultural Services)*

Duet for Two Hands, about a concert pianist who loses his hands in an accident then mistakenly has the hands of a murderer grafted onto him with appropriately *Guignol* results, came to typify the English approach to the genre. This approach later found its way onto cinema screens, and into the consciousness of filmgoers everywhere, when Hammer Film Productions released its first and vastly influential foray into *Grand Guignol, The Curse of Frankenstein,* in 1957.

The Curse of Frankenstein was *Grand Guignol* in the gruesome French style, but it also carried on the English Gothic tradition as well, emphasizing period atmosphere and costuming, castles and psychodrama. *Curse's* characters were not simply puppets brought on screen solely for the grisly kill—the gore films of Herschell Gordon Lewis would soon reinstitute that tradition. Hammer's early efforts, beginning with *The Curse of Frankenstein,* were a wedding of both French and English *Grand Guignol* styles.

As influential as Hammer's films were to become within this budding screen genre, however, they were not the first to portray realistic, gory effects on-screen for the purpose of astonishing audiences. On the contrary, gory effects had popped up in the movies as far back as 1916.

And that was when trouble with the censors began.

Silents and Censors

The face of an innocent, Roscoe "Fatty" Arbuckle. And innocent he was too—of murdering starlet Virginia Rappe. Nevertheless, his scandal helped pave the way for screen censorship. (*Museum of Modern Art/Film Stills Archive*)

The years 1908 through 1922 were the most uninhibited the movies have enjoyed until today. From 1922 until approximately the mid-1960s, however, they continually ran afoul of those who would censor them. And the reason for that is only too plain. Almost from their inception, the movies have always been too damn popular.

D. W. Griffith directed his first film in 1908. It was called *The Adventures of Dollie,* and its reception by the public sparked not only a brilliant career for Griffith, but the maturing of an art form and the birth of the motion picture industry worldwide as well.

Beginning with *Dollie,* Griffith employed every technique devised for the cinema thus far—pans, close-ups, dramatic lighting—to create what he called a "grammar" of film. Many of his short films and his subsequent feature-length films were among the most popular, powerful, and controversial of the silent-film era. With the release of *The Birth of a Nation,* he became the directorial giant of his day. A man who could do anything. And who did.

In *Intolerance* (1916), his epic but ill-timed hymn to world peace, which was released on the eve of America's entry into World War I and died at the box office because of it, Griffith elected to portray the history of man's inhumanity to man throughout the ages. The film, which told four stories concurrently and ran for over three hours, examined every aspect of human intolerance imaginable, but with a major emphasis on sex and violence. There are many scenes of women in partial stages of undress scattered throughout the film's orgiastic Babylonian sequences. Likewise, there are almost as many scenes of explicit gore. Half-naked ladies audiences had seen before. Gore they had not.

During the spectacular siege of Belshazzar's palace by the invading Persian hordes, for example, Belshazzar's loyal bodyguard, the Mighty Man of Valor (Elmo Lincoln), brutally chops off the head of an armed foe in full view of Griffith's camera. This happens not once, but *twice.* Later, Griffith offers us glimpses of boiling water being poured on people, arrows thudding into soldiers's chests, and a spear being slowly driven into a soldier's naked stomach, blood bubbling out of the wound as the point sinks in inch by inch. Griffith was obviously not fooling around. He wanted his battle scenes to have the sting of authenticity, to be both brutal and shocking. The results were unprecedented for the movies: scenes not just of violence, but of explicit gore—or the human body being realistically mutilated. From the moment they appeared, they caused trouble for the infant medium.

Thereafter, sex and violence ran riot throughout the movies of the silent era, particularly those of Griffith's fellow pioneer, the flamboyant Cecil B. DeMille. The sex frequently revealed itself in scenes of partial female as well as male nudity. Sexual intercourse and its related passions were left, however, to suggestion, though very often the suggestion was quite blatant. An amusing example occurs in *Intolerance* when the love-

sick Mountain Girl (Constance Talmadge) is seen mooning over the man of her dreams while she is milking a cow. The more dreamy-eyed she gets, the more energetic her stroking of the cow's udder becomes. The sexual connotation, I'm sure, was not lost on Griffith's audience.

Ironically, it was an incident from real life that finally brought the wrath of the country's would-be censors down on Hollywood's head. The year was 1921. At a wild bash hosted by world-famous funnyman Roscoe (Fatty) Arbuckle at the plush St. Francis Hotel in San Francisco on Labor Day of that year, a young actress named Virginia Rappe died under mysterious circumstances. It was ascertained later that she had died of a ruptured bladder. Arbuckle himself was accused of causing the rupture with the pressure of his enormous 250-pound weight as he'd tried to rape her. Arbuckle denied everything, but there were guests who testified that they had seen Arbuckle disappear into one of the bedrooms and that later they had heard screams. No one had actually seen Arbuckle commit the crime; nevertheless, he stood accused and was tried three times. The first trial ended in a ten-to-two vote for acquittal, as did the second. The third jury acquitted Arbuckle in six minutes, issuing a statement that said: "Acquittal is not good enough for Roscoe Arbuckle. We feel a great injustice has been done to him and there was

Elmo Lincoln as the Mighty Man of Valor who is prone to decapitating his enemies in D. W. Griffith's *Intolerance* (1916). (*Museum of Modern Art/Film Stills Archive*)

11

not the slightest proof to connect him in any way with the commission of any crime."

The public and the news media didn't buy the verdict, however, and proceeded to vilify Arbuckle as a symbol of all that was evil and dangerous about that Sodom by the Sea, Hollywood. No matter that Arbuckle was, in fact, innocent. No matter that much evidence had been falsified against him. He became a scapegoat. City mayors and other state government officials ruled unconstitutionally that Arbuckle's films were not to be shown in their communities. Films of his that were not yet in release were promptly shelved. Arbuckle's career was finished.

Even before the Arbuckle affair had had a chance to die down, however, an even bigger scandal broke. The same year that Arbuckle was finally acquitted of having murdered Virginia Rappe, well-known film director William Desmond Taylor was shot dead in his opulent Hollywood home by a person or persons unknown. The case has never been solved. But the public furor that erupted over it, combined with the furor over the Arbuckle scandal, sealed Hollywood's fate. The movies, it was shouted from headlines and pulpits across the land, were a corruptive influence on the lives of anyone they touched. They *had* to be censored; the only remaining question was how.

Acting out of a sense of survival, the movie industry decided that it had better take steps to protect itself. An organization called the Motion Picture Producers and Distributors Association of America (MPPDAA), which had been created in 1921 in the wake of the Arbuckle debacle to help foster a better image for Hollywood, was given the power to draft a list of "dos and don'ts" the industry swore it would follow from then on in the making of its films. At the head of the MPPDAA stood Will H. Hays, a former U.S. postmaster general under President Warren G. Harding, and a deeply religious man. He took his job quite seriously. And for a time, he did manage to keep the public off the back of Hollywood.

By 1930, however, the public was once again clamoring for a federally sponsored law to censor the movies. This was due to the string of anarchic and very brutal Warner Bros. gangster movies starring either Jimmy Cagney or Edward G. Robinson that had begun to appear on America's movie screens. To get the public off its back this time, the industry allowed a strict Motion Picture Production Code to be written. The Code was adopted in March that same year, but for all intents and purposes virtually ignored. Four years later, however, following intense pressure from the newly created Catholic Legion of Decency and other groups such as the Federal Council of Churches, the industry finally promised that it would deny distribution to any of its films that did not receive the Code's "seal of approval." Censorship of the movies had at long last become a reality.

They're young, they're in love, and they kill people. Faye Dunaway and Warren Beatty as *Bonnie and Clyde* (1967). (© *Warner Bros., Inc.*)

William Holden as Pike Bishop gets his
in the bloody finale to Sam Peckinpah's
landmark western, *The Wild Bunch*
(1969). (© Warner Bros., Inc.)

The Production Code touched on every possible area: violence, sex,
crime, vulgarity, obscenity, profanity, provocative costuming, suggestive
dancing, religion. But the main focus was, as always, on sex and
violence. In the area of sex, the Code strictly forbade any scenes showing
excessive or lustful kissing, nudity, realistically portrayed seduction or
rape, or sexual perversion. The list of don'ts for violence was equally
long. The technique of murder, it said, was to be presented in a way that
would not inspire imitation; brutal killings were not to be presented in
any detail; revenge in modern times (as opposed to, say, Babylonian
times) was never to be justified; repellent subjects such as hangings or
electrocutions, brutality or gruesomeness, or surgical operations were all
to be treated within the careful limits of "good taste."

For over three decades, the Motion Picture Production Code remained the chief arbiter of what audiences were allowed to see up on the
silver screen. Many of its principles were even adopted worldwide. But

by the late sixties, the Code had about run its course. With the 1968 release of Roger Vadim's *Barbarella,* which had been granted a Code seal of approval despite it's being loaded with explicit sexual content as well as scenes of Vadim's then wife, Jane Fonda, romping about in the nude, the Code finally bit the dust and was soon replaced by our present rating system of G, PG, R, and X.

The road back to full freedom of expression for the movies had been a long and circuitous one, marked by a gradual whittling down of restrictions, particularly toward matters of sexual content and language. The fight to portray violence on the screen with the same realism Griffith had once used had been waged much more quietly, however. There had been no noisy test cases such as the one involving Michelangelo Antonioni's *Blow-Up,* which had been released by MGM in 1967 without a Code seal because Antonioni had refused to make certain cuts in the film's explicit sex scenes in order to comply with Code standards. On the contrary, the graphic portrayal of violence had creeped back into the movies virtually unannounced. The release of *Bonnie and Clyde* (1967) finally served as a resounding announcement, however.

Morally ambiguous (to some anyway) and graphically violent, *Bonnie and Clyde* was a tremendous box-office smash. It was also a hit with most critics. That kind of acceptance helped to relax some of the Code's standards on the treatment of violence on the screen. Sam Peckinpah's *The Wild Bunch* (1969), released after the Code had been abolished, sorely tested the new classification system, almost earning an X rating until certain cuts in the film were made. Still, its critical and popular success helped to relax restrictions even more. Together, these two watershed American movies broke the ground that made it possible for the splatter movies of today not just to be made, but, more importantly, to earn widespread release and acceptance in the industry, to become *legitimate cinema,* unlike, say, the exploitation films of gore master Herschell Gordon Lewis, which the industry has never embraced as legitimate and which have seldom gotten decent bookings.

Still, what films had actually served to soften the ground that *Bonnie and Clyde* and *The Wild Bunch* later broke? Well, there was Hitchcock's *Psycho* (1960), of course, with its celebrated shower murder. And then there were the *Psycho* imitators that followed, such as William Castle's *Homicidal,* released a year later.

But before any of them . . . there was Hammer.

CHAPTER 4

Hammer Horror

"We're in the business to make money, not to win Oscars. If the public were to decide tomorrow that it wanted Strauss waltzes, we'd be in the Strauss waltz business."

Sir James Carreras, Founder and President, Hammer Film Productions Ltd., 1946—1972

"I feel inclined to apologize to all decent Americans for sending them a work in such sickening bad taste."

C. A. Lejeune, *London Observer*, 1957 (Upon release of Hammer's *Horror of Dracula*)

Above: Hammer's *Curse of Frankenstein* (1957) was *Grand Guignol* in the traditionally Gothic British tradition, but with a dash of the French thrown in. (© *Hammer Films*)

On the trip home from an Adirondack mountain weekend with my family in the summer of 1957, my young, monster-movie-addicted eyes were quick to spot a series of starkly lettered handbills that had been tacked to the trees and telephone poles that lined our route:

STARTS WEDNESDAY
THE CURSE OF FRANKENSTEIN
AND
X THE UNKNOWN
STRAND THEATRE, ALBANY

Well, by the end of that trip, my imagination was so stirred up that I couldn't wait until Wednesday night rolled around so that I could feast my eyes on that double feature. Fortunately, it took very little effort to persuade my dad to take me, since he was a horror film fan himself.

Wednesday morning, I threw open the newspaper to the movie page to get a peak at the Strand's ad. The names in the ad meant nothing to me: Hammer Film Productions, Peter Cushing, Anthony Hinds, Jimmy Sangster, Terence Fisher. But by the end of the day, I had committed those names to memory, for I sensed that they were going to play an important part in my life. I wasn't wrong. When my dad and I emerged from the theater that night, those names were indelibly imprinted on my consciousness. *The Curse of Frankenstein*, the first Frankenstein film I had ever seen in color (because it *was* the first), had succeeded in scaring the pants off me. And *X the Unknown*, though in black and white, had claimed the socks as well. *Curse*, especially, was deliciously gruesome fun—colorful in its period decor, elegantly costumed, and acted with dignity and total conviction by a first-rate troupe of British performers led by the accomplished Peter Cushing, who quickly became my hero and with whom I soon began corresponding.

Apart from the scare factor (admittedly a big plus to a kid of thirteen), this landmark double feature affected me in two very specific ways: it created a passion for the films of this minor British film company that lasted for almost six years, and more importantly, it marked the beginning of an affection for them that has lasted to this very day. I am not alone. Today, twenty-seven years later, the name Hammer Film Productions Ltd. is world-famous, as well-known as Warner Bros., MGM, or Paramount—in some circles, perhaps, even more well-known. And even though Hammer has not produced a feature-length horror or fantasy film since *To the Devil—A Daughter* in 1976, devotees of Hammer's vastly influential low-budget series of grisly but stylish "Hammer Horrors" of the late fifties, sixties, and early seventies continue to grow in number.

For example, Hammer fan clubs continue to sprout up in Europe,

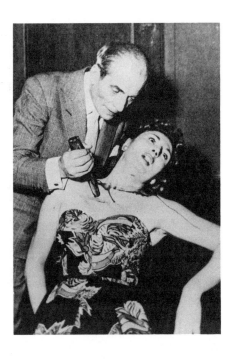

The influence of French-style *Grand Guignol* on Hammer's Gothic thrillers of the fifties is easily discerned in these remarkably similar photographs. The photo above is from a *Théâtre du Grand Guignol* horror play called *Le Vampyre*. The photo at left—from Hammer's *Hound of the Baskervilles* (1959). (*Above: French Cultural Services; left: © Hammer Films*)

Left: David Peel as the mom-fixated vampire in *Brides of Dracula* (1960). (© *Hammer Films*)

Right: Baron Meinster revenges himself on his mother (Martita Hunt) by turning her into an undead. From *Brides of Dracula* (1960). (© *Hammer Films*)

Japan, and the United States. Fan magazines devoted to covering the activities of Hammer past and present, like Dick Klemensen's *Little Shoppe of Horrors,* continue to be published. The films themselves remain a staple of Saturday afternoon and late night television, earning new young fans each year. And, of course, Hammer's influence is still being felt in contemporary film circles; many of Hammer's youthful fans of yesteryear have grown up to become big-time movie makers themselves, many of them bent on creating a whole new breed of horror and fantasy films for yet another generation of fright film fans to get hooked on. This list includes such luminaries as Steven Spielberg *(Jaws),* John Carpenter *(Halloween),* George Romero *(Dawn of the Dead),* and, especially, George Lucas, the force behind the phenomenally successful *Star Wars* (in which, perhaps as a nod of affection to Hammer, he cast Hammer stalwart Peter Cushing as one of the film's chief villains, the evil Grand Moff Tarkin).

From 1957 to 1973, the years of its golden age, Hammer Films turned out over one hundred feature films in almost every conceivable category. Over fifty percent of its output, however, was horror, science fiction, or fantasy, genres for which the studio is best remembered and for which its name has since become synonymous. Budgets for these films seldom rose above $300,000 and were often half that amount, but to quote composer Malcolm Williamson, who wrote the score for one of Hammer's best early films, the stylish *Brides of Dracula* (1960), ". . . there is always the lavish Hammer quality about these films . . . the craftsmanship, the editing, and the music mixing, for example, the casting of the small parts, the artwork are all of an outstanding high order."

This description is quite accurate and sums up the Hammer method perfectly. Though essentially small-budgeted exploitation movies, Hammer's films were always designed to look far more lush and expensive than they were. As a consequence of this ploy, the company managed to attract the attention of the major Hollywood studios. Contracts were signed with Universal, Warners, Columbia, and others to release Hammer's films in the United States and abroad. As very few of these films ever lost money, the ailing British film industry, whose films—with rare, but notable exceptions—seldom achieved much notoriety outside the British Isles, received a solid shot in the arm.

In the wake of Hammer's explosion upon the world, British films in general soon became very popular with audiences everywhere, but particularly in America. Previously denied all but the most prestigious British fare (Laurence Olivier's *Hamlet*, for example, or the internationally flavored productions of J. Arthur Rank and Alexander Korda), Americans were soon getting a taste of native British humor in satires like *I'm All Right Jack* (1960) and *The Wrong Arm of the Law* (1961), starring a young comedian named Peter Sellers. Fresh from the theater and BBC television, young directors like Tony Richardson, Karel Reisz, and John Schlesinger got the chance to make their feature film debuts with slice-of-British-life dramas such as *Look Back in Anger* (1959), *Saturday Night and Sunday Morning* (1961), and *A Kind of Loving* (1962), films that the critics and American filmgoers alike received quite warmly. Hammer Films in no small way helped make this brief resurrection of the ailing British film industry possible.

Hammer was also having an impact on the American film industry as well—in the form of American-International Pictures. AIP had been making cheap horror/exploitation films since 1955. But there was a marked difference between AIP's approach to the genre and Hammer's. AIP also capitalized on familiar horror names such as Frankenstein and Dracula, and stock horror subjects such as zombies and werewolves, in order to lure jaded American teenagers away from their TV sets and back into the theaters (chiefly drive-ins). But whereas Hammer's equally low-budget Gothic thrillers were lavishly mounted in color, nicely crafted, and well played by a seasoned stock company of professional actors, invariably AIP's were shot in black and white, and almost always on location, utilizing patchwork sets, and boasting a cast of young unknowns, many of whom had never been before a camera. Frequently, AIP chiefs James H. Nicholson and Samuel Z. Arkoff would initiate and sell one of their films on the basis of a splashy advertising campaign alone—and *then* begin work on the script. Though financially successful in a modest way, AIP's films were mainly looked upon by the industry as an aberration, or as a joke. Like Rodney Dangerfield, they got no respect.

Independent producer-director Roger Corman, who frequently

worked for AIP, was quick to perceive that if AIP was to emulate Hammer's success, it had to emulate the company's formula as well. And so he persuaded Nicholson and Arkoff to undertake production of an elaborately mounted, studio-shot, period thriller loosely based on a well-known short story from the pen of a more homegrown source of Gothic terror, Edgar Allan Poe. *House of Usher* (1960) was budgeted between $300,000 and $500,000 and featured the experienced and respected Vincent Price. It turned into a bonanza for AIP, boosting the studio's coffers considerably and giving it some badly needed industry prestige in the bargain. Corman followed up this film with the even more successful *Pit and the Pendulum* (1961). And the rest, as they say, is movie history.

In 1968, Hammer Films was given the Queen's Award for Industry in recognition of the role it had played over the years in raising the fortunes of the British film industry and, consequently, those of the Empire as well. The announcement came as a surprise to many in Britain, but particularly to Hammer itself, whose films had seldom been regarded favorably either by the British press or by the industry whose health it had done so much to enliven. The press in particular had always taken an especially harsh attitude toward the company. Upon the release of *Curse of Frankenstein*, for example, *London Observer* film critic C.A. Lejeune commented: "I put it among the half-dozen most repulsive films I have ever encountered." And a year later, she had this to say about Hammer's even more popular *Horror of Dracula:* "I feel inclined to apologize to all decent Americans for sending them a work in such sickening bad taste." In light of all that's come since, it's hard to imagine how anyone could have considered Hammer's now rather tame horror thrillers of those years to have been either sickening *or* in bad taste. And yet, Ms. Lejeune's attitude was the prevailing one among critics at the time. *The Curse of Frankenstein, Horror of Dracula, The Revenge of Frankenstein* (1958), *The Mummy* (1959), *The Hound of the Baskervilles* (1959), *The Brides of Dracula* (1960), *The Curse of the Werewolf* (1961), *The Phantom of the Opera* (1962) were all hailed upon release as being in the vanguard of a very dubious new wave: explicit horror and violence in the cinema. Other critics (not just in Britain) termed the films "For Sadists Only" and categorized them as being both depressing and degrading. The fact that the company's films were successful with the public only served to increase their hostility. After the Queen's Award, however, many of these same critics began to revise their opinions. Today, more than a few of these once hostile reviewers look upon Hammer's early films with so much fondness and nostalgia that they have even begun calling them "classics."

Eventually, even the elitist British Film Institute came around and saluted Hammer by holding a retrospective of its films at the BFI's exclusive Thames-side theater complex, a spot usually reserved for showcasing the works of Bergman, Fellini, Hawks, and the most obscure

European or Third World directors. Thus, this one-time black sheep of the British film industry finally achieved respectability.*

Success for Hammer had been a long time in coming. The company had been in existence since 1934, created by a former jewelry shop owner named William Hinds. Hinds adopted the name Will Hammer, a former vaudeville moniker, when he went into film production and distribution, registering his new company under his stage name as well. Among Hammer's partners was theater owner Enrique Carreras, whose son James and grandson Michael, along with Hammer's own son, Anthony Hinds, were to be instrumental in making the name Hammer Film Productions Ltd. world-famous twenty-three years later.

For the first two decades of its existence, Hammer's films were basically "programmers," B pictures aimed exclusively at the domestic British market. Some of its films—such as *The Mystery of the Marie Celeste* (1936), starring Bela Lugosi—did achieve a wider distribution, but not until Hammer's release of *The Quatermass Xperiment* in 1955 did they find box-office success on a much grander scale.

Based on a highly successful BBC television serial by Nigel Kneale, *The Quatermass Xperiment* employed science fiction trappings to tell what was essentially a monster-on-the-loose horror story. Hammer went so far as to advertise the film's "X" certificate (for horror) by incorporating it

*Ironically, in 1979, a similar fate befell American-International Pictures when New York's Museum of Modern Art offered a similar retrospective of that company's once scorned films, beginning with *I Was a Teenage Werewolf* (1957) and culminating with the premiere of AIP's latest shocker, *The Amityville Horror* (1979). By then, however, James H. Nicholson had died; co-founder Samuel Z. Arkoff accepted the kudos alone.

A fine sense of Gothic atmosphere was one of the hallmarks of Hammer's period thrillers—as exemplified in this shot from *Brides of Dracula* (1960). (© *Hammer Films*)

Above: Occasionally Hammer would spice up the gore in its films for the Japanese market. Here's a clip we never saw Stateside: the undead Jonathan Harker (John Van Eyssen) lying in repose. From *Horror of Dracula* (1958). (© *Hammer Films*)

Opposite page: Dracula (Christopher Lee) rots away in the sunrise in Hammer's *Horror of Dracula* (1958), a film that *London Observer* film critic C. A. Lejeune considered to be in sickening bad taste. (© *Hammer Films*)

into the film's title. The film was a phenomenal success, even in America, where its title was changed to *The Creeping Unknown* (1956).

Three more science fiction/horror films followed, two of which were also based on successful television plays by Nigel Kneale. Each was modestly successful, but none proved to be the box-office bonanza Hammer was seeking to put it over the top in the global marketplace.

The year 1957 changed all that, however, for it was then that the company finally struck its richest vein. Science fiction was set aside in favor of a more homegrown formula, that of *Grand Guignol* done in the traditionally Gothic British style, but with a dash of the French thrown in. Black and white was scrapped in favor of color in order to enhance the lush period settings and costumes as well as a new ingredient—blood. Subjects with names like Frankenstein and Dracula in them, names already familiar to moviegoers the world over, were selected in order to create a ready audience up front for the company's new product.

The Curse of Frankenstein, Hammer's maiden effort, cost around $160,000 to make. When James Carreras screened the film for Warner Bros. executives, the response was immediate and enthusiastic—though it's been reported that Jack Warner personally hated it. Warners picked up *Curse* for worldwide release, and the film went on to gross in the neighborhood of $5 million, making it Hammer's most triumphant success up until that time and proof positive that its newly discovered formula was a solid one.

Horror of Dracula, which followed a year later, was influenced even more heavily by the French style of *Grand Guignol.* It was bloodier, its effects of stakes being driven through human hearts and Dracula rotting away in the sunrise far more graphic and spectacular. And it proved to be an even bigger success. For Hammer, no further proof was needed. *Grand Guignol* meant very big business indeed.

Though Hammer had decided to harken back to the classic Universal horror films of the thirties for its subject matter, neither *The Curse of Frankenstein* nor *Horror of Dracula* could actually be called remakes of the James Whale and Tod Browning films that had preceded them, and neither were they unduly influenced by their forebears. Director Terence Fisher, in fact, had gone out of his way to avoid screening the earlier films for fear of duplicating them in any way. He was after a totally different approach, and *Grand Guignol* provided it. The Universal films were much more influenced by German fairy tales and legends in the tradition of the Brothers Grimm and by the silent expressionist cinema of Murnau and Lang than by either French *or* British *Grand Guignol.*

Revenge, a major recurring theme throughout the brutal French puppet shows of a century earlier and the *Grand Guignol* plays that followed, showed up as the central plot thrust of most of the early Hammers and many of the company's later films as well. The word itself was even included as part of the title of the company's second Franken-

Above: Hammer's dynamic duo, Christopher Lee and Peter Cushing, go at it once more in *The Mummy* (1959). (© *Hammer Films*)

Right: Christopher Lee prepares to have his tongue ripped out in a flashback sequence from *The Mummy* (1959). (© *Hammer Films*)

stein film, *The Revenge of Frankenstein*. Consistent with *Grand Guignol*, this revenge was usually exacted in Hammer's productions in some violent form, the avenger occasionally biding his time for years (or, in the case of *The Mummy*, for centuries) to claim his just and grisly due.

In *Brides of Dracula*, for example, Baron Meinster (David Peel) turns his own mother (Martita Hunt) into a vampire because she'd kept him imprisoned by her side for years in order to prevent him from putting the bite on anyone else in the neighborhood. Later Meinster goes on a rampage, claiming as his bride every able-bodied girl he meets, until he is finally stopped by a pretty schoolteacher (Yvonne Monlaur) and that obsessive vampire hunter, Dr. Van Helsing (Peter Cushing).

In *Curse of the Werewolf*, begger Richard Wordsworth is also imprisoned, unjustly so, by a villainous Spanish marquess (Anthony Dawson). Years later, having degenerated into an animal, he too takes revenge by raping a servant girl (Yvonne Romain), who later gives birth to a werewolf (Oliver Reed). The servant girl then claims revenge for both herself and the begger by stabbing the marquess to death, while Reed later exacts an even more extreme form of revenge on behalf of his father and mother by terrorizing the countryside and slaughtering both animals *and* people. In the end, he is released from his torment when he

Right and above: The unfortunate Leon (Oliver Reed) begins and completes his transformation into the title character of *Curse of the Werewolf* (1961). (© *Hammer Films*)

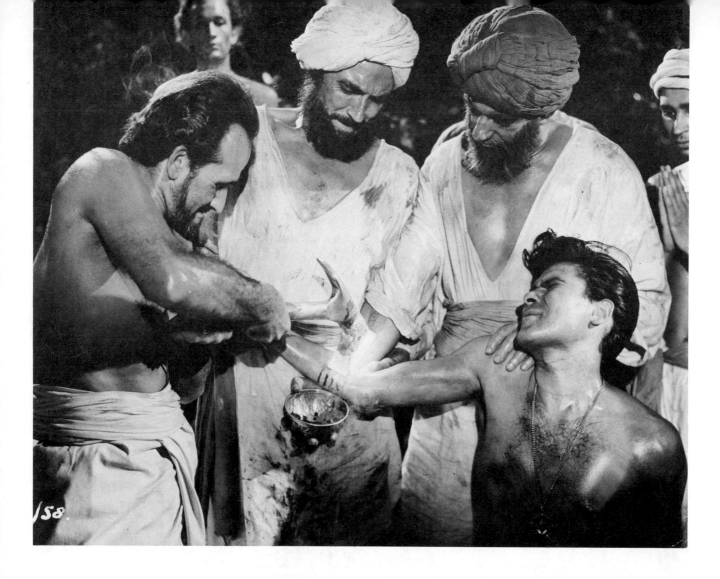

French-style *Grand Guignol* often found its way into Hammer's non-horror films too, such as Terence Fisher's *Stranglers of Bombay* (1960), an action drama about the Thuggee reign of terror against the British in India of the 1850s. (© *Hammer Films*)

is shot down with a silver bullet fired by his adoptive father (Clifford Evans).

The revenge elements implicit in the plot of Hammer's last Universal-inspired horror film, *The Phantom of the Opera* (1962), are, of course, only too obvious—the phantom terrorizes the opera house and kills people because he has been wronged by a villainous impresario (Michael Gough).

Another interesting characteristic of these early Hammers is that the supernatural elements were always pushed as far into the background as possible even if the films themselves had an obviously supernatural theme. It was almost as if Hammer (or, more precisely, director Terence Fisher) felt that audiences would not accept scenes of gory realism in films of an overtly fantastic nature. In *Horror of Dracula*, for example, the king of the vampires (Christopher Lee), while given a supernatural presence (his footsteps make no sound), is denied the traditional power to alter his shape. He is also given an obvious sexual charisma; both his behavior and the nature of his appeal are made to seem more like a perversion than anything else. This emphasis on "realism" was echoed even more strongly in *Brides of Dracula,* where the cause of Baron Meinster's affliction is attributed not to supernatural forces, but to his having been "corrupted at school," an obvious reference to homosexuality. That Meinster directs his revenge chiefly at his mother, and then other women, would seem to bear this out.

Although Hammer's early productions were traditional horror films in many ways, they were also quite adventurous in the emphasis they placed on character development and motivation. The two flowed as freely as the blood throughout these early efforts, the graphic realism of the one serving, perhaps, as an impetus for the other to develop as well.

The abundance of rich acting talent available in England, combined with the unsnobbish willingness of that talent to work even in low-budget horror films such as those made by Hammer, doubtless had much to do with the high caliber of characterization found in Hammer's early films. Actors and actresses such as Richard Wordsworth, Leo McKern, Martita Hunt, Hazel Court, Gordon Jackson, Lionel Jeffries, Robert Urquhart, Michael Ripper, Guy Rolfe, and Michael Gough among many others brought a wealth of experience on stage and screen (both large *and* small) to their work for the company. And Hammer, of course, reaped the rewards of all this experience in the form of delightful bits of pure characterization sprinkled throughout its films that served to flesh them out and many times lift them a cut or two above the norm.

One actor, however, stands out above all as having provided the single most important contribution to the success of Hammer's initial experiments in *Grand Guignol*. He is Peter Cushing.

Playwright Barré Lyndon's *The Man in Half Moon Street* was a *Grand Guignol* drama in the restrained British tradition. But for its second film incarnation, Hammer's *The Man Who Could Cheat Death* (1959), it was given a distinctly French *Grand Guignol* flavor. (© Hammer Films)

In Hammer's *Hound of the Baskervilles* (1959), the fanatical Sherlock Holmes (Peter Cushing) even endangers the life of his client (Christopher Lee) to solve the case. Dr. Watson (Andre Morell) looks on. (© *Hammer Films*)

Already forty-four when he made his debut as the screen's most fiendish scientist, Baron von Frankenstein in Hammer's *The Curse of Frankenstein*, Cushing had acquired a solid reputation in England for his diversified peformances on stage and especially on television during the early fifties. Outside of England, however, he was a virtual unknown, even though he had spent some years in Hollywood prior to World War II. There, he'd secured some minor roles in films such as Laurel and Hardy's *A Chump at Oxford* (1940) and one major role opposite Carole Lombard and Brian Aherne in George Stevens's prestigious 1940 drama about life in a provincial English hospital, *Vigil in the Night*. But the war had interrupted everything.

The Curse of Frankenstein, however, brought Cushing worldwide fame. Although Christopher Lee would become equally well-known and just as strongly identified with Hammer, it is Peter Cushing who remains etched in the minds of most—even now—as the chief icon of Hammer's early films. His series of characterizations served not only to clearly define the burgeoning genre now known as Hammer Horror, but provided the next link in a chain that included Hammer's introduction of French-style *Grand Guignol* to the cinema, and began with the brutal French puppet shows of a century before. As portrayed by Peter Cushing, Baron von Frankenstein, Dr. Van Helsing, and to some extent even Sherlock Holmes, were as heartless a trio as Punch, Judy, or *Guignol* themselves had ever been.

28

Cushing acknowledges that his portrayal of the amoral Baron von Frankenstein was patterned after the real-life anatomist Dr. Robert Knox of Burke and Hare infamy. But Cushing's baron is decidedly more pitiless in his obsessive quest for knowledge than Knox ever was. In his quest to create life—to duel, as it were, with God—Cushing's baron seems instead much more like Herman Melville's equally obsessed and pitiless hero, Captain Ahab, whose hatred of the white whale that has bested him sparks Ahab's long voyage of vengeance.

Cushing's Baron von Frankenstein also seems bent on vengeance, in that he is compelled by some twisted inner drive to beat nature at its own game. His quest to create life is in effect a quest to become an equal with God. Like Ahab, the baron views the power of God as a monstrous insult to him as a man. Cushing's baron is ruthless and cruel and even a murderer—more a monster, in fact, than the mindless, feeble creature (Christopher Lee) that he succeeds in giving life.

In Hammer's second *Frankenstein* film, the baron's amorality becomes even more pronounced as he uses a clinic for the poor as a sort of flesh and blood garden from which he plucks whatever organs he needs for his experiments. He gives no thought whatsoever to the poor wretches whose lives and anatomies he destroys in the process. Ironically, his experiment results in his giving life to a creature with cannibalistic tendencies—not unlike himself.

Peter Cushing even brought elements of his Frankenstein and Van Helsing personas to the character of Sherlock Holmes in *Hound of the Baskervilles* (1959). (© *Hammer Films*)

Peter Cushing as Dr. Van Helsing, the neurotic vampire destroyer in *Horror of Dracula* (1958). He pounds stakes through human hearts without even batting an eyelash. (© *Hammer Films*)

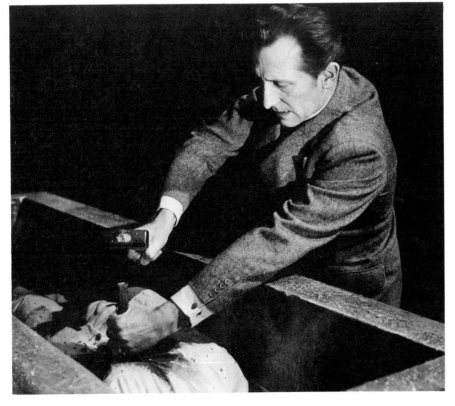

Equally significant is Cushing's performance as the neurotic vampire-destroyer Dr. Van Helsing in Hammer's follow-up film, *Horror of Dracula*. Again his character is one bent on an obsessive quest for vengeance—this time against the King of Vampires, Count Dracula. In his pursuit of Dracula, Van Helsing pounds stakes through human hearts without batting an eyelash, just as Baron von Frankenstein before him had wallowed up to his elbows in human blood and body parts without exhibiting the slightest qualm. So intense is Van Helsing's determination to "rid the world of this unspeakable evil" that eventually Dracula himself is made to seem like the underdog. In the film's final shot, after he has finally turned Dracula to dust, Cushing's demeanor suggests not a feeling of final victory, but one of overwhelming defeat and sadness, for by having destroyed his nemesis, he has really destroyed himself. Of what need is God when the threat of the devil is no longer present? Again, the pervasive tone is one of heartlessness. Even success brings only pain and anguish.

Peter Cushing even brought elements of his Frankenstein and Van Helsing personae to the character of Sherlock Holmes in *The Hound of the Baskervilles*. Little seems to matter to his Holmes save the solution to the mystery. Cushing's Holmes is not simply cerebral and dispassionate, qualities we have come to accept as defining the character of Sherlock Holmes, but, like Frankenstein and Van Helsing, obsessive and, at times, even fanatical in his quest to attain the powers only God may possess—at one point he endangers the life of his client, Sir Henry Baskerville (Christopher Lee), in a last-ditch effort to solve the mystery of the phantom hound that has cursed and killed the Baskerville line for centuries.

Hammer has since faded from the filmmaking scene. It no longer holds any influence over either the horror film genre or the splatter movie sub-genre that, for the moment, seems to have replaced the traditional horror film. Hammer itself never really made splatter movies as such. Its productions, though occasionally quite gruesome, were more in keeping with the psychological tone of splatter movies as personified chiefly by the characters played by Peter Cushing.

Hammer probably lost its position of influence simply because the competition became too stiff. Roger Corman's Poe films and Amicus's anthology films soon glutted the market with Gothic horror. By 1970, when Hammer finally decided to spice up its own output with the release of *The Vampire Lovers*, nudity had become a fixture even in mainstream movies, and scenes of explicit gore had found their way into Hollywood movies such as *Bonnie and Clyde* and *The Wild Bunch*, thereby pulling the rug out from under Hammer altogether. With the release of Alfred Hitchcock's *Psycho*, even the face of *Grand Guignol* had changed. The British tradition of castles and costumes now no longer seemed to appeal to audiences. They preferred instead to have their horrors take place in run-down motels or decaying Southern mansions. Once a leader, Hammer had become a follower. Today, though still active, the company is mostly a memory.

Still, the significance of Hammer to film history cannot be underestimated. When Hammer started showing blood in its films, other companies soon started showing it in theirs. In the ten-year interval between Hammer's release of its watershed *The Curse of Frankenstein* and the explosive appearance of *Bonnie and Clyde*, the rules of censorship pertaining to scenes of explicit gore and violence on the screen had become considerably relaxed. Hammer had played no small part in bringing about that relaxation. Furthermore, for good or ill, Hammer had paved the way for the splatter movies of today by providing them with an essential ingredient in their development—a visible link to their *Grand Guignol* past.

Andy Warhol's Frankenstein (1972), one of the most freakish of the new wave of splatter movies that began hitting movie screens in the early seventies, acknowledged splatter's debt to Hammer in full. Produced by

By the time *Frankenstein and the Monster From Hell* (1973) appeared, Hammer had lost its power to compete. Here Dave Prowse plays the gorilla-like final creation of the mad Doctor F. (© *Hammer Films*)

The grotesque finale to Paul Morrissey's homage to the viler implications of the Frankenstein legend, *Andy Warhol's Frankenstein* (1972), filmed in 3-D. (*Bryanston Pictures*)

Carlo Ponti on a budget of $500,000, the film seemed to be almost a homage to the gore in Hammer's Frankenstein films and to the viler implications of the Frankenstein legend at large.

Directed with an eye toward the completely revolting by Warhol's house director, Paul Morrissey, it dealt with a Baron von Frankenstein (Udo Kier) who is more obsessed than Hammer or Peter Cushing could have ever imagined. In love with his sister (Monique Van Vooren), with whom he has spawned two very strange children, this Frankenstein seems to have only one desire in life: to paw, grope, and fondle every internal organ the human body contains. At one point, he tears open a lengthy stitch in the side of his gorgeous female creature (Delila Di Lazzaro) and, mounting her, announces to his assistant in all panting seriousness that "to know death, Otto, one must first fuck life in the gall bladder." In the end though, the baron gets his comeuppance when his male creature (Srdjan Zelenovic) runs a spear through him, tearing out his own gall bladder. For added effect, this *Frankenstein* was shot in 3-D, so that the baron's innards wind up dangling about three feet from his nose and about two inches from ours.

Warhol's follow-up, *Blood for Dracula* (1973), which was again directed by Morrissey, sacrificed some of its outlandish gore for comedy of an equally bizarre nature. In the film, Udo Kier plays a Count Dracula who can only sup on the blood of virgins (otherwise he throws up). To find these virgins, he abandons Transylvania for Roman Catholic Italy, settling down next to a plush villa inhabited by a nobleman (Vittorio De Sica), his three nubile daughters, and a lascivious handyman (Joe Dallesandro) who speaks with a Brooklyn accent and who winds up saving the daughters by deflowering them moments before the vampire can sink his teeth in. As it always must be in a true splatter movie, however, gore triumphs at the film's conclusion: Dracula is "staked out," but not until he's had both his arms and legs chopped off.

At the conclusion of *Blood for Dracula* (1973), the vampire (Udo Kier) is finally staked out, but not before he's had both his arms and legs chopped off. (*Bryanston Pictures*)

CHAPTER 5

Sam Peckinpah and The Wild Bunch

Director Sam Peckinpah on the set of his landmark western, *The Wild Bunch* (1969), the film that remains the Pandora's Box of on-screen splatter. (© *Warner Bros., Inc.*)

Sam Peckinpah's *The Wild Bunch*, released domestically in the summer of 1969—at the close of one of the most violent decades in modern American history—tore down the last remaining barriers to showing explicit violence on the screen. Released with an R rating (it almost got an X until some cuts were made), the film was greeted by some outraged critics and filmgoers as a mindless exercise in cinematic mayhem. The headline of Rex Reed's scathing review of the film in a now-defunct entertainment magazine (the title of which I can't recall) screamed: MR. PECKINPAH, YOU STINK! Other critics and filmgoers, however, called it a masterpiece, a bonafide classic of the genre, a film destined to take its place alongside John Ford's *The Searchers* (1956) and a few other select westerns.

The Wild Bunch is clearly not a splatter movie. It is an extremely violent film that draws its power from an emphasis on action rather than gore. Similarly, its occasional nods to past westerns—particularly John Huston's *The Treasure of the Sierra Madre* (1948)—are there for a purpose (as I shall make clear), not simply to rip off their plots. But just as clearly, *The Wild Bunch*, more than any other film, helped make the splatter movie possible. It remains the Pandora's box of screen violence because the overall acceptance—by audiences, critics, and the MPAA ratings board—of its graphic depiction of bloodletting and carnage within the context of a film designed for mass consumption made it possible for filmmakers everywhere to begin exploiting these same elements more openly in their own films.

Over the years there has been much revisionist thinking about *The Wild Bunch*. Testifying to its enduring status as an important work of American filmmaking, reappraisals of it are continually popping up, many of which are no longer favorable, a fact due in large part, I feel, to Peckinpah's precipitous decline as a vital and innovative filmmaker during the decade that followed *The Wild Bunch*'s release. Many of his subsequent films—*The Getaway* (1972), *Bring Me the Head of Alfredo Garcia* (1976), *Convoy* (1978)—border on being grotesque parodies of the very films that made his reputation, particularly *The Wild Bunch*. Others, such as *Pat Garrett and Billy the Kid* (1975), which admittedly was subjected to quite a bit of studio tampering prior to its release, and *The Killer Elite* (1977), are downright unwatchable.

The Wild Bunch, however, remains not only a landmark film in terms of screen censorship, but an astonishing cinematic achievement as well. Despite the abundance of graphically violent films that have followed in its wake, it remains not only the most violent film ever made, but one of the very few such films that actually says something important *about* violence. It does not wallow in bloody effects for their own sake, but uses these effects to clarify its point of view about why the human animal has not managed to drive this ugly instinct from its psyche after millions of years of evolution. This viewpoint is drawn considerably from

Above: One of the bunch bites the dust during the explosive gun battle between Pike's gang and the railroadmen that opens *The Wild Bunch* (1969). (© *Warner Bros., Inc.*)

Left: The grim aftermath of the opening massacre, which has claimed the lives of many innocent townsfolk caught in the crossfire. (© *Warner Bros., Inc.*)

the work of anthropologist and screenwriter (*Khartoum*, 1966) Robert Ardrey, whose controversial studies on violence and territoriality in animals had a profound impact on Peckinpah. While making *The Wild Bunch* in Mexico, Peckinpah was shown a copy of Ardrey's *African Genesis* by actor Strother Martin. The book, which poses the theory that man's continued fascination with war and weaponry is the result of his being descended from killer apes, seemed to Peckinpah an affirmation of one of the major themes of *The Wild Bunch*. Ardrey's *The Territorial Imperative*, which Peckinpah read later, had an even greater impact on him, so much so that he used the book's thesis as the foundation of his script for *Straw Dogs* (1971).

Born in 1926 in California, Sam Peckinpah is every inch a Westerner. His relatives include homesteaders, cattlemen, superior court judges, miners, and an aunt who was a full-blooded Paiute Indian; his grandmother reportedly knew Calamity Jane well enough to call her "a dirty, drunken woman who smelled bad." With this background, it comes as no surprise that Peckinpah's best films have always dealt with western themes. Even his work in television,* where his career as a writer-director began, was marked by a strong desire to explode the myths of the Old West by portraying the era with realism and honesty.

Following his television internship, Peckinpah moved into feature films, a medium with which he was not entirely unfamiliar, as he had previously worked as an assistant to Don Siegel (*Invasion of the Body Snatchers*, 1954) and Jacques Tourneur (*Wichita*, 1955). He had also adapted a cult novel by Charles Neider about the exploits of Pat Garrett and Billy the Kid called *The Authentic Death of Hendry Jones*. His script was altered considerably and subsequently made in 1961 as *One-Eyed Jacks*, directed by and starring Marlon Brando.

In 1962, Peckinpah made his feature film debut as director of *The Deadly Companions*, a western starring Brian Keith and Maureen O'Hara. But Peckinpah's scripting efforts were ignored and his original cut of the film was scrapped. Seen now only on television, the film makes little sense. But its story of mutually hostile types forced together by circumstances to accomplish a common goal formed a pattern for his subsequent work. And one scene in particular, the accidental shooting of O'Hara's little boy during a wildly chaotic bank robbery, clearly calls to mind the melee that opens *The Wild Bunch*.

Ride the High Country, made for MGM the same year, proved more successful, however. Critics not only took notice, they were even kind. What's more, its story of two aging gunfighters-cum-lawmen, Gil Westrom (Randolph Scott) and Steve Judd (Joel McCrea), who pair up to

Sam Peckinpah, Robert Ryan (not in costume), and William Holden discuss a story point in the midst of a Mexican village, one of the many stark locales used to lend authenticity to *The Wild Bunch* (1969). (© *Warner Bros., Inc.*)

---

*Peckinpah wrote over a dozen *Gunsmoke* episodes, created three television series (*The Rifleman* with Chuck Connors, *Klondike*, and *The Westerner* with Brian Keith), and wrote as well as directed a number of segments for Dick Powell's anthology series, *Four Star Theatre*.

bring a shipment of gold safely across the mountains to a bank, formed the basis of a theme that found its ultimate expression in *The Wild Bunch*.

In *Ride the High Country*, Peckinpah played havoc with the traditional appearance of the movie western. The film's characters looked as if they were part of the land, towns were shown in the ramshackled throes of construction, streets were thick with dust. And Westrom and Judd were not the typical white knights of past westerns, but real human beings, old-timers struggling for survival as the twentieth century advanced upon them, and full of contradictions. Overall, the film seemed like a moving daguerrotype of the past.

Such an emphasis on realism was certainly not new to the movie western, of course. William S. Hart had done similar things in his silent horse operas, and both John Ford and Howard Hawks had experimented along the same lines in the sound era as well. Yet *Ride the High Country* was perceived by critics as being the first significant step in bringing the curtain down on the archetypal western (Andrew Sarris, for example, called it an "anti-western"); and so critics everywhere began either to praise Peckinpah or damn him, depending upon their individual sense of nostalgia for the traditional genre.

In his next film, *Major Dundee* (1965), Peckinpah introduced his preoccupation with Mexico, its people, and the relationship of its history to that of our own American West. The story again is about two men, former friends like Westrom and Judd, who join together to accomplish a mutual goal. Major Dundee (Charlton Heston) is the commander of a

Faced with being sent back to prison if he doesn't hunt down Pike's gang, Deke Thornton (Robert Ryan) must reconcile himself to being aided in his mission by low life bounty hunters Coffer (Strother Martin) and T. C. (L. Q. Jones). (© *Warner Bros., Inc.*)

Union prisoner-of-war camp who finds it necessary to use Confederate prisoners and their leader, Captain Tyreen (Richard Harris), to track down an Apache cutthroat, Sierra Charriba (Michael Pate), who has been preying on nearby settlers. To do this, Dundee and Tyreen are forced to cross into Mexico, where they come into conflict with Emperor Maximilian's troops and Juarista rebels.

From the beginning, *Major Dundee* ran into trouble. Shortened shooting schedules and incessant script changes hastened its completion. Prior to its release, Peckinpah's cut was shorn by the studio of a number of scenes, including careful daubs of character and motivation, in order to bring the film down to a more acceptable running time of two hours. Basic plot and action remained, but like *The Deadly Companions*, gaps are noticeable. The fight Peckinpah put up to save *Major Dundee* earned him a reputation as a recalcitrant director. It was with this reputation that he started work on *The Cincinnati Kid* (1965) for Martin Ransohoff, a producer well known for his own persistence of vision. (Ransohoff's associations with Tony Richardson on *The Loved One* (1965) and Roman Polanski on *The Fearless Vampire Killers* (1967) ended with both directors requesting that their names be removed from the credits of their films.) Disagreements arose quickly between Peckinpah and Ransohoff, and on the fourth day of shooting, Peckinpah was fired—reportedly for having shot some unauthorized nude scenes involving star Ann-Margret—and subsequently replaced by Norman Jewison.

Unable to get work as a director, Peckinpah turned wholly to screenwriting. A script he had written based on Hoffman Birney's cavalry novel, *The Dice of God*, was purchased by Laven-Gardner-Levy Productions (producers of Peckinpah's old *Rifleman* television series) and released in the summer of 1965, directed by Arnold Laven, as *The Glory Guys*. Its death was quick and merciful. His second script, *Villa Rides* (1968), was one that Peckinpah obviously would have liked to direct himself. Its story of an American flyer (Robert Mitchum) who gets involved in Pancho Villa's (Yul Brynner) struggle with the Federales and his own superior, General Huerta (Herbert Lom), contains many of Peckinpah's favorite themes. The flyer's growing friendship with Villa as well as his belief in the Mexican's cause, and his ultimate inability to betray either closely parallels the relationship of the "wild bunch" and its Mexican member in the later film.

That same year, Kenneth Hyman, an independent producer (*The Hill*, 1965; *The Dirty Dozen*, 1967), was appointed vice-president in charge of production at Warner Bros.-Seven Arts. A great admirer of *Ride the High Country*, Hyman contacted Peckinpah and asked him to direct a pet project of his called *The Diamond Story*. Peckinpah agreed, but when plans fell through due to casting problems, Peckinpah was allowed to go ahead with his own project, *The Wild Bunch*.

* * *

In an article about John Huston and *The Treasure of the Sierra Madre* written for *Life* magazine in 1950, critic James Agee described the character of Gold Hat (Alphonso Bedoya), the Mexican bandit who dogs the trail of the three down-and-out American prospectors, as "a primordial criminal psychopath about whom the most fascinating and terrifying thing is his unpredictability." This description also fits Peckinpah's "wild bunch."

To live, Pike Bishop and his gang steal. When they find the encroachment of civilization—law and order—to be endangering this way of life, they flee to revolution-torn Mexico circa 1913, where everything more closely resembles the lawless, easily preyed upon American frontier of their recent past. There they plan to make one last score and "back off."

Pursued into Mexico by Deke Thornton—a parolee and former friend and associate of Bishop's—and his posse of ex-bounty hunters, gunmen, and common street trash—each of whom has been offered either a pardon, money, or a job within the law in exchange for capturing Bishop and his men—the bunch makes the acquaintance of General Mapache, a tequila-soaked Federale officer bent on stealing guns from one of the U.S. Army supply depots across the border, provided he can do so without jeopardizing the already delicate relations between his country and the United States. Bishop presents the solution. In exchange for $10,000 in gold, he and his men will rob the train.

After the robbery, Bishop and his men warily return to Mapache's headquarters to deliver the guns—all except for one case, which the Mexican member of the bunch, Angel (Jaime Sanchez), has given to the Villistas in his Federale-devastated village. Complications arise when Angel is taken prisoner by Mapache and tortured. The film climaxes when Bishop and the others forsake the gold, strap on their guns, and confront Mapache, demanding that Angel be returned to them. Mapache agrees, but a split second later, cuts Angel's throat. Reacting instinctively, Bishop's men gun down the general. Then both the outlaws and the Mexican soldiers freeze. Slowly Bishop and the others break into a triumphant grin, for they have momentarily achieved the impossible: they are holding Mapache's entire army at bay.

The stand-off is finally broken when Bishop impulsively shoots the German munitions expert who had been Mapache's aide, and both sides open fire. What follows is one of the most anarchic, graphically bloody and violent gun battles ever staged for a film, as the "wild bunch" howlingly greets its own extinction in an impossible attempt to annihilate the odds-on foe. Virtually everyone is killed. A wind blows up. The smoke clears. And Thornton's posse arrives to find a bullet-ridden, bloodstained camp full of corpses and feasting vultures.

The posse, scavengers also, gathers up the gang's remains prior to returning north. Thornton, however, decides to stay behind. Shortly

One of the many moments of tension during which violent tempers flare on all sides in *The Wild Bunch* (1969). (© *Warner Bros., Inc.*)

thereafter, shots resound from the hills. Later, Freddy Sykes, the sole survivor of Bishop's gang, shows up with a small band of Villistas from Angel's village; they have stopped Thornton's posse in its tracks. Freddy invites Thornton to join his ragtag band of aging bandits and machete-wielding young boys ("It ain't like it used to be, but it'll do."). Adopting the same "Why not?" attitude characteristic of his former partner's behavior, Thornton agrees, and this new but even more out-of-date wild bunch rides off to meet its own inevitable doom. As the dust blows up around them, Freddy and Thornton break into loud, raucous laughter, echoing the finale of *Sierra Madre* when Old Howard (Walter Huston) and Curtin (Tim Holt), their greedy partner Dobbs (Humphrey Bogart) dead, his murderer jailed, and the gold dust carried back to the mountains by the wind, find themselves laughing uncontrollably at the joke that fate has played upon them.

The plot of *The Wild Bunch* (co-written by Walon Green and Peckinpah), like Huston's (from B. Traven's novel), is spare, yet the overall film is breathtaking in its detail. The evocation of time and place is meticulous—compare it with the atmospheric inadequacies of George Roy Hill's similarly themed, but more Hollywood-ized (and popular) *Butch Cassidy and the Sundance Kid*, released the same year. Lucien Ballard's photography (he also did *Ride the High Country*) possesses the you-are-there quality of Timothy O'Sullivan and Matthew Brady photographs come to life.

Most remarkable of all, however, is the film's sense of characterization: William Holden is superb as Pike Bishop, an over-the-hill outlaw whose legs are so scarred from a lifetime of fast getaways that he can barely mount his horse without help; Edmond O'Brien puts himself in a class with Walter Huston as the grizzled, garrulous Freddy Sykes, who has seen his kind come and go so often that he can't help but view life as something that must not be taken too seriously; Mexican film director Emilio Fernandez flawlessly portrays the stupid, unpredictable Mapache, whose very pores seem to ooze venom and alcohol; and Robert Ryan as Deke Thornton, the film's subtlest characterization, perfectly conveys a man who is deeply troubled by having to turn on his friend, yet who is terrified of being sent back to prison if he does not. His relationship to Bishop echoes the bond between Steve Judd and Gil Westrom in *High Country* (as well as the bond between Major Dundee and Captain Tyreen); his final decision to take up Bishop's banner, knowing that he too will someday share the same bloody fate, significantly parallels Westrom's decision to bring in the gold rather than steal it when his more honest partner is killed.

Sam Peckinpah made *The Wild Bunch*, in part, as a response to Richard Brooks's *The Professionals* (1967), a turn-of-the-century western in which four American men of action who have been successfully duped by their devious American employer succeed in outwitting an entire army of Mexican bandits on the Mexicans' own turf. Peckinpah, like Huston, sees a similar situation quite differently. As the opening sequence of *The Wild Bunch* suggests, the fate of Peckinpah's men of action more closely resembles that of a scorpion placed on a hill of red ants— overwhelmed, it chooses to sting itself to death. Similarly, Huston's Fred C. Dobbs, who is unable to get by in his familiar Tampico, takes to the Sierra Madres in search of gold only to be done in by the change in his surroundings. Sudden wealth turns the consistently impoverished Dobbs into a violent paranoid who sees everyone as being after his "goods," especially the Mexican bandit, Gold Hat. But when Gold Hat traps him beside a water hole, Dobbs's error of judgment proves fatal, for the bandit's only aim is murder. As Dutch (Ernest Borgnine) explains to Bishop: "We ain't nothing like them [the Federales]; we don't *hang* nobody!" A moot point, but a decisive one.

The Wild Bunch was shot and edited during the spring and summer of 1968, a period that saw the assassination of Martin Luther King, Jr., the burning of many American cities that followed in the wake of the national trauma, the murder of Robert Kennedy, the gunning down of students in Mexico City, and the madness of the Democratic National Convention in Mayor Daley's Chicago. Unquestionably, these events and the questions they presented about the rising tide of violence around the world had a significant influence on Peckinpah's approach to his film. Arthur Penn's *Bonnie and Clyde* had established a precedent with its graphic depiction of killing and had been severely criticized for doing so.

Angel (Jaime Sanchez) saves Dutch's (Ernest Borgnine) life during the railroad heist. (© *Warner Bros., Inc.*)

Peckinpah knew that he would be similarly criticized, not to mention accused of jumping on a questionable bandwagon, but he went ahead anyway. Whereas Penn's film emphasized the painful aftermath of violence, Peckinpah took the tiger by the tail, determined to explore what he felt to be the real face of violence—the genuine need it appears to serve for some people.

As the film opens, a group of temperance marchers is caught in the middle of a gun battle between the law and Bishop's gang, and the marchers are impotent in the face of such violence. Unlike the scenes of violence in Penn's film, where the killing escalates with the precision of a pagan rite, Peckinpah's massacre reaches its apex with spontaneous combustion. Unable to get out of the way, the do-gooders are ravaged.

From here the wild bunch heads for Mexico and safety. Yet even when they are alone, the gang members fight among themsleves. Peckinpah, with the help of his thoroughly convincing set of actors, never lets the audience forget even for a moment that these men are *dangerous;* with them, violence is always around the corner, ready to erupt. But when Bishop and his gang meet up with Mapache even they grow uneasy, for, like Gold Hat, the instincts of the general and his men cannot be calculated.

In this measured way, the film builds inexorably to its finale, when

42

Bishop and the others strap on their guns to go fetch Angel. Like warriors, the bunch enters Mapache's compound and within seconds the carnage begins. With wild abandon, Dutch starts tossing grenades while Lyle and Tector Gorch (Warren Oates and Ben Johnson, respectively) take turns on a machine gun. Women and children are caught in the crossfire; some even take part in the fighting. Horses are stampeded by the explosions. Geysers of blood spray everywhere; bodies are torn asunder—all to the accompaniment of Lyle Gorch's frenzied screams of pain and excitement. The scene is overwhelming in its combination of horror and visceral excitement, its power drawn substantially from Peckinpah's (and editor Lou Lombardo's) use of flash cuts of real time alternated with slow motion, a cinematic technique that has since become a much overworked cliché. While serving with the marines in China during World War II, Peckinpah witnessed the death of a Chinese coolie, who had been felled by sniper fire, and recalls the moment as being "the longest split second of my life." The climactic battle (annihilation might be a better word) in *The Wild Bunch* clearly reflects this impression.

After its initial release in New York and Los Angeles in the summer of '69, Warner Bros. cut *The Wild Bunch* down from its original 148-minute running time to 135 minutes. This was done primarily to enable

Dutch (Ernest Borgnine) and Pike (William Holden) pause to catch their breath before losing their lives in the film's climactic gun battle—annihilation might be a better word. (© *Warner Bros., Inc.*)

Left: Pike (William Holden) ferociously greets his own extinction while attempting to annihilate the odds-on foe. (© *Warner Bros., Inc.*)

Opposite page: "Give 'em hell, Pike!" Dutch shouts at William Holden, who has opened fire on Mapache's army with a machine gun. Seconds later, both men will be dead, literally shot to pieces in a hailstorm of bullets. (© *Warner Bros., Inc.*)

exhibitors to squeeze in a second showing of the film each evening. Cuts included some very important flashbacks explaining the Pike Bishop/ Deke Thornton relationship as well as a major battle sequence that served to flesh out Mapache's character by revealing in him a capacity for leadership and bravery. These scenes remain, however, in the European release prints.

When it was televised nationally on CBS, *The Wild Bunch* was cut still more by the network censors, who pared the film down to 127 minutes by excising most of the graphic violence. In doing so, they rendered much of the film incomprehensible. It is this 127-minute version that subsequently went into syndication and remains the one by which most people now judge *The Wild Bunch*—regrettably. This callous treatment recalls another comment James Agee made about *The Treasure of the Sierra Madre* not long after that film was released: "And yet I doubt that many people fully realize, right away, what a sensational achievement, or plexus of achievement, it is . . . the story itself—a beauty—is not a kind which most educated people value nearly enough, today."

CHAPTER 6

The Godfather of Gore: Herschell Gordon Lewis

"Blood Feast I've often referred to as a Walt Whitman poem—it's no good, but it's the first of its type and therefore it deserves a certain position."

Herschell Gordon Lewis*

Inactive as a feature filmmaker since 1971, Chicago-based independent producer-director Herschell Gordon Lewis nevertheless holds a preeminent position as the man who brought the splatter movie into full being. He literally was *the first*. And however crude many of his films appear to us today, they remain outstanding examples of splatter cinema in its purest form.

Prior to H. G. Lewis, splatter movies had but inched forward in their march toward becoming a full-blown movie genre. After him, they seemed to mature almost overnight into a powerful source of expression (and revenue) for filmmakers everywhere. And the tide has not yet ebbed, for today Lewis's type of film is flourishing in a way that Lewis himself probably never would have thought possible, a fact that must both please and depress him—the former because it assures him of his place as a pioneer, the latter because his metier is now more closely associated with others—like George A. Romero and David Cronenberg.

A one-time professor of English at the University of Mississippi, H. G. Lewis began his career in film in the late fifties. The owner of a chain of movie theaters in the Chicago area, he also headed up his own advertising agency. Both jobs provided good experience for his future endeavors: the former revealed to him the ins and outs of film distribution and exhibition, while the latter gave him a working knowledge of film production—in the form of thirty- and sixty-second television spots produced for his various clients.

One interest fed the other until, inevitably, he decided to combine them under a single umbrella. Together with partner Dave Friedman, he formed Mid-Continent Films, and in 1960 produced his first low-budget feature film, *The Prime Time*, prints of which apparently no longer exist. The film was not a big success. Mid-Continent's second outing, *Living Venus* (1961), a *cinema à clef* that dealt with a girlie-magazine publisher patterned very loosely after *Playboy*'s Hugh Hefner, was likewise unsuccessful, though prints of it have survived. Nevertheless, *Living Venus* did spur Lewis to the realization that if he was to survive in the filmmaking business, if he was to compete successfully for theater space with Hollywood's bigger budgeted, classier, and far more professional-looking productions, then he had better develop some kind of a hook for his films—some gimmick that would pull audiences in because they couldn't get it elsewhere, not even from Hollywood. And so he began making nudies.

Lucky Pierre (1961), his first, was shot in only four days with Friedman acting as producer and soundman and Lewis as writer-director and cameraman. The film starred a local Chicago comedian named Billy Falbo, whose forte was slapstick, and, as Lewis puts it, "six of the ugliest

---

*Kings of the Bs by Todd McCarthy and Charles Flynn (New York: E.P. Dutton, 1975), page 352.

46

girls you've ever seen." When the film earned back its cost and then some, Lewis and his partner knew they were on the right track. They abandoned the idea of doing "serious" films (which, despite their many failings, both *The Prime Time* and *Living Venus* were intended to be) and became makers of exploitation films instead.

Nature's Playmates (1962), *Daughters of the Sun* (1962), *B-O-I-N-N-N-G!* (1962), and *Goldilocks and the Three Bares* (1963) followed in quick succession. But in 1963, nudity of the tame sort Lewis and Friedman had been using to sell their films had begun to creep into Hollywood's product as well. Streetwise filmmakers by now, the pair quickly perceived that a relaxation of censorship laws toward nudity and sex on the screen would soon deprive them of their competitive edge. Cued not only by the success of Hammer's modestly gruesome series of horror films, but by the success of Hitchcock's *Psycho* and its host of imitators, and by his own marketing instincts as well, Lewis decided to move in an entirely different direction. He replaced sex with gore.

Blood Feast (1963), produced, directed, photographed, and scored by Herschell Gordon Lewis, holds the distinction, however dubious, of

Say what you will about him, Lewis is not a sentimentalist. From *Blood Feast* (1963), Lewis's mindless, virtually plotless, but high-spirited orgy of gore for gore's sake. (*Courtesy Hollywood Book & Poster*)

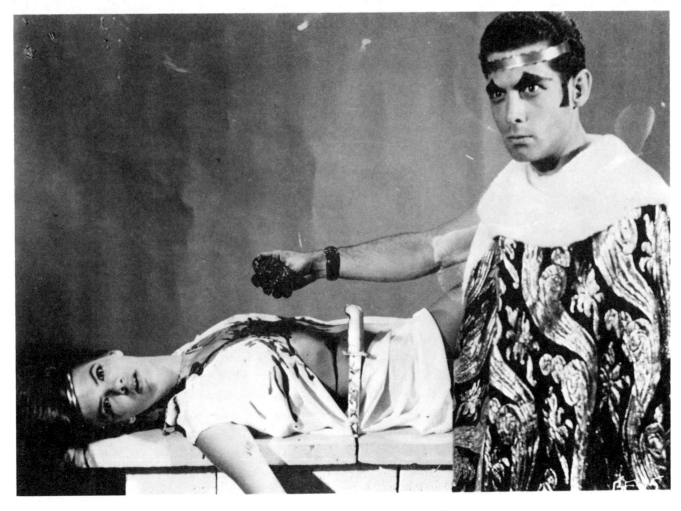

Blood Feast (1963) holds the distinction, however dubious, of being the cinema's first full-fledged splatter movie. Here a girl's brains have been torn out. (*Courtesy Hollywood Book & Poster*)

being the cinema's first full-fledged splatter movie, though Lewis himself refers to it as a "gore film," which amounts to the same thing. Filmed in only nine days on location in Miami for well under $70,000, the film deals with the revivification of a long-dead Egyptian princess by a lunatic who thinks he's a sort of modern Dr. Frankenstein.

Spinning off somewhat from Hammer's Frankenstein films, Lewis has his madman "hero" collect the spare parts he needs for the job not from any morgue or graveyard but from a number of voluptuous young girls who are still quite alive and breathing. In fact, so zealous is this nut to replace his princess's moldy old parts with new ones that he doesn't even wait for his victims to die before he starts ripping off limbs and scooping out internal organs. In medium shot and, for the most part, without editing, Lewis reveals to us how to rip a girl's tongue out of her head. He also shows us another girl's brains being torn out, and still other flesh and blood female "puppets" are sequentially hacked to shreds in all kinds of ways. Say what you will about him, Lewis is not a sentimentalist.

As Lewis intended, *Blood Feast* was a mindless, virtually plotless, but high-spirited orgy of gore for gore's sake, which, upon its initial release to drive-ins in the South, managed to shock both the popcorn-eaters and the neckers alike into wide-eyed, openmouthed attention. Its effects had never been seen before in a commercial feature film.

Scorned by furious critics who deemed the film "amateur night at the butcher shop," *Blood Feast* nevertheless went on to become Lewis's first huge success and his biggest hit ever. It was followed by *2000 Maniacs* (1964), a bigger-budgeted, more serious effort on Lewis's part, which tells the story of a Southern town ravaged by Yankee troops during the Civil War that claims its revenge a hundred years later when its citizens kill and dismember a group of tourists visiting from the North. One sees in the story line revenge that breaks the barriers of time in ironic fashion—a hazy reflection of Rod Serling's television series *The Twilight Zone*, which seems to have had some influence on Lewis in the way that he occasionally blends a basically science fiction theme with a supernatural one. *The Twilight Zone* influence would crop up again two years later in *Monster-A-Go-Go* (1965), a film about an American astronaut who returns to earth as an overgrown radioactive monster, and in *The Wizard of Gore* (1971), which deals with a magician whose bloody stage illusions become equally grisly realities hours after they have been performed.

Lewis went all out in promoting *2000 Maniacs*, even to the extent of writing a novelization of his screenplay, which was eventually published to tie in with the film's release. But for some reason the public did not respond to *2000 Maniacs* as strongly as it had to *Blood Feast*. In fact, not until the release of *She-Devils on Wheels* in 1968, a film about an all-girl gang of motorcyclists who, perhaps responding to *Blood Feast*'s overt sexism, decapitate and mutilate only men, would another Lewis gore film hit the jackpot at the box office. But by then Lewis had dissolved his partnership with Dave Friedman and was making films on his own. Friedman meanwhile went on to become president of the Adult Film Association of America and a distributor of porno films and videocassettes.

Southern hospitality from *2000 Maniacs* (1964), a bigger-budgeted, more serious film according to Lewis. (*Courtesy Hollywood Book & Poster*)

Left: These two are a real barrel of laughs—though not to the guy inside the barrel. Notice the absurdly fiendish grins on their faces, a Lewis trademark. (*Courtesy Hollywood Book & Poster*)

Below: More southern hospitality from *2000 Maniacs* (1964). (*Courtesy Hollywood Book & Poster*)

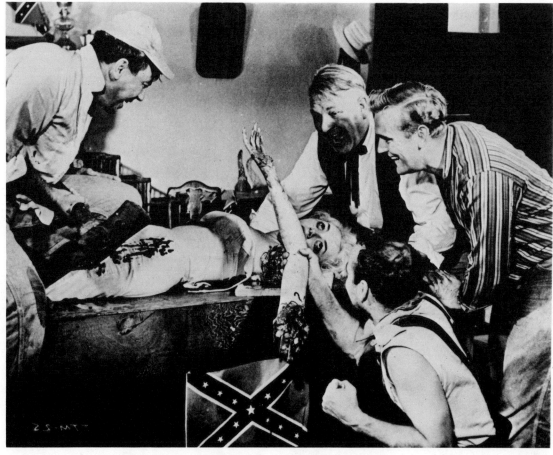

It is indeed ironic that while Lewis's films proved a potent influence in setting the ground rules to be followed by today's plethora of splatter movies, Lewis himself never rose above his position as a loner on the edge of cinema's lunatic fringe. As a director, he has never been considered seriously—except in France, of course, where just about everyone gets exalted by the critics at one time or another (especially if his films are banned there, which Lewis's were as late as 1975).

Lewis's last gore film, *The Gore Gore Girls* (a.k.a *Blood Orgy*, 1971), is almost as crudely acted as his first. Technically, however, many of his films possess the polish of a competent made-for-TV movie. Lewis's modern Dracula story, *A Taste of Blood* (1967), for example, won for Lewis an invitation of work from Roger Corman. And *She-Devils on Wheels* was almost picked up for distribution by American International until Lewis's partner, producer Fred Sandy, nixed the deal.

Due to budgetary limitations, Lewis was frequently forced to shoot many of his sequences silently, adding music or voluminous quantities of narration later to cover the lack of sound. Lighting for night scenes was often accomplished using one or possibly two photofloods. He was seldom able to use any camera movements except for an occasional pan. And sound effects that were post-synchronized onto the track later were occasionally over-amplified. Sometimes, a sound effect was even left out. This occurs specifically in *Monster-A-Go-Go*—a film credited to director Bill Rebane (*The Giant Spider Invasion*, 1975), but which also bears the stamp of its producer and additional dialogue writer Sheldon Seymour (Lewis)—when, at one point, an overzealous army colonel scrambles to answer a phone that isn't even ringing.

Monster-A-Go-Go is a bad-movie junkie's dream, for it is awful in almost every way, a fact due in large part to the unusual circumstances under which the film came about. Lewis describes the situation this way: "*Monster-A-Go-Go* was eighty thousand feet of film I bought from Bill Rebane, figuring there had to be a feature in there somewhere. Bill had blown his brains out on this picture (shot in glorious black and white), cut off the slates, and given up. I picked it up as a second half for *Moonshine Mountain* (1965). I was wrong. There wasn't a picture in there. We shot some close-ups to make it releasable. Surely, I wouldn't have excreted a film with that plot line starting from scratch."

The reason why Lewis foisted *Monster-A-Go-Go* on the filmgoing public when even he knew it was an embarrassingly dreadful bomb derives from his greatest weakness as a filmmaker, as well as his greatest virtue as a businessman. Quite simply, he would release anything in order to recoup his investment. "Herschell had the capacity to do a good job," says Dan Krogh, who worked as an assistant to Lewis on such extravaganzas as *The Wizard of Gore* and *The Gore Gore Girls*. "He *knew* how to do a good job, but at a certain point, he was a financial pragmatist. If it meant getting the film done or not getting it done, he would rather have a halfway goofed up job than no job at all. In other words, when the chips were down, it was *any* way to get an image on film, *any* image. But if he had the time and the resources—actors who were pretty good, a good script, then I think he had the capacity to be very good. You must understand that for Herschell, professionalism has as much to do with bringing a picture in at or below budget and making money at the box office as it does with artistry. That these films *always* turned a profit was what he was most proud of."

As for the quality of the acting in Lewis's films, well, the less said about that the better; even Lewis admits that solid acting is not one of the hallmarks of his work, as his casts are most often made up of friends, relatives, ex-Playboy bunnies, Playmates-of-the-Month, and other non-professionals. Lewis himself even appears in a featured role in *A Taste of Blood*, posing as, of all things, an Englishman. This came about when the actor he'd originally signed for the part, another non-professional, failed to appear for shooting.

"Lewis used to get all sorts of things for nothing, not just actors," says Dan Krogh. "The way he would do this was by acting much more big-time than he actually was. People would let us shoot in their homes for nothing, supply us with things. Even the police departments cooperated with us. Herschell used to say that he'd never use actors to play cops in his films because real cops were cheaper.

"The weird thing that strikes me about Lewis all the time is the fact that because he did things so cheaply, there is this incredible amount of physical or objective realism about his films. There's never a set—or hardly ever. If you see two guys talking about dismembered bodies in a fried chicken restaurant, well, that's a real fried chicken restaurant, and you can bet that besides being allowed to shoot in there for nothing, he probably got the owner to cater lunch for the whole crew for the two weeks of shooting."

One significant result of Lewis's devil-may-care attitude toward filmmaking, however, is that his films appear more outrageous than either shocking or offensive. Possessed of a sharp sense of humor about his work (responding to a film magazine's suggestion that his work was a subject worthy of further research, Lewis remarked that the same could also be said of cancer), Lewis imbues his films with an offbeat sense of the absurd. It's as if, knowing that his work is schlock, he calls deliberate attention to the fact, serving up dialogue that is intentionally ridiculous and situations that are so excessive in their bloodthirstiness that they too seem ridiculous.

Monster-A-Go-Go, which borrows its "plot" quite liberally from Hammer's *The Creeping Unknown* and MGM's *First Man into Space* (1959), offered audiences a ten-foot-high radioactive monster (played by an actor with the improbable name of Henry Hite) who sucks the life out of earthlings, leaving them with faces resembling dried prunes in the

"Take *that*, you hussy!" Backwoods justice dispensed Lewis style in *Moonshine Mountain* (1965). (*Courtesy Daniel Krogh*)

throes of a scream. At one point in the drama, the off-screen narrator clues the audience in on all the action that's been happening behind the scenes with this typically Lewisian monologue:

"Dr. Logan did know where the giant was—in a storeroom in that very building. Logan had learned that massive doses of the antidote brought about an almost human appearance, but with such unpredictable side effects that enough tranquilizers to subdue ten ordinary men had to be given each day. This day it was late. Logan knew that each passing minute might mean a return to violence. As it turned out, he was too late. Like his brother, the scientist had an intuitive knowledge of the situation. *Thus an extraordinarily bad sense of timing.*"

One does not need to be a film critic to realize that Lewis is sending his film up in this ridiculous monologue. Likewise, the orgies of gore in *Blood Feast* and his other films serve much the same purpose. They defuse these films of their psychological grimness, turning them into exercises in outrageousness and absurdity. If it weren't for this sense of their own absurdity, in fact, Lewis's films would be little more than Nazi death camp films re-staged as entertainment. Audiences will accept quite a lot from splatter movies, but they will not accept being psychologically trampled by them—at least not repeatedly. Lewis understood this from the start and in his films he seemed to be saying that realism has its

Religious symbolism? Nope. Just a little vengeful sport from Lewis's *This Stuff'll Kill Ya!* (1971). (*Courtesy Daniel Krogh*)

limits, folks. Go too far with it, and it ceases to be realism at all. Dan Krogh confirms this: "Herschell's attitude towards his films and his audiences was always very good-natured. I remember being in the screening room looking at the rushes of *The Gore Gore Girls* with him and him chuckling and saying, 'Well, that'll make 'em sick out in the drive-ins.' But it wasn't a malevolent attitude at all. He never *really* wanted to make anybody sick. Behind his films, there was always a very sly smile."

Lewis's very clear and intuitive message about the limited effectiveness of showing graphically violent events on the screen would not be lost on George A. Romero, as we shall see in the next chapter. If splatter cinema were to continue to develop, it would require something more than realism alone to sell itself. Otherwise, it would soon repel audiences rather than draw them in. Here, too, Herschell Gordon Lewis pointed the way. Ironically, he would never really gain from his insight, as his mantle would soon fall to others. As the genre grew, he would, like Hammer Films, lose the power to compete.

Very few of today's splatter moviemakers acknowledge their debt to Lewis—most, in fact, don't even acknowledge his existence. One who does, however, and does so with gusto, is Baltimore's John Waters, the bad-boy director of such notorious splatter hits as *Pink Flamingos* (1972) and *Female Trouble* (1974). Water's films are also notable for their outrageousness and absurdity, not to mention their cheerful bad taste. He makes, he says, exploitation films for the art house crowd. And in his engaging, offbeat, and frequently hilarious autobiography, *Shock Value*, he makes no bones about the affection he holds for the work of the Godfather of Gore. "I discovered his monstrous trilogy, *Blood Feast*, *2000 Maniacs*, and *Color Me Blood Red*, at my local drive-in," Waters says. "And when I saw teenage couples hopping from their cars to vomit, I knew I had found a director after my own heart." Waters later went on to pay homage to the work of Lewis in a film called *Multiple Maniacs* (1970), a splatter-filled satire on the Manson family that starred Waters's favorite leading "lady," a 300-pound actor and female impersonator named Divine.

After murdering her husband, Divine goes totally nuts and is raped by a fifteen-foot lobster. Here's the aftermath . . . from *Multiple Maniacs* (1970), John Waters's salute to the films of Herschell Gordon Lewis. (© *1970 New Line Cinema*)

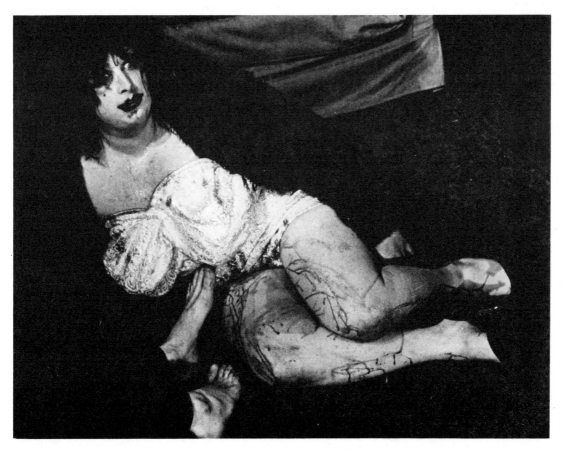

55

The Splatter Movies
of Herschell Gordon Lewis

Blood Feast (1963)
A Friedman-Lewis Production (Box
Office Spectaculars)/Color/75 minutes
Producer: David F. Friedman
Director/Photographer: Herschell Gordon
Lewis
Screenplay: Allison Louise Downe
Editing: Robert Sinise, Frank Romolo
Music: Herschell Gordon Lewis
Cast: Connie Mason, Thomas Wood, Mal
Arnold, Lyn Bolton, Scott H. Hall, Toni
Calvert

2000 Maniacs (1964)
A Friedman-Lewis Production (Box
Office Spectaculars)/Color/75 minutes
Producer/Art Director: David F. Friedman
Director/Photographer/Writer: Herschell
Gordon Lewis
Editing: Robert Sinise
Music: Larry Wellington and The Pleasant
Valley Boys
Cast: Connie Mason, Thomas Wood,
Jeffrey Allen, Ben Moore, Shelby
Livingston, Vincent Santo, Gary
Bakeman, Mark Douglas, Michael Korb

Color Me Blood Red (1964)
A Box Office Spectaculars Production/
Color/74 minutes
Producer: David F. Friedman
Director/Photographer/Writer: Herschell
Gordon Lewis
Assistant Photographer: Andy Romanoff
Editing: Robert Sinise
Cast: Don Joseph, Candi Conder, Scott
H. Hall, Elyn Warner, Patricia Lee,
Jerome Eden, Jim Jaekel

Monster-A-Go-Go (1965)
a.k.a. *Terror at Halfday*/B.I.&L.
Releasing Corp./B & W/70 minutes
Producer/Additional Dialogue Writer:
Sheldon Seymour (H.G. Lewis)
Director: Bill Rebane
Screenplay: Jeff Smith, Bill Rebane, Don
Stanford
Photographer: Frank Pfeiffer
Cast: Phil Morton, June Travis, George
Perry, Lois Brooke, Henry Hite

Moonshine Mountain (1965)
B.I. & L. Releasing Corp./B & W/
Producer/Director: Herschell Gordon
Lewis

Writer: Charles Glore
Production Manager: Andy Romanoff
Assistant Director: J. G. Patterson, Jr.
Editing: Robert Sinise & Ron Closky
Crew Chief: Bob Vercruse
Cast: Chuck Scott, Adam Sorg, Jeffrey
Allen, Bonnie Hinson, Carmen Sotir, Ben
Moore, Pat Patterson, Mark Douglas,
Karin March, Gretchen Eisner

The Gruesome Twosome (1966)
A Mayflower Production
Executive Producer: Fred M. Sandy
Producer/Director/Photographer: Herschell
Gordon Lewis
Screenplay: Allison Louise Downe
Music: Larry Wellington
Cast: Elizabeth David, Chris Martel,
Gretchen Welles, Rodney Bedell

Something Weird (1966)
A Mayflower Production/B & W/83
minutes
Producer/Writer: James F. Hurley
Director: Herschell Gordon Lewis
Photographer: Andy Romanoff
Cast: Tony McCabe, Elizabeth Lee,
William Brooker

A Taste of Blood (1967)
a.k.a. *The Secret of Dr. Alucard*/An
Alucard Production/Color/120 minutes
Executive Producer: Sidney J. Reich
Producer/Director: Herschell Gordon
Lewis
Screenplay: Donald Stanford
Photographer: Andy Romanoff
Editing: Richard Brinkman
Music: Larry Wellington
Cast: Bill Rogers, Elizabeth Wilkinson,
Thomas Wood, Otto Schlesinger, Eleanor
Valli, Lawrence Tobin, H. G. Lewis

She-Devils on Wheels (1968)
A Mayflower Production/Color/83
minutes
Executive Producer: Fred M. Sandy
Producer/Director: Herschell Gordon
Lewis
Screenplay: Allison Louise Downe
Photographer: Ray Collodi
Editing: Richard Brinkman
Music: Robert Lewis, Sheldon Seymour
(H. G. Lewis)
Cast: Betty Connell, Pat Poston, Nancy
Lee Noble, Christie Wagner, Rodney
Bedell, Ruby Tuesday, John Weymer

The Wizard of Gore (1968)
A Mayflower Production/Color/96
minutes
Producer: Fred M. Sandy
Director: Herschell Gordon Lewis
Screenplay: Allen Kahn
Photographer/Editor: Eskandar Ameripoor
Music: Larry Wellington
Cast: Ray Sager, Judy Cler, Wayne Ratay,
Phil Laurensen, Jim Rau, John Elliott,
Don Alexander

The Gore Gore Girls (1971)
a.k.a. *Blood Orgy*/A Lewis Motion Picture
Enterprises Production/ Color/ 90 minutes
Producer/Director: Herschell Gordon
Lewis
Screenplay: Alan Dachman
Photographer/Editor: Eskandar Ameripoor
Music: Sheldon Seymour (H. G. Lewis)
Cast: Frank Kress, Amy Farell, Hedda
Lubin, Russ Badger, Nora Alexis, Phil
Laurensen, Frank Rice, Ray Sager,
Henny Youngman

This Stuff'll Kill Ya! (1971)
Ultima Productions, Inc./Color/100
minutes
Producer/Director/Writer: Herschell
Gordon Lewis
Associate Producer: Allison Louise Downe
Assistant Director: Raymond Szegho
Production Manager: John Sezonov
Editing: Alex Ameripoor
Photographer: Eskandar Ameripoor
Second Unit Photographer: Daniel Krogh
Crew Chief: Scott Kranzberg
Sound Recordist: Paul Dickinson
Cast: Jeffrey Allen, Tim Holt, Gloria
King, Ray Sager, Erich Bradley, Terrence
McCarthy, Ronna Riddle, Larry Drake,
John Garner, Bill Mays

Opposite page: Responding, perhaps, to
the overt sexism of Lewis's previous
films, the girls start to get even in *She-
Devils on Wheels* (1968), the story of an
all-girl gang of motorcyclists that calls
itself "The Man-Eaters." The film
turned out to be Lewis's biggest box
office success since *Blood Feast* (1963),
proving, after all, that there really is a
market out there for women's pictures.
(*Courtesy Movie Star News*)

CHAPTER 7

The Dawn of Romero

"Just because I'm showing somebody being disemboweled doesn't mean I have to get heavy with a message."

George A. Romero*

EC horror comics remain a profound influence on Romero, as this cover of EC's *Vault of Horror* comic clearly shows. (© 1983 William M. Gaines)

The release of George A. Romero's independently made *Night of the Living Dead* in 1968 ushered in the era of splatter cinema. It also ushered in the era of the filmed comic book, for in Romero's hands the two became synonymous.

Romero perceived very early on in his career, as Herschell Lewis had before him, that graphic violence portrayed on the screen with unrelenting seriousness and unflinching realism produced a negative effect on an audience rather than a positive one. It seemed that when coupled with scenes of hideous violence stretched forty feet or more in width over a huge screen (and in stereophonic sound), *Grand Guignol*'s themes of heartlessness and unrelieved terror began to turn an audience off psychologically, not on. It became clear to him then that if splatter cinema were to continue to evolve as a significant sub-genre of the horror film, if realism itself were to continue to be employed and even expanded upon by directors as a powerful cinematic tool, then the negative factors implicit in splatter cinema had to be fashioned into positive ones. Lewis had tried to achieve this feat with the self-mocking crudity of his films. Romero, in every way the superior craftsman, sought a different approach.

For many contemporary American fantasy writers and filmmakers who spent their adolescence during the fifties, William M. Gaines's EC horror comics *(Tales from the Crypt, Vault of Horror,* and so on) remain not only a vivid memory, but a potent creative influence. Certainly this is true of the forty-four-year-old Romero.

Published for a brief time during the fifties, EC horror comics were eventually put out of business when their flamboyantly grisly content and frequently graphic scenes of gore began to arouse the ire of parents and the concern of the Comics Code Authority. Innocent enough by today's standards, EC horror comics were then considered to be exerting a harmful effect on the youth that read them. Juvenile delinquency, then on the rise in America, was believed to be an alarming confirmation of this. A scapegoat was needed and everything from rock'n'roll to television to movies to poor old EC horror comics was blamed. Only EC horror comics succumbed, however. Now, a quarter of a century later, they are back. Not on the printed page, but on the big screen—in the form of splatter movies. And George Romero is the man chiefly responsible for their resurrection.

Born in the Bronx in 1940, George A. Romero is a bonafide member of the film generation, having made his first 8-mm films while still in his teens. He went on to Carnegie-Mellon Institute to study art, design, and theater, graduating in 1961 with a B.A. He has remained in Pittsburgh ever since, finding the area far more receptive to his independent style of filmmaking than the more corporate climes of Hollywood.

---

*"Dawn of the Dead," by David Bartholomew, *Cinefantastique*, Vol. 9, No. 4, page 78.

Above: The Silent Majority finally goes on the march in *Night of the Living Dead* (1968), Romero's Agnew-era horror film debut. (© *Laurel Entertainment*)

Left: Splatter master George A. Romero (left) and his literary counterpart, best-selling novelist Stephen King, on the set of their first collaboration, *Creepshow* (1982). (© *Warner Bros., Inc.*)

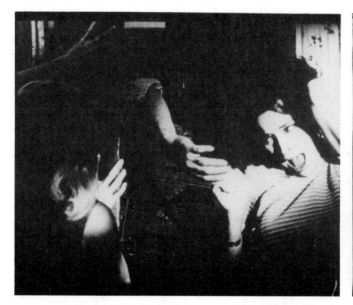

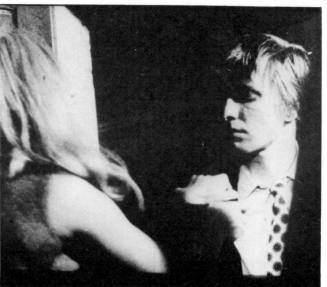

60

Like Herschell Lewis, Romero began his career in advertising. His Pittsburgh-based company, Latent Image, was geared to the production of industrial films and television commercials. In 1967, however, he teamed Latent Image with another Pittsburgh advertising firm, Hardman Associates, to produce a low-budget, feature-length horror film that he hoped would serve as his ticket into the film industry.

A number of ideas as well as titles *(The Flesh Eaters, Night of the Flesh Eaters, Night of Anubis)* were tossed about before Romero and his associates finally struck upon the ideal story line and approach for their film, which would eventually be called *Night of the Living Dead.*

Significantly, the story line Romero and his group came up with—a small band of humans, survivors of some mysterious plague that has animated the corpses of the dead, fight to save themselves from their blood-drinking, flesh-eating attackers—borrowed liberally from Richard Matheson's novel *I Am Legend* without crediting it as a source. Not until after the film's release, in fact, would Romero or his co-writer, John A. Russo, acknowledge their debt to Matheson's book. This policy of ripping off ideas or whole scenes from other people's books and films as a method of dispensing with plot in order to concentrate more readily on effects would become standard operating procedure for splatter moviemakers in the years to follow. Romero's film can perhaps be excused for having helped inaugurate the process if only because it remains the best "unofficial" version of Matheson's book yet filmed. The two official adaptations, *Last Man on Earth* (1964) and *The Omega Man* (1971), were artistic as well as commercial duds by comparison.

While a number of hands had an influence in the making of *Night of the Living Dead,* including producers Karl Hardman and Russell Streiner, each of whom played roles in the film, Romero's influence remains the most profound. He not only co-wrote the film, he directed, photographed, and edited it. And by his own admission, what emerged was exactly what he had intended—an EC horror comic on film. Even the absurdly lurid title was a throwback to those that had appeared in the comic books.

Romero spent little time in the film explaining either the genesis of the epidemic that has brought the dead to life or how it works. In keeping with the pace of EC horror comics, he merely unleashed the horrors and allowed the action to begin at first frame.

When the film was released it caused a modest stir in the press. *Variety*'s reviewer, for example, was appalled not just by the film's graphic gore, but by what he called its "amateurism of the first order." Scenes in the film of grotesquely decaying zombies scooping up human entrails and devouring them elicited sharp attacks from local newspaper critics all across the country as well. Still, the film had a very successful initial engagement, playing almost exclusively at drive-ins, not just in the South, but all over the country. Then it found its real home: indoor theaters coast-to-coast began playing it on Friday and Saturday nights as a midnight show. At one theater in Boston, for example, *Night* played in this manner for two solid years. Ticket sales spiraled and the film became a cult favorite. It also began to garner good reviews, particularly in Europe, where the prestigious *Sight and Sound* magazine published by the British Film Institute cited it as one of the ten best films of the year. Romero was off and running. His first time at bat, he had hit a home run.

Disinclined, despite many pressures, to do a sequel right away, or even another horror film, Romero decided to abandon the EC horror comics/splatter approach altogether and opted for a straight love story, a romantic comedy called *There's Always Vanilla* (a.k.a. *The Affair*, 1971), which he also filmed in Pittsburgh. The film was a resounding financial flop—as well as an artistic one, as Romero himself admits.

His next film, *Jack's Wife* (1972), another non-splatter film that had some occult overtones, was picked up for distribution by Jack *(The Blob)* Harris, who then re-cut the film and retitled it *Hungry Wives* for quick payoff. It too died at the box office.

With *The Crazies* (1973), Romero returned somewhat to the formula that had made his first film such a huge success. The plot—a chemical agent designed to produce madness is being developed by the U.S. Army as a weapon and is accidentally dumped in a community's water supply—is a straight live-action comic book, recalling not only EC horror comics, but some of EC's other publications as well, including *Weird Fantasy* and *Weird Science*. Working with a bigger budget and using color for the first time, Romero kept the pace of the film just as frantic as *Night*'s had been. Technically much slicker than any of Romero's first three films, certainly more so than *Night of the Living Dead, The Crazies* was nevertheless very unevenly acted (a failing even of Romero's later films) and, worse still, devoid of either cohesiveness or tension. It did receive wider distribution and promotion than either *There's Always Vanilla* or *Jack's Wife*, but it still lost money. Retitled *Code Name Trixie*, it was quickly sold to television, where it now turns up from time to time on the late, late, late show.

With one hit behind him and three flops, Romero was no longer leading a charmed life. Financing was not so readily available, and so he devoted more of his time to advertising work. The same year *The Crazies* was released and died, however, Romero's luck took a turn for the better. He met and formed a partnership with a New York stockbroker named Richard Rubinstein. The association would eventually prove quite fortuitous.

Calling their new company the Laurel Group, Romero and Rubinstein proceeded to develop a series of sports-related documentaries, profiles of athletes such as Reggie Jackson, which they succeeded in selling to network TV. Flush once again, Romero then decided to tackle another horror film, this time with Rubinstein acting as producer. It was

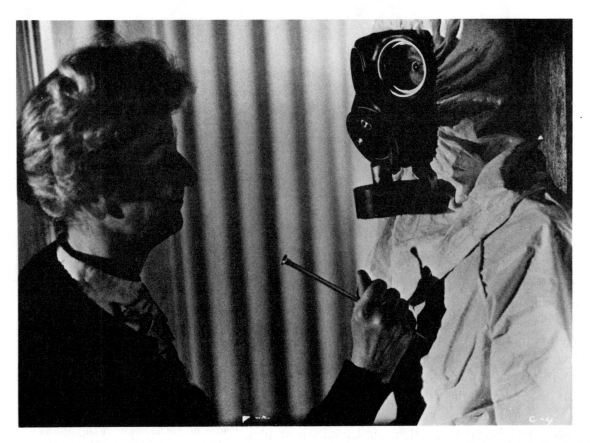

Romero's *The Crazies* (1973) reflected an image of America's Vietnam war experience on the homefront as viewed through a funhouse mirror. (*Courtesy Cinemabilia, Inc.*)

to be a modern vampire story, again in the EC mold and again liberally laced with splatter. He called it *Martin*.

Martin was completed in 1976 but did not secure American distribution until two years later. In Europe, however, where it got widespread distribution strictly on the basis of Romero's name and the still-potent reputation of his *Night of the Living Dead, Martin* netted Romero his best reviews, as well as his best box office, since *Night*.

Martin is a most untraditional vampire story, though all the traditional trappings of the genre are present in it—garlic cloves, crosses, wooden stakes, and so on. By film's end, we still don't know if Martin (John Amplas) is truly a vampire of the supernatural variety or just a psycho youth with a yen for blood. Martin himself doesn't even seem to know the answer, for at one point he claims to be older than Tati Cuda (Lincoln Maazel), the relative who has taken him in as a boarder, but at other times he admits that "there is no magic" at the root of his condition. He is simply driven, for whatever reason, to sedate his victims with a needle, slash them with a razor blade, then drink their blood. Whatever the explanation for his sickness, Martin does have a sense of humor about it. Because the superstitious Cuda firmly believes him to be a *nosferatu* out of folklore, Martin occasionally plays up to the old man, taunting him by donning a cape and snapping a set of store-bought fangs at him. On the whole though, *Martin* is no joke.

Despite its EC horror comics intonations, Romero's film has an almost clinical air to it, somewhat like *Jack's Wife*. It is also a very brooding film (on the order of Roman Polanski's *Repulsion* [1965]), a study of loneliness and breeding psychosis set against the background of a decaying Pennsylvania manufacturing town called Braddock, where even the church has decided it's time to pull up and move on. Braddock is the perfect place for a psycho like Martin to prey on, for there is no longer any spiritual strength present to thwart him. In the end, only Cuda recognizes him for the monster that he genuinely is. And even Cuda, perhaps, has done so for all the wrong reasons.

Even before *Martin* had finally gained American distribution, Romero and Rubinstein had begun preparation on Laurel's next film, Romero's long-avoided sequel to *Night of the Living Dead*. Released in the spring of 1979, eleven years after the debut of *Night*, *Dawn of the Dead* became Romero's biggest box-office hit ever, putting him over the top as the most successful as well as the most well-known American filmmaker working outside the Hollywood system. He is determined to maintain that status. His most recent films, *Knightriders* (1981) and *Creepshow* (1982), were again made entirely in the Pittsburgh area.

As I have written in the introduction to this book, Romero's splatter movies possess an underlying layer of social satire that separates his work from and makes it more interesting than that of most of his contemporaries. This does not mean, however, that his films are any more serious. *Dawn of the Dead* pokes fun at our age of consumerism by pushing the implications of that lust to its grotesquely absurd limits. And *The Crazies* does reflect an image of America's Vietnam War experience on the homefront as viewed through a funhouse mirror. But that's the extent of the social implications of these films. Despite their flamboyant grisliness, they remain only playful exercises. In no way can they be viewed as the political films many critics portray them to be—and Romero would be the first to admit it. Robert Aldrich's *Twilight's Last Gleaming* (1977) is a political film disguised as a thriller. *Night of the Living Dead*, despite its engaging implications of what would happen if Spiro Agnew's Silent Majority ever did go on the march, is not. Romero's films are live-action comic books, and the satire in them is precisely of the comic book

Above, left: A haunting shot of the vampire youth (John Amplas) in *Martin* (1978), the first Romero/Rubinstein collaboration. (© 1977 Braddock Associates)

Above, right: The requisite cross is wielded against the vampire by Tati Cuda (Lincoln Maazel) in *Martin* (1978). (© 1977 Braddock Associates)

Opposite page, above: Sexual psychopath, confused youth, or vampire? Probably a little of each, Romero seems to be telling us in his modern vampire tale, *Martin* (1978). (© 1977 Braddock Associates)

Opposite page, below: Another victim of the vampire in *Martin* (1978), the film that netted Romero his best reviews, as well as his best box office since *Night of the Living Dead* (1968). (© 1977 Braddock Associates)

Above: Consumerism pushed to its grotesquely absurd limits in Romero's *Dawn of the Dead* (1979), the film that finally put him over the top as an established and sought after independent filmmaker. (© *Dawn Associates, 1978/K. Kolbert*)

Right: Special effects for *Dawn of the Dead* (1979). A zombie's blood bag is wired to explode on cue. (© *Dawn Associates, 1978/K. Kolbert*)

Opposite page: Romero's sense of the absurd is evidenced by this shot from *Dawn of the Dead* (1979) in which the heroine arms to the teeth to protect herself against a nun with a very bad habit—cannibalism. (© *Dawn Associates, 1978/K. Kolbert*)

66

variety. He did not coin the term "splatter cinema" to describe his own *oeuvre* for nothing. The term rings with a lighthearted absurdism that the term *gore film* simply does not. With *Dawn of the Dead* particularly, Romero turned the entire notion of realism in films inside out, rendering realism, through excess, patently unrealistic.

The violence in *Dawn of the Dead* is so broad, in fact, that it comes across almost like slapstick, the difference being that instead of taking pies in the face, the butts of Romero's mayhem get shot, decapitated, or run over. At the same time, however, there is one scene in which Romero actually does let his zombies take pies in the face—hurled at them by members of a marauding gang of motorcyclists. Completely unexpected, this very telling scene is a comic gem, summing up perfectly the spirit in which Romero obviously wants the entire film to be taken.

Romero's first-time-out success with *Night of the Living Dead* served as an inspiration for beginning filmmakers everywhere. If he could do it, so could they. And so *Night* imitations popped up everywhere, rivaled in number only by those imitations that have followed the recent release of John Carpenter's even more successful, independently made, *Halloween*. Two of *Night*'s spawns stand out, however, not only as barometers of how much influence Romero's approach to making splatter movies was to have in the coming years, but as studies in contrasts as well. They are Wes Craven's *Last House on the Left* (1973) and Tobe Hooper's *The Texas Chainsaw Massacre* (1975).

Left: Even the fanzines hated Wes Craven's newsreel-like tale of rape, murder, and revenge, *Last House on the Left* (1972)—the only splatter movie on record to claim Ingmar Bergman as its source of inspiration. (*Courtesy Larry Edmunds Bookshop*)

Right: Hard place to keep clean, huh? Dig the armchair in the background. It's literally just that. From Tobe Hooper's successfully EC-ish *The Texas Chainsaw Massacre* (1975). (© *New Line Cinema*)

Craven's first feature, written by himself and newcomer Sean *(Friday the 13th)* Cunningham, lifted its plot from Ingmar Bergman's lugubrious medieval tale of rape and revenge, *The Virgin Spring* (1960). Shot in Connecticut, the film was updated to the present. A trio of degenerate thugs rape and murder a young girl in the woods. Later, the girl's parents entice the killers into their home for the express purpose of revenge. The father slaughters two of his victims with a chainsaw. The mother castrates the third with her teeth and allows him to bleed to death.

Devoid of Romero's comic book approach and redeeming sense of humor, *Last House on the Left,* shot in color and blown up from 16mm, has the gritty look of a newsreel and is a complete downer. Craven wanted not only the explicit violence but the entire atmosphere of his film to be almost too painful for the audience to endure. He succeeded. The film is psychologically repulsive in a way that Romero's films are not. Promoted heavily by its distributor, Hallmark Releasing, *Last House on the Left* did meet with some commercial success. But the reviews were scathing. Even the fanzines called it "foul-minded," "sick," and "loathesome." Craven learned from this lesson and adopted the Romero approach for his next splatter film, *The Hills Have Eyes* (1977), which intermingled the grotesque with the absurd in true EC horror comics style.

Tobe Hooper's *The Texas Chainsaw Massacre* (1975), in contrast, adopted the Romero approach right off and achieved by far the greater success of the two films—even garnering some good reviews. Loosely based on the true story of Wisconsin mass murderer Ed Gein, the cannibal-killer whose exploits also served as the basis for Robert Bloch's novel *Psycho, Chainsaw* is nowhere near as splatter-filled as its title would suggest. This is Hooper's cleverest ploy. The title alone has the audience cringing before it enters the theater.

Instead of one cannibal-killer, Hooper offers four, three of them brothers, the fourth their blood-sucking skeleton of a grandfather who lives with them in an out-of-the-way farmhouse that is filled with the bones and flesh of the quartet's past victims. An armchair located in the living room of the farmhouse, for example, is literally just that—which indicates just how closely Hooper was following in Romero's footsteps. Hooper's subsequent films followed this ghoulishly humorous approach as well. *Eaten Alive* (1976), *Salem's Lot* (made for television, 1980), *Funhouse* (1981), and *Poltergeist* (1982), all bear the unmistakable stamp of the very same source that gave rise to the dawn of Romero himself: William M. Gaines's EC horror comics.

Romero's greatest weakness, apart from the generally low caliber of

Shades of Romero? Only on the surface. From *Zombie* (1980), directed by Lucio Fulci, Italy's reigning king of spaghetti splatter. (© *The Jerry Gross Organization*)

Aunt Bedelia (Viveca Lindfors) takes part in a grisly Father's Day celebration in the opening segment of Romero's *Creepshow* (1982). (© *Warner Bros., Inc.*)

the acting in some of his films, is his inclination to write his own scripts. He is a director of great imagination and remarkable ingenuity, as well as being a superb editor, but he lacks the writer's instincts for strong character development, cohesive plotting, and dialogue that is both representative of the characters who speak it and vital to the momentum of the plot itself. His best-written film to date is *Night of the Living Dead*. Significantly, the screenplay of that film, though based on a story by Romero, was written by a professional writer, John A. Russo, who has since established a reputation in his own right as the author of a number of well received though minor horror novels, including *Midnight, The Majorettes, Limb to Limb,* and *Black Cat.*

Romero's weakness for writing his own scripts may be the result of something more than ego or carelessness, however. He shares this flaw with many of today's younger directors, all of whom are a part of the same film generation to which Romero himself belongs. The cause of the problem may very well lie in the belief most members of this group hold that the director is the person chiefly responsible for how a film looks, how it moves, and, above all, what it says; that he or she is the film's *auteur.* Undeniably, this belief is valid. Its general acceptance, in fact, among not just film directors but critics as well, has helped to fashion an aesthetic focal point for the art of film appreciation that was badly needed. Still, it does have a negative aspect, for what it has done is to push many of today's young and even established directors into becoming excessively credit-conscious. The urge to write as well as direct their own scripts so as to firmly establish authorship beyond all question has become of paramount importance to many of them, regardless of how their films are affected. Romero is as much a victim of this urge as he is guilty of it.

Still, there is hope for him. His much-publicized alliance with best-selling novelist Stephen King on a number of projects to be directed by Romero but written by King over the next decade suggests that he is not unaware of his limitations as a writer-director. On the surface, this pairing seems ideal, for King's own work *(Carrie, Salem's Lot, The Dead Zone)* is as heavily influenced by EC horror comics as Romero's is. King, an excellent storyteller, is superb at creating characters who breathe, which Romero is not. Likewise, whereas King's work often lacks originality and surprise, Romero's does not.

Creepshow, the first Romero/King collaboration, is Romero's most expensive film to date and his first to boast a cast of name professionals, including Hal Holbrook, Leslie Neilsen, Adrienne Barbeau, E.G. Marshall, and Viveca Lindfors. The film unfolds like an old EC horror comic, consisting of five terror tales presented in rapid-fire progression

'Tell him to call you Billie!" shouts husband Hal Holbrook, off-screen, to his obnoxious wife, Adrienne Barbeau, as she opens the deadly crate in *Creepshow* (1982). (© *Warner Bros., Inc.*)

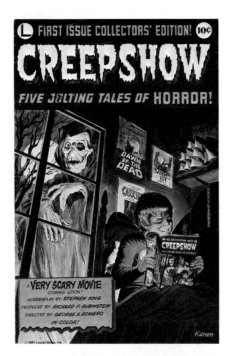

In *Creepshow*, Romero, with the help of scriptwriter Stephen King, pushed his concept of comic book horror to the limit. (© *1981 Laurel Show, Inc.*)

with actual comic book ads separating them. The opening sequence shows an unsympathetic father finding his son reading a horror comic called *Creepshow* and throwing it into the garbage, where the wind begins flipping through the pages, bringing each of the stories to life. This provides the context for the film, which ends with the boy getting even with his dad with a voodoo doll that he has ordered with a coupon from the *Creepshow* comic book.

King has already completed the screenplay of his bulky novel of Armageddon, *The Stand,* which Romero aims to direct in the not-too-distant future. Prior to that, however, Romero will solo with the concluding chapter of his zombie trilogy, tentatively titled *Day of the Dead.* Very likely, the teaming of Stephen King and George A. Romero will succeed in pushing Romero's unique brand of splatter cinema that vital next step beyond.

The Splatter Movies of George A. Romero

Night of the Living Dead (1968)
An Image Ten Production (Continental Films)/B&W/90 minutes
Producers: Russell Streiner, Karl Hardman
Director/Photographer/Editor: George A. Romero
Screenplay: John A. Russo
Production Designer: Vincent D. Survinski
Lighting Supervisor: Joseph Unitas
Special Effects: Regis Survinski, Tony Panatello
Cast: Judith O'Dea, Duane Jones, Karl Hardman, Russell Streiner, Keith Wayne, Judith Ridley, Marilyn Eastman, Kyra Schon

The Crazies (1973)
a.k.a *Code Name Trixie*/A Lee Hessel Presentation/A Pittsburgh Films–Latent Image Production (Cambist Films)/Color/104 minutes
Producer: Alvin C. Croft
Director/Photographer/Editor: George A. Romero
Screenplay: George A. Romero, based on an original script by Paul McCollough
Cast: Lane Carroll, W. G. MacMillan, Harold Wayne Jones, Lloyd Hollar, Richard Liberty

Martin (1978)
A Laurel Group Presentation (Libra Films)/Color, B&W/95 minutes
Producer: Richard Rubinstein
Director/Writer/Editor: George A. Romero
Photographer: Michael Gornick
Music: Donald Rubinstein
Special Effects and Make-Up: Tom Savini
Cast: John Amplas, Lincoln Maazel, Christine Forrest, Elayne Nadeau, Tom Savini, Sarah Venable, Fran Middleton, Al Levitsky, George A. Romero

Dawn of the Dead (1979)
A Laurel Group Presentation (United Films)/Color/127 minutes
Producer: Richard Rubinstein
Director/Writer/Editor: George A. Romero
Photographer: Michael Gornick
Music: The Goblins with Dario Argento
Special Effects and Make-Up: Tom Savini
Cast: David Emge, Ken Foree, Scott Reiniger, Gaylen Ross

Creepshow (1982)
A Laurel Production/A United Film Distribution Release/Color/122 minutes
Producer: Richard Rubinstein
Director: George A. Romero
Writer: Stephen King
Photographer: Michael Gornick
Editor: Michael Spolan
Production Design and Scenic Special Effects: Cletus Anderson
Sepcial Effects and Make-up: Tom Savini
Cast: Hal Holbrook, Adrienne Barbeau, Fritz Weaver, Leslie Neilsen, Carrie Nye, E.G. Marshall, Viveca Lindfors, Ed Harris, Ted Danson, Stephen King

CHAPTER 8

David Cronenberg

"The Brood I've often described, only half jokingly, as my version of Kramer vs. Kramer.*"*

David Cronenberg (in a conversation with the author)

Writer-director David Cronenberg on the set of *Videodrome* (1983), his ghoulish tale of the power of television to alter human perception. (© *1983 Universal*)

The very *Guignol* films of Canada's David Cronenberg advanced the phenomenon of splatter cinema its logical next step forward. Through excess and the application of his EC horror comics style, George A. Romero had succeeded in winning a wider audience for his splatter movies by making the horrendously real on the screen seem absurdly unreal and at times even comically absurd. Cronenberg reversed the process. Beginning with *They Came From Within* (a.k.a. *The Parasite Murders* and *Shivers*, 1976), he transformed the absurdly unreal through a similar use of ghoulish excess into something that seemed grotesquely real indeed.

In *They Came From Within,* for example, a man leans over a balcony railing and vomits a parasite, which has mysteriously invaded his body, onto the umbrella of a female passerby below. In *The Brood* (1979), a psychologically disturbed woman named Nola (Samantha Eggar) succeeds in externalizing her inner rage so completely that this rage actually manifests itself as a developing fetus clinging to her thigh. And in *Scanners* (1981), a villainous telepath (Michael Ironside) causes another man's head to explode in a shower of blood and brains through the power of his own intense concentration. Unreal? Absurd? To be sure. But through his meticulous staging of these unreal events, Cronenberg makes them seem horribly vivid and very real indeed. Real and deeply disturbing, the stuff of genuine nightmare.

Cronenberg admits that his own nightmares are very often the source for his films. This is not surprising, for his films seem to work on the same level as both nightmares and dreams—the level of symbol and metaphor. On the surface, his films appear to be straightforward horror stories. But that surface is often a mask for some deeper and more unsettling meaning.

In *The Brood,* Nola, the victim of a broken home and parental abuse, attempts to visit the same kind of treatment as an adult on her own daughter Candy (Cindy Hinds). Separated from her husband (Art Hindle), who has taken custody of the child, she wills her manifested inner demons, the brood, to claim revenge on them both. Her plan doesn't quite work, but then it doesn't entirely fail either. The ending of the film shows us that small sacklike bumps are beginning to swell up on Candy's arm as they once had on Nola's—telltale signs of another brood yet to come. Abused as a child, Candy is in all likelihood destined to become an abusing parent. The vicious circle draws closed; the victim becomes the victimizer.

Cronenberg's wry comment at the head of this chapter about *The Brood* being his version of *Kramer Vs. Kramer* is really quite apt. Both films are about the trauma of divorce and its impact on parents and their offspring. *The Brood* is a much gloomier study, however, for it also raises the specter of child abuse. "It's basically a horror soap opera," Cronenberg has said. "It is very autobiographical and horrific, the story of my

Second City Television's Andrea Martin (extreme left) is reluctant to dig into the evening's repast: the body of her boyfriend. From Ivan Reitman's *Cannibal Girls* (1970), the box office success of which prompted Cronenberg to pursue a wider audience for his own films. (*Courtesy Hollywood Book & Poster*)

last few years. A not uncommon domestic situation in which all the paranoid fears of one of the partners are suddenly realized. More than realized. It is worrying that perhaps your wife, or your husband, is going mad and will kill your child, which you know is ridiculous, except finally you realize that it is not only quite possible, but actually true beyond your wildest dreams." Of course, the major difference between *The Brood* and *Kramer Vs. Kramer* is that Cronenberg has chosen to tell his story of the perils of divorce and parental responsibility not in the manner of a social worker, but in the manner of Edgar Allan Poe.

Born in Toronto in 1943, David Cronenberg was a late-bloomer as far as today's generation of filmmakers go. Unlike George A. Romero, for example, he didn't take to the viewfinder until he was well into his twenties. Prior to that, he'd thought of himself as a potential novelist. Cronenberg's father, a fairly well-known Canadian writer of pulp fiction and comic books, had been a strong influence on him, and so the progression seemed quite natural. But then the film bug bit.

Cronenberg had entered the University of Toronto in 1962 to major in science. Preferring the metaphor of science to the reality of it, however, he switched a year later to the university's English language and literature program. Awarded a grant from the Canadian Arts Council for his writing, he then spent a year traveling and writing in Europe, primarily in Copenhagen.

Returning to the university in 1966 to complete his degree, he discovered film instead and quickly proceeded to shoot his first one, despite little knowledge of the craft of filmmaking itself. Called *Transfer*, the seven-minute film told the story of a patient whose relationship with his psychiatrist becomes the only meaningful bond in his otherwise fractured life. Much later in his career, Cronenberg would deal with this same theme in *The Brood*.

A devotee of horror comics and movies since his childhood, Cronenberg continued in this vein with his next film, *From the Drain*, the story of a secret agent and a biological warfare expert who are done in by a slime creature that emerges from guess-where to attack them both.

Graduating with a B.A. in English, history, and philosophy, Cronenberg managed to win yet another grant from the Canadian Arts Council: this one for a film. With it, he wrote, produced, directed, edited, and photographed a 65-minute film called *Stereo*, the plot of which, like *Scanners*, deals with the perils of ESP. Shot in 35mm, *Stereo* was shown at a number of film festivals in Canada and abroad.

A year later, Cronenberg made another 65-minute film, *Crimes of the Future*, the story of a strange disease that causes people to bleed fluid from their noses and eyes. The disease has an even odder effect on those around the bleeders, however, for it compels them to try to devour the running liquid. Similar elements would again show up in Cronenberg's *Rabid*.

Uncontrollable violence and bizarre sexual behavior are the frightening results of a deadly parasitic disease in David Cronenberg's *They Came From Within* (1976). (© Trans-America)

In 1970, Cronenberg received a third Arts Council grant and with it he returned to Europe, spending nine months in France writing and shooting several documentary fillers, which he sold to the Canadian Broadcasting Corporation upon his return. By this time, however, Cronenberg had become disenchanted with the low-budget, experimental film scene. His desire to make a film that would not only win wider distribution, but provide him with his first commercial success, had become acute. The opportunity came in 1973 when he met Ivan Reitman, the producer-director of a low-budget Canadian horror film, *Cannibal Girls* (1970), which had been released worldwide by American International with some success. Reitman's accomplishment now became Cronenberg's chief goal.

They Came From Within, the first Reitman–Cronenberg collaboration, took two years to get off the ground. Major financing was eventually secured from the Canadian Film Development Corporation, heretofore the sponsor of documentaries and educational short subjects (Cronenberg's script, which had a working title of *Orgy of the Blood Parasites*, was definitely neither). Nevertheless, the Corporation bankrolled the film, which was released in Canada by Cinepix under the title *The Parasite Murders* and then *Shivers*. It proved to be the financial success Cronenberg was looking for, achieving quite a bit of notoriety in the bargain. Canadian newspapers and magazines attacked its subject matter viru-

Above: A youthful Cronenberg (center) discusses an upcoming scene with actor Alan Migicovsky on the set of *They Came From Within* (1976). (*Courtesy Hollywood Book & Poster*)

Right: Alan Migicovsky is outfitted with a fake chest appliance for the special-effects sequence in *They Came From Within* (1976) where one of the parasites bursts from his stomach. (*Courtesy Hollywood Book & Poster*)

lently. There was even a debate in the Parliament over the Corporation's use (or misuse) of the public funds to finance such a film. All this was very good for business, however, and *Shivers* was picked up for U.S. distribution by American International, who retitled it *They Came From Within* for its American release.

They Came From Within deals with an obsessive scientist (the first of many in Cronenberg's films) who creates a sexual parasite capable of stimulating the sexual appetite of its human hosts out of all control. The parasites grow in number, sweeping like a strain of venereal disease through a plush Montreal apartment complex, where they inhabit the bodies of many of the residents, young and old alike, turning them into sexual crazies. The film is heavily laden with splatter, but for audiences of the time, it was splatter of a kind very different from what they had been used to seeing. For example, when one of the malevolent parasites bursts from the stomach of actor Alan Migicovksy and latches onto the face of co-actor Joe Silver, who, while attempting to pull it off with a pair of pliers, turns his face into a raw, bleeding jelly, audiences were again pummelled into openmouthed silence, but this time by a new and even more astonishing addition to the *Grand Guignol* bag of tricks. Cronenberg's violent set piece had sprung forth wholly unexpected, catching the audience completely off-guard. His sexual parasite was no knife-wielding assassin or flesh-craving zombie whose bloodthirsty deeds could be anticipated, but a bizarre, almost comic creation, whose grisly explosions of violence permitted no foreshadowing at all. Thus a new and perhaps even more viscerally disturbing form of splatter cinema was born. Cronenberg has made it his special province ever since.

Cronenberg's brand of splatter cinema is a unique blend of the absurd and the physically revolting. His films revel in scenes detailing the utter corruption of the human body. As will become clear in the conversation with Mr. Cronenberg that follows, however, this emphasis is not altogether self-serving and gratuitous, for it directly relates to a very consistent theme in all of his films to date: the inability of human beings to come to terms with the fact of their own mortality; to confront their fear of death.

Cronenberg's splatter movies are also distinctively marked by a blessed absence of endless cinematic quotes and homages to other director's films, which tend to glut the films of most of his contemporaries both in and out of the splatter field. If his films bear resemblance to the work of any director at all, it is perhaps to that of French filmmaker George Franju, whose 1960 *Les Yeux Sans Visage (Eyes Without a Face)* has much in common with all of Cronenberg's films.

Les Yeux Sans Visage deals with a brilliant plastic surgeon (Pierre Brasseur) whose beloved daughter (Edith Scob) is horribly disfigured in a car accident brought on by his own reckless driving. The surgeon, obsessed with the idea of restoring the girl's features, claims a number of

Alan Migicovsky makes splatter movie history, as the sexual parasite that has mysteriously invaded his body begins its bloody exit. From *They Came From Within* (1976). (*Courtesy Hollywood Book & Poster*)

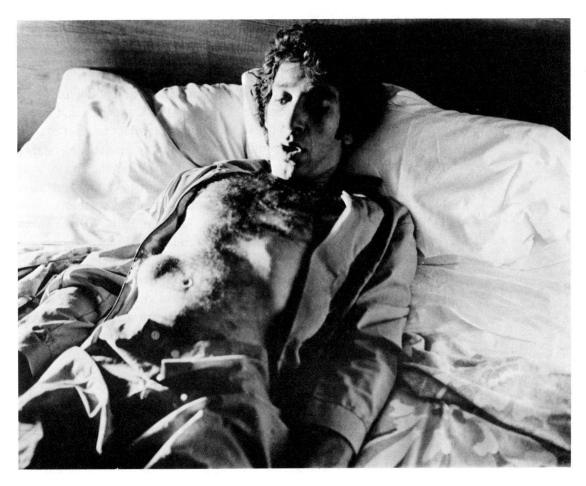

Georges Franju's *Les Yeux Sans Visage* (1960), the story of a surgeon's daughter (Edith Scob) who has been horribly disfigured in a car accident, has much in common with Cronenberg's work. (*Museum of Modern Art/Film Stills Archive*)

female victims who resemble her and literally (as well as gruesomely) tries to graft their faces onto his daughter's own, but without success. In the end he too is mutilated—by the vicious dogs he uses to guard his estate.

One can see a definite link between Franju's film and Cronenberg's work as evidenced by these common threads: the brilliant doctor whose obsessions lead him to the practice of a kind of voodoo science that brings about his own end; the inability of the characters to face the fact of their mortality in any form; the comic book plot that is nevertheless staged with a relentless, deadpan seriousness; and the blend of the absurd with the physically revolting. However, these similarities go beyond mere influence. They can instead be traced to the origins of splatter cinema itself on the stage of the *Theatre du Grand Guignol* in Paris. *Les Yeux Sans Visage* is not only a clear cinematic descendant of France's gruesome theatrical tradition, but a sort of hymn to it. It is also a French film, one of the few such films, in fact, ever to have been made in France, due to that country's strict policy of censoring scenes of graphic violence on the screen. It is no coincidence, I think, that when Cronenberg's very French *Grand Guignol* thriller, *They Came From Within*, was first released in Canada, it enjoyed its greatest popularity among French-Canadian moviegoers, who even saw the film under a French title, *Frissons*. Obviously a familar cord had been touched.

By some strange and sinuous path, French-style *Grand Guignol*, now no longer a fixture in the country of its origin, had reached its full expression in the films of a remarkably kindred spirit in a country with a common national bond.

A Conversation with David Cronenberg

I've interpreted The Brood *as really being about the effects of child abuse. Would you agree?*

Oh, yes. Definitely. *The Brood* I've often described, only half jokingly, as my version of *Kramer Vs. Kramer.* It's sort of the nightmare side of that movie in which everyone was relatively polite, reasonable, understanding, and compassionate—something that very rarely happens in a situation like that really. It's about the character played by Samantha Eggar being abused by her mother and she, in turn, abusing her own child, psychologically as well as physically, with the understanding at the end that there's another generation yet to come.

Your films have often been interpreted as political statements too. I'm thinking specifically of They Came From Within, *which some critics have seen as being a political movie on the level of Don Siegel's* Invasion of the Body Snatchers, *which kind of symbolized the sickness of McCarthyism rampant in America at the time it was made. Do you see your films this way?*

Well, I would say really that *Invasion of the Body Snatchers* could be interpreted politically—as the French tend to interpret anything they want to get excited about. For example, French critics tend to like left-wing fascist politics even in their cinema. And, in fact, they were very heavy in their interpretation of *They Came From Within* as politics because they wanted to see the disease that spread throughout this extremely bourgeois, uptight high-rise as sort of a disease of the middle classes and so on. And there's no denying that certain ideas do lend themselves to this kind of interpretation at times. But *Body Snatchers* I would never interpret politically—certainly when I was a kid I didn't. I prefer to interpret it on an emotional level as being about people who feel that they are outside of society for whatever reason and that they have to conceal what they are from society at large because that society is becoming more monolithic and capable of pushing them more and more to the side if they expose themselves. In a sense, though, I suppose that's a political statement too. But I prefer to see it as a sort of portrait of the artist. You know, the feeling that something about you gives you power and with it vulnerability. As you begin to find that this power you have—this talent or insight—is not readily appreciated by society, you learn to cover it, you hide it, and yet, at the same time, you learn ways of expressing it. I think you can interpret *Body Snatchers* that way, as you can *They Came From Within. Scanners,* in a way, is even that much more upfront about that aspect of its narrative. It's about a group of people who have a very specific power which is misunderstood by society at large and even by itself at first. But gradually these people learn to pass as normal until they can figure out some way to make use of the potential this power has given them.

I can't help but think that you're describing yourself and the way many critics have received your films. True?

I don't really think of my reception by the critics in quite those terms. I mean however good or bad they are as critics, they're also writers and they also go to movies, and so I have more in common with them than I do with some people who don't understand writing, don't go to movies.

How would you answer your critics then—the ones I mean who actually see some value in splatter movies and yet call They Came From Within, *for example, or* Rabid, *loathesome or disgusting?*

Well, I must say I think such reactions are really very subjective. I mean the scenes that they're talking about I tend to think of as being either quite funny or exhilarating, or cathartic, or beautiful. I certainly understand what people mean when they say loathesome and disgusting, but it's very subjective. I can't argue with them. If someone says: "I find that repulsive," I don't say: "No, you don't." Undoubtedly there are scenes in some of my films which even I feel are repulsive in some ways and yet this is all part of my general feelings toward not only horror films, but—as you call them—splatter films. They are films of confrontation. They aren't films of escape. And what it is that the audience is forced to confront are some very hard truths about the human condition, which have to do, in my films particularly, with the human body and the fact of aging and death and disease and the loss of people close to you. These things are inevitable and yet very hard to

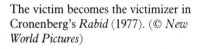

The victim becomes the victimizer in Cronenberg's *Rabid* (1977). (© *New World Pictures*)

come to terms with. And they are things that horror/splatter films force you to confront.

Do you think the kinds of things people are being forced to confront in horror films these days have changed much over the years? Or has the method of presenting them changed?

I think the subject matter is incredibly constant. Not just in films, but in horror literature as well, which goes back to the beginning of time really. It's the basic material of the unconscious. It's style and fashion and censorship in both literature as well as film that have changed. I don't think that the basic stuff has changed. And it's kind of boring really because it would be much more exciting, I'm perfectly willing to admit, if the preponderance of splatter movies which we are now seeing were really a reflection of something current that's happening to society, but there's really nothing that new in them. Every age has its incredible frustrations and anxieties and feelings that the world is about to end, that apocalypse is now and so on. *Götterdämmerung.* Even the words are from other ages.

You've been quoted as differentiating your splatter movies from George Romero's in this manner: his deal with childhood fears, yours with adult fears. Do you still believe that?

Well, my comment there was really just a response to the fact that I feel my approach to horror, or splatter, is very different from Romero's. Once he had said that his films deal in childhood fears. The truth is that the fears of childhood and the fears of adulthood are basically the same at bottom. It's just that your perceptions of them change as you get

In David Cronenberg's *Rabid* (1977), porno star Marilyn Chambers took time out from her X-rated romps to play a straight dramatic role, that of Rose, the victim of a motorcycle accident, whose life is saved by a doctor who uses a daring and experimental surgical technique. The operation has an unfortunate side effect—it leaves Rose with a ravenous appetite for blood. Soon she begins spreading the disease to others, passing it on to them in a unique and grisly way. (© *New World Pictures*)

older. When you're a child, you might be worrying about your pet. The pet gets run over, and for children—in North America fortunately—that's usually their first confrontation with death. Then when you become a parent, you worry about your own child and your friends, your parents, and yourself in the same manner you had once worried about your pet. Your perceptions of things change. But I think it's simplistic to say it's the fear of a dark room, for example, that works on you when you see a horror film. That's not even nearly close to what it's all about.

Has horror literature always had a special appeal for you?

Not more than other kinds. I've always been very eclectic. It's the same with the films. I see everything. I know that there are a lot of young filmmakers today who are very obsessed with the horror and science fiction films of their youth and who are constantly trying to remake them, or, more appropriately, relive them. I've seen all those films too and have certainly been enchanted by them and scared by them, but I've also seen all the comedies, cop, and war movies, and I have been influenced by them. It's just a matter of my own sensibility, I suppose, that when I sit down to write something, what comes out is not just a regurgitation of what's gone in.

True. I don't see constant references to this director and that film in your work.

No. And it's not that I'm disrespectful—to Howard Hawks, shall we say. Oh, there is one slight reference to *Forbidden Planet* in *The Brood*. I have a school in the film called the Krell Street School. It just came to me when I was writing the script. Of course, I knew what it was from, but I didn't realize how particularly apropos it was until after I was shooting the movie because in a sense the plot of *Forbidden Planet* and the plot of *The Brood* are very similar; having to do with creatures from the id, the unconscious being made manifest and so on. Such a reference couldn't have been completely accidental, of course. But in this case, it was not meant to be an *homage* or an in-joke. It just came out. And it's about the only thing like that I've done in any of my films.

Yes, it strikes me that if something is truly influential and it shows up in one's work, one is seldom conscious of it at the time.

I agree. That's the truest type of influence. We've all seen what happens to guys like Peter Bogdanovich when they make a conscious effort to pay homage. The same thing is happening with Brian De Palma. I mean, is it plagiarism or is it influence? It's the synthesis of the influence that's important, not just the mimicking of it, turning it around and having it appear exactly as it came in.

The psychologically disturbed Nola (Samantha Eggar) gives birth to one of *The Brood* (1979), a manifestation of her inner rage. (© *New World Pictures*)

There's a particular shot from Rabid *that amuses me. It shows this creature, the one which causes people to become rabid, emerging from the main character's armpit; she in fact is the one who is spreading the disease. The creature reminded me of the head of a penis, and it amused me that you had chosen as your leading lady porno star Marilyn Chambers. Was that an in-joke?*

No, that whole concept was in the script long before Chambers came on the scene. But these sort of ironies do happen all the time. And I quite like them. Actually, I had originally wanted Sissy Spacek for the Chambers role. She was unknown at the time. I had seen *Badlands* and had admired her tremendously in it. But my producers were worried that she, in their words, had a Texas accent and too many freckles. They told me to forget it. Of course, two months later, she showed up on the cover of *Newsweek* magazine for being in *Carrie*, and they regretted having told me to forget it.

Had you actually discussed the part with Spacek?

No. I was just pushing for her. I was saying: "Look at this lady. She's going places!" But it all fell on deaf ears. Of course, I didn't even know

Michael Ironside as the villainous telepath in Cronenberg's *Scanners* (1981). (© *Embassy Pictures*)

if she would have been interested in playing the part. I never got as far as asking. The problem was we didn't have a very large budget and it was felt that it would really help us if we had some kind of a name. But we couldn't afford the fifty thousand or hundred thousand dollars it would have taken us to get a name. Then Ivan Reitman, one of the film's producers, heard that Marilyn Chambers was going to do a movie in New York with Rip Torn to be directed by Nicholas Ray, and that certainly sounded bizarre. Anyway, it fell through and Marilyn was still looking to do a movie that wasn't an X. She was willing to work relatively cheaply to establish that she could, in fact, act. I hadn't seen any of her movies—still haven't except for *Rabid,* but I did think she was the most interesting of the porno stars. Ivan said, "Look, if she's terrible, we don't have to go with her, though it would be nice if she could act—it would be a good selling point." When I auditioned her, I was surprised that she really could act, and so I cast her. Simple as that.

It's been reported that you've dropped the idea of doing your version of Frankenstein, *which to me has always been the* Hamlet *of splatter. What attracted you to the idea of doing the film in the first place?*

Well, it seems that there are maybe three films that are the basic horror films. One is *Frankenstein,* one is *Dracula,* and the third is probably *Dr. Jekyll and Mr. Hyde.* Those three are the closest to the "primal stuff." *Frankenstein* was first proposed to me—it was not my idea—because my films had a lot in common with *Frankenstein,* more certainly than with the other two. And it's true. A lot of my films—all of them, in fact, up to and including *Videodrome*—have to do with creators, people who create monster children in some sense and who have to deal with their own creation once it comes back to them. And so I thought, maybe it might be illuminating and challenging to go back to that source and see what would happen if I tried to tell that story.

I've always felt that if Mary Shelley's book were ever filmed as written, it would probably be unbearable to watch. Because of its theme of loneliness and responsibility—that man has been put on earth by God and left to wander.

That's right. Dr. Frankenstein is really the father of the creature and yet he rejects him. And what are the consequences of that? That as a theme interests me a great deal.

Scanners *was your first film with a substantial budget. Did that make things easier for you?*

I wrote a first draft of the script in three weeks, and we went into production right after that. I spent a lot of time during the shoot writing and rewriting the script. And even during post-production, we went back and reshot some things. I prefer to write four or five drafts of a script before I shoot because it's much cheaper to try things out on paper. *Scanners* had a budget of about four million. But I can't say that made things easier, no.

The Canadian film industry is really booming these days. How does it resemble Hollywood? Is it simply a reflection of Hollywood—the deal is the thing and so on?

Yes, there's a lot of that. A lot of the real movie producers of Hollywood have left there so that the town has been taken over by accountants and agents; they're running the show now. And in Toronto, leaving out the agents, of which there are very few, there are a lot of accountants and lawyers who have gotten into the film business because the tax shelter laws encourage people to invest in movies. And so they've turned themselves overnight into producers, movie people. The problem is that they are more into the deal than they are into the film. They're not prepared once the film is through to take on the hassle of getting decent distribution, fighting off censors, and doing all the things you really have to do to see a film through. That's the bad side of it. On

Frank (Art Hindle) is too late to save Ruth (Susan Hogan), who has been brutally murdered by *The Brood* (1979). (© *New World Pictures*)

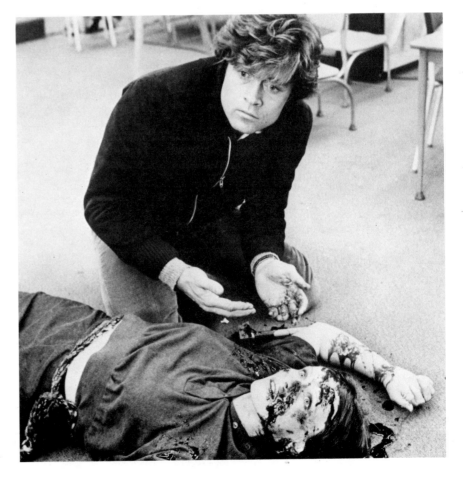

the other hand, there's also a lot of money around for people who really do make movies.

You were certainly in the vanguard of the burgeoning Canadian film industry.

Yeah, I certainly started before this latest wave.

How does that industry look upon you now—as sort of a favorite son?

(*laughs*) Not exactly! Well, actually, I must say that lately things have improved. Producers like me because my films have made money. They know that I'm known and that they can sell me in a package. That's my strength in the Canadian film industry. I'm halfway to real respect, I suppose, though still not totally there at all.

The Splatter Movies of David Cronenberg

They Came From Within (1976)
a.k.a. *The Parasite Murders, Shivers*/A
DAL-Reitman Production (A
Trans-America Release)/Color/94 minutes
Executive Producers: John Dunning,
Andre Link, Alfred Pariser
Producer: Ivan Reitman
Director/Writer: David Cronenberg
Photographer: Robert Saad
Editor: Patrick Dodd
Make-Up: Joe Blasco
Music: Ivan Reitman
Cast: Paul Hampton, Joe Silver, Lynn
Lowry, Alan Migicovsky, Susan Petrie,
Barbara Steele, Ronald Mlodzik

Rabid (1977)
A Cinema Entertainment Enterprises Ltd.
Production (New World Pictures
Release)/Color/91 minutes
Executive Producers: Ivan Reitman, Andre
Link
Producer: John Dunning
Director/Writer: David Cronenberg
Photographer: Rene Verzier
Editor: Jean Lafleur
Make-Up: Joe Blasco, Byrd Holland
Music: Ivan Reitman
Cast: Marilyn Chambers, Frank Moore,
Joe Silver, Howard Ryshpan, Patricia
Gage, Susan Roman

The Brood (1979)
A New World Pictures Release/Color/90
minutes
Executive Producers: Pierre David, Victor
Soinicki
Producer: Claude Heroux

Director/Writer: David Cronenberg
Photographer: Mark Irwin
Editor: Allan Collins
Make-Up: Shonagh Jabour
Music: Howard Shore
Cast: Oliver Reed, Samantha Eggar, Art
Hindle, Cindy Hinds, Nuala Fitzgerald,
Henry Beckman, Susan Hogan, Bob
Silverman

Scanners (1983)
An Avco-Embassy Pictures
Release/Color/104 minutes
Executive Producers: Pierre David, Victor
Solnicki
Producer: Claude Heroux
Director/Writer: David Cronenberg
Photographer: Mark Irwin
Editor: Ron Sanders
Make-Up: Dick Smith, Tom Schwartz,
Chris Walas, Stephen Dupuis
Music: Howard Shore
Cast: Stephen Lack, Jennifer O'Neill,
Patrick McGoohan, Michael Ironside,
Robert Silverman, Adam Ludwig

Videodrome (1983)
A Universal Release/Color/87 minutes
Executive Producers: Pierre David, Victor
Solnicki
Producer: Claude Heroux
Director/Writer: David Cronenberg
Photographer: Mark Irwin
Special Make-Up Effects: Rick Baker
Editor: Ron Sanders
Music: Howard Shore
Cast: James Woods, Deborah Harry,
Sonja Smits

Above: Christopher Lee as the revenge-seeking Kharis in *The Mummy* (1959). (© *Hammer Films*)

Right: Christopher Lee makes his entrance as the bloodthirsty Count Dracula in Hammer's *Horror of Dracula* (1958). (© *Hammer Films*)

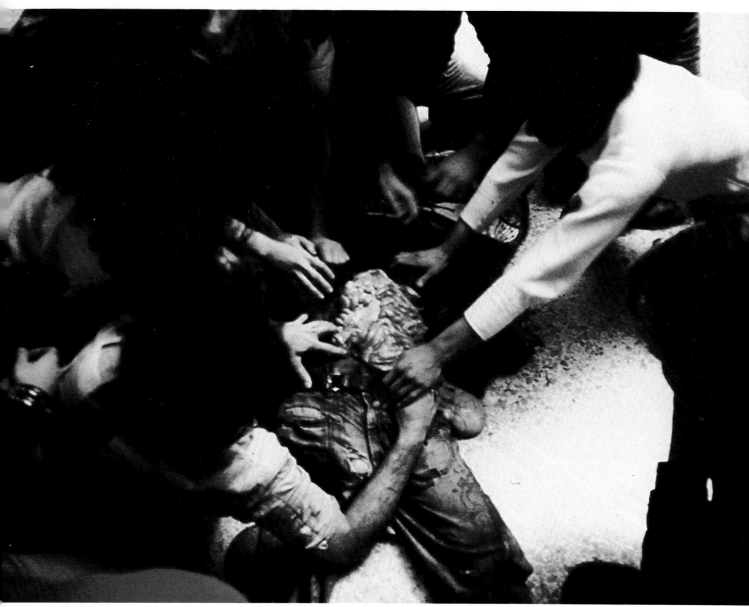

Opposite page, above: Montag the Magnificent (Ray Sager), master of illusion and on-stage gore, adds a little body snatching to his repertoire in Herschell Gordon Lewis's *The Wizard of Gore* (1970). *(Courtesy Daniel Krogh)*

Opposite page, below: Herschell Gordon Lewis (center) calls out directions to his actors and crew on the set of *Year of the Yahoo* (1972), a non-splatter movie about political corruption and media manipulation. *(Courtesy Daniel Krogh)*

Above: The zombies partake of a hot lunch in George A. Romero's *Dawn of the Dead* (1979). *(© Dawn Associates, 1978/K. Kolbert)*

Above: At the conclusion of *The Texas Chain Saw Massacre,* poor Marilyn Burns is tied up, terrorized, and beaten with a hammer by the crazies for the benefit of their virtually mummified Grandpa. Then Leatherface (Gunnar Hansen) proceeds to force feed Gramps using Marilyn's bloodstained fingertip for a spoon. *(Courtesy Edwin Neal)*

Opposite page, above: If David Lean had directed *Blood Feast* (1963), the result might have been a lot like this scene from *An American Werewolf in London* (1981), the cinema's first multi-million dollar *sleaze epic.* *(© 1981 Universal)*

Opposite page, below: One of the high points of *Damien–Omen II* (1978) is this "creative death" in which a doctor who has caught on to Damien's secret is done away in a spectacular (and noisy) elevator accident that results in his being cut in half. *(© 1978 Twentieth Century-Fox)*

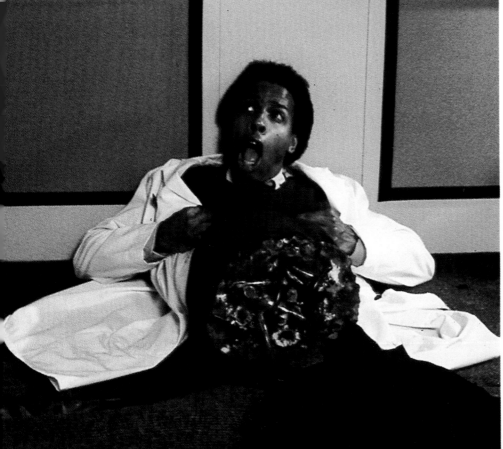

Above, left: Jason, the drowning victim whose death prompts the revenge massacre of the counselors of Camp Crystal Lake in Sean Cunnigham's *Friday the 13th* (1980). Special make-up by Tom Savini. (*Courtesy Foto Fantasies*)

Above, right: Savini first got hooked on becoming a movie make-up master when he saw *The Man of a Thousand Faces* (1957), the biography of Lon Chaney. But Chaney's make-ups were never like this. From *Dawn of the Dead* (1979). (© *Dawn Associates, 1978/K. Kolbert*)

Right: The Rats Are Coming! The Werewolves Are Here! (1972) was one of Andy Milligan's bargain-basement period thrillers made in England for between $7500 and $20,000.

Above: When Torrance (Jack Nicholson) unburdens himself to Lloyd the bartender (Joe Turkel) in the Overlook's ornate restaurant and Lloyd provides all the right reassurances, Torrance is really reassuring himself. (© *Warner Bros., Inc.*)

Left: A terrified Wendy (Shelley Duvall) screams in terror as her husband starts breaking down the bathroom door to get at her. No storybook marriage this! (© *Warner Bros., Inc.*)

*The Evil Dead, 1983 (© 1983 New
Line Cinema)*

Max (James Woods) prepares to become part of the "new flesh" in Cronenberg's *Videodrome* (1983). (© *1983 Universal*)

CHAPTER 9

Acting in Splatter: The Making of The Texas Chainsaw Massacre

"I don't want to be Clark Gable. I want to be Strother Martin. Or L. Q. Jones. A character actor."

Texas Chainsaw's Ed Neal (in a conversation with the author)

Ed Neal, as the crazy middle brother of a family of four cannibal-killers, terrorizes Marilyn Burns, the sole survivor of a group of vacationers, during the horrific conclusion of *The Texas Chainsaw Massacre* (1975). (© *New Line Cinema*)

Those who have seen *The Texas Chainsaw Massacre* may or may not be familiar with the name Ed Neal, the actor who plays one of the film's three principal psychopaths, but they are more than familiar—perhaps uncomfortably so—with his work. Neal is the first of the cannibal killers introduced to us on the screen, and his nerve-rattling debut as the scarfaced middle brother who revels in his job at a local slaughterhouse and further gets off on self-mutilation, sets the tone of relentless derangement that continues to rip like the saw of the title throughout the remainder of the film.

Ed Neal's *tour de force* performance *(Chainsaw* remains his first and only film so far) as the hitchhiker who is rescued from the sweltering Texas sun by a van-load of vacationing young people who later fall prey to him and his meat-loving family, raises the hairs on the back of the neck because of its unsettling mixture of both comic and terrifying craziness. My first reaction to Neal was that this was no actor at all, but a bonafide backwoods Texas lunatic who had escaped from his asylum and somehow managed to land a part in the movie. As I watched him, I found myself thinking: "Where did they get this guy?" Gunnar Hansen and Jim Siedow's equally persuasive performances as the two other crazy brothers who appear later on only served to confirm this opinion. By the end of the film, I was convinced that all three of them were, in fact, bloodlusting maniacs, who, hopefully, had been locked up securely as soon as the film had been completed. Subsequent research into the making of *Chainsaw* proved to me, of course, that my fears were groundless. Each of these gentlemen just happens to be a good actor. But they're not the only good actors in the film.

The consistently high caliber of the acting throughout *Chainsaw,* in fact, is one of the reasons why the film is so terrifyingly effective and why it continues to stand head and shoulders over most other splatter movies that have followed in its wake. Because the film was such a big box-office success, it's hard to understand why none of its cast members have gone on to bigger things. Marilyn Burns (the sole surviving victim of the meat fanciers), for example, appeared in director Hooper's next film, *Eaten Alive* (1976), and had a featured role as Manson family member Linda Kasabian in the TV adaptation of Vincent Bugliosi's bestseller, *Helter Skelter* (1976), but has done little else since. Paul Partain (Burn's brother in the film) had a cameo in the Warren Oates/Peter Fonda occult biker movie *Race with the Devil* (1975). Gunnar Hansen ("Leatherface") made one other film, *The Demon Lover* (1976), then gave up acting altogether. Yet, ironically, the director who guided them through the *Chainsaw* experience, Tobe Hooper, is now making multimillion-dollar splatter movies *(Poltergeist,* 1982) in collaboration with cinema's reigning King Midas, Steven Spielberg. How could this be? In a fascinating two-part article about the making of *Chainsaw* written for the *Los Angeles Times* by freelance journalists Ellen Farley and William K. Knoedelseder, Jr., one can find a good deal of the answer.

Director Tobe Hooper (left) and camera-man Daniel Pearl line up a shot in the sweltering 100°-plus Texas heat. (*Courtesy Edwin Neal*)

"The story of what happened to *The Texas Chainsaw Massacre*," write Farley and Knoedelseder, "is at once a best and worst possible case of independent filmmaking in America. The movie succeeded, both critically and commercially, beyond the Texans' wildest expectations. It should have made them all rich. But after two years of distributing *Chainsaw* to an estimated worldwide box office of at least $20 million, Bryanston (the releasing company) mysteriously disappeared from the movie business in 1976, owing the Texans millions of dollars in profits. Worse, *Chainsaw* had passed into the black hole of the movie-distribution business. Its prints, negatives, and various distribution rights were held by Bryanston creditors—distributors, exhibitors, and film labs around the world. So far, there have been at least twenty-five *Chainsaw* lawsuits, involving more than twice that many attorneys. For a time, the legal fees succeeded in draining off more money from the profits than the filmmakers themselves received. Internecine warfare broke out among the disappointed Texans, who took to suing one another for slander, malfeasance, and more."

Bill and Ellen are planning to expand their riveting story about "The Real Texas Chainsaw Massacre," a tale fraught with more bizarre incidents than the film itself, into a book, so I shall avoid going into details here. Suffice it to say that the facts behind how *Chainsaw* actually got made and became a success should dispel forever anyone's doubts that making a movie, even a low-budget splatter movie, can be a frustrating, grueling, and frequently heartbreaking experience. To find out firsthand what it was like to be a part of the process in *Chainsaw*'s case, it seemed useful to contact not the director, nor the writer or producer, but one of the troops: the frequently unsung hero of the splatter moviemaking process—the *actor*.

A Conversation with Ed Neal

Before we get into the harrowing details surrounding the making of Chain-saw, *why don't you tell me a little about your acting experience to that point.*

Well, up to that point, and since, I've been involved in virtually every phase of show business there is. I went to junior college up in Jacksonville, Texas, for two years and toured there with Sandy Duncan doing Shakespeare. I just worshipped the ground Sandy walked on. She just had "hit" written all over her. We toured shows at Methodist colleges, schools, and churches all around Texas for about two years. She was one of the first people I worked with—and I'd been doing theater for five to eight years—who made a tremendous big impression on me—like, hey, if I work hard enough maybe I could be that good. From there I went to the University of Texas in 1966 and I got a scholarship there to work in the publicity department. And I also started to do shows there. The first role I did was probably my favorite of all time, the Jimmy Porter role in John Osborne's *Look Back in Anger*, a role I've always wanted to repeat because at that time I didn't have the technique, the abilities I think I have now after having had the opportunity to work with and learn from some really super people over the years.

From Shakespeare to John Osborne. What else have you done?

I've done musical comedy—I love musical comedy. And at U.T., I also got into commercials. People from the advertising world found me; they'd come backstage and ask me to do ads for them. And so I evolved into specialty advertising, doing specialty voices—animation voices, trick voices, imitations, and so on. I really enjoyed that. It not only paid well, it was fun. I went from there to doing stand-up comedy and toured with a guy named Tommy Taylor. He's been touring the country for the last eight or nine years as Woody Guthrie in his play *The Child of Dust*. It's played in New York at the Cherry Street Theater; it's played all over the world. We were a team for a while. A real great guy. We specialized in taking old vaudeville jokes and modernizing them. Our specialty was to take a box of props on stage and improvise skits around them. We did that in a small cabaret theater down on Sixth Street in Austin, which is now a real jumping, trendy place, but back then it was just beginning. I've been in Austin since '65, during which time the population has just about doubled.

After that I did Vietnam and when I came back I got into graduate school. I already had one degree in drama education; I was going to be a teacher. Basically, I was pursuing that direction because I was under a lot of pressure from my folks, who kept saying, "You need a real job, a real job!" My mother used to cut want ads and tape them to my door: "Court reporters make $5.75 a month. . . and UP!" She always wanted me to be a court reporter. Every time they'd raise the price, she'd post another one to my door: "Court reporters now make $8.75 a month!" I used to have a whole box of court reporter clippings.

Tell me about the audition for Chainsaw.

It was quite interesting. We were downstairs in the Green Room at U.T.—a place where actors gather to tell each other how wonderful they are or aren't—and some campus cut-up stuck his head in and said, "Hey, they're making a movie upstairs. They're looking for weird guys; you guys are pretty weird, why don't you try out? Ha! Ha!" So we decided to check it out. Now the last thing you want to tell a group of drama students is that you're looking for weird people because it's like pushing a button: we just walked in to audition and acted completely off-the-wall. They handed us a script, and I just read a few lines, and said, "Hey, I'm home!" We didn't take it very seriously because the script was *so* weird and *so* strange. And the guys that were auditioning us—Kim Henkel and Tobe Hooper—were so straight, low-keyed, and serious, it was like somebody had handed them the wrong script. Unbeknownst to us, they had been working years on this. But we didn't know that; we thought: "Boy, this is a dog, this is just some grand tax write-off scheme." So we just got up and acted silly. And I looked over and the sillier I got, the more Kim and Tobe seemed to dig it. Wow, I thought, these guys are really getting off on this! So I got weirder and starting rolling my eyes around, etcetera. Afterwards, there

Screenwriter Kim Henkel on the set with "Grandpa." (*Courtesy Edwin Neal*)

92

were thank-yous and don't-call-us-we'll-call-yous and we all went out the door doing pratfalls. Then, later, up comes Kim Henkel: "Ed, we'd like to use you in this film. We're going to pay you a couple of hundred dollars up front, Ed. In cash." And I thought: "Good grief, they're going to pay me money to do this silly script?" Then Kim said, "And then we're going to give you a percentage of the profits, Ed, because we think it's going to be. . . a *big* hit." Well, I still have the scar on the inside of my cheek where both sets of teeth completely bit through from trying to stop laughing. Kim was a very nice guy and I didn't want to hurt his feelings. So I said, "Okay." I thought really that afterwards, they'd give me a couple of hundred bucks, we'd get a couple of scenes in the can, and that'd be the end of it; they just wouldn't finish the film because it was really such a dog. But then I started working on the film and really got into it because a lot of really neat people were involved. Gunnar Hansen was a lot of fun to work with. Tobe was weird and he was fun to work with. Kim was really laid back and mellow, so he was a lot of fun to be around. A good mix of people. Bill Vail, who'd been my roommate for awhile, was in it too.

Were most of the people in the movie fellow students?

A lot, yes. Gunnar was teaching at U.T., an English teacher. Did you ever see a picture of him without his "Leatherface" mask on?

No.

Gunnar's a real good-looking guy. But they wouldn't allow any pictures taken of him without his mask because it would have ruined his image.

He's a teacher now, isn't he? In Maine?

I don't know whether he's teaching up there or not; I've lost contact with him. I know he was building houses for awhile. He's a carpenter, and a very good poet by the way. He had a very successful little poetry magazine here in town for awhile called *Lucille*.

He's only done one other film since Chainsaw. The Demon Lover.

That's true. But then again, all I've done since, film-wise, have been industrial films and things like that. I'll fly out to Los Angeles and do an industrial and fly back. I've never really pursued films because I've been so busy with the commercial stuff. And I've been doing "Esther's Follies," a comedy group here in Austin, for about three years. We do six shows a week. And so that's been keeping me kinda busy. I've also got a couple of companies. One buys and sells movie memorabilia, The Texas Movie Emporium; I tour with that to movie conventions. And I have a little company called Tight Spots where we write comedic advertising. I work seven days a week, so as a result I've never really pursued the movie thing. I've had a lot of people interested, but nothing came up that I really wanted to do. Though I did hear—and I don't know whether it's true or not; but as it never happened, it doesn't really matter—this story from Kim Henkel. Kim called me in the middle of the night to say that the Disney casting director was trying to get in touch with me. Kim had been over to Tobe's apartment in L.A., and he saw a note from the Disney casting director, saying that he wanted to talk to Ed Neal. Kim asked Tobe what that was about, and Tobe told him that the Disney casting director was trying to get in touch with me about some part. So Kim said, "Well, why don't you call Ed?" And Tobe said, "Well, I can't find his number." So Kim, bless his heart, called me immediately, told me, and the next day my agent called the Disney casting office and was told that the role had already been filled. They had been trying to find me, but being unable to, they filled the part with another actor. I still don't know what the part was for. I do know that at the time, they were casting *The Black Hole*, but whether that was the film or not, I still don't know.

Prop man Robert Burns's prop table. Just what the doctor ordered for the grisly farmhouse sequence. (*Courtesy Edwin Neal*)

Having co-written and produced what turned out to be a fabulously successful first film, what's Kim Henkel doing now?

Kim went out to L.A., wrote screenplays, and, I think, didn't get anything else started, so now he's back in Rockport, Texas. I've seen him a few times, but not lately. At one time there was talk of a sequel to *Chainsaw*—the ending was left open for one—but the problem is they've been fighting over who owns the rights. A major battle. And all I can tell you is that there are a *lot* of really bad people involved.

Prior to working in Chainsaw, *had you been interested in getting into the movies, splatter or otherwise?*

Well, I've always been interested in anything theatrical. And I've always been a movie buff. I've been collecting film memorabilia for about twenty years. So, I've got in my personal collection over 85,000 posters and over 400,000 eight by ten stills. I've got one of the largest Disney and Reagan collections in the country.

So splatter movies, apart from their theatricality, are not necessarily your thing.

Well, I was a fifties child, and I grew up with the monster movies of the time. I loved them; they were so bad they were good. Monsters with wires on them, and zippers on them; I've got about four hundred science fiction posters of the first order in my collection. But splatter movies per se, well, no. You see, *Chainsaw* in my opinion moved away from the "so bad it's good" into the "so real, it's *too* real." And it was one of the first movies to do that. It's so real it polarizes you to a gut feeling you really don't want to have. It's like the feeling you might have when you've been walking through an alley to save some time, and you trip over a drunk; then you turn around to say you're sorry and suddenly there's three or four of them standing there with ball bats. *"Oh, shit!"* That kind of feeling. And I have a great delight now when I see the film; I no longer watch the film itself, I watch the audience because I know what's going on on the screen, and it's more interesting to watch the audience reactions. You can learn a lot about your work that way—what you do that elicits certain responses. I went to a lot of colleges—I still do—and a lot of conventions where I would be a guest speaker and show the film and answer questions. The kids always got off on that because they always had so many questions. "Why did you do that? What did this mean?" Etcetera. Because if you watched a horror or science fiction film in the fifties, you always got a pretty good handle on it right away. But *Chainsaw* was different. It didn't have good and bad people in it. It just had stranger and stranger.

It was relentless.

Right. It never let up. Not all the kids in the film were good, not all were bad. Even the crazies themselves had degrees of personality. Like, I think one of the most interesting characterizations was Jim Siedow's. Jim's an older actor from Houston who came down to audition and got the part. He was supposed to play our father in the film, but wound up playing a sort of older brother. What was interesting about his character was that he *wanted* to kill the girl (Marilyn Burns), he *wanted* to hurt her, but he kept pulling himself back because he wasn't quite as far gone as the other guys. And that kind of characterization is really interesting, and you don't see it a lot of times in splatter-type movies. Like you watch *Halloween I, II* or *III;* I had to be woken up after they were over. There's no characterization. It's pubescent T&A. Who *is* this guy that's killing people? You don't care about him. He never says anything. He never does anything.

In Siedow's case, who brought that nuance of character to his part? Was it Siedow himself, or Tobe Hooper?

Siedow. Tobe was so interested in the technical side of it that he didn't really work with us very much. Most of the people who did good work in the film did it on their own. I mean that not as a slam against Tobe because, my God, the man had ten million problems every single day. We didn't have enough money, we were behind schedule, we were over budget. You know, we were working under primitive circumstances. Like, we'd need thirty-five feet of dolly track? Well, we had *eight*. Sometimes it would take three and a half to four hours to set up for just a two-minute shot because we didn't have the equipment, couldn't get it, couldn't afford it. We'd have to find ways around everything. And Tobe and people like Danny Pearl, the cameraman, did yeoman's work. They'd invent ways to get shots. But, you see, that was also one of the

Cameraman Daniel Pearl begins setting up the tripod for another difficult shot to be taken on yet another of *Chainsaw's* many trying locations. (*Courtesy Edwin Neal*)

95

At the film's conclusion, poor Marilyn Burns is tied up, terrorized, and beaten with a hammer by the crazies for the benefit of their virtually mummified grandpa. Then Leatherface (Gunnar Hansen) proceeds to force-feed Gramps using Marilyn's blood-stained fingertip for a spoon. (*Courtesy Edwin Neal*)

most delightful experiences too. Here were people—some had been to film school; Tobe'd done a lot of commercials, and he'd shot a little film called *Eggshells,* so he had experience, but not an abundance of it; and the cast, for the most part, had done theater and some commercials—who were all learning together, and that was very exciting. There were these mountainous problems, and we'd all pitch in to solve them. I found myself never wanting to leave the set.

How long did the film take to shoot?

Months and months and months. And then editing took even more months.

Where did you find that farmhouse that the crazies live in?

The farmhouse is right outside Austin in a place called Hutto, Texas, a small farm community. In reality the farmhouse is right down the street from the house where the kids go first, but the film was shot in such a way that they seem miles apart.

Getting back to some of the difficulties involved with shooting the film, and some of the hostilities that flared up afterward, you were quoted once as saying, "If I ever see Hooper again, I'm gonna kill him." True?

It was taken out of context. What was left out was all the background of what went on before. Obviously I had no intention of killing Tobe. He did what he had to do to get his film done, and I mellowed after awhile. That interview took place right after all the problems had occurred, so it created a lot of animosity.

Chainsaw *was such a success for him, why didn't he ever use any of you in any of his subsequent films?*

Well, he did use Marilyn Burns in *Eaten Alive,* or whatever that film was eventually called. But, you see, after *Chainsaw,* most of us were angry with him because we felt he'd used us; we felt he knew a lot more about the bad contractual deals we were all getting than he ever let on. *Chainsaw* was his stepping-stone to Hollywood, and he would have done anything to get that film made. Nobody knows how much that film has grossed, including Tobe. The film has never been out of release since it was made. It went from Bryanston, who played it all over the world, to Joseph Brenner, who played it again all over the world, to New Line Cinema, who's still playing it. It plays somewhere on the college circuit in sixteen millimeter every single day. And on videocassette, it became one of the top sellers. So, it's never really been out of distribution since 1974. That's incredible!

Did you ever make any money out of your so-called percentage deal?

Not very much. I do get checks all the time, but instead of checks for fifteen thousand dollars or twenty thousand dollars, they're for one hundred dollars, fifty dollars, seventy-five dollars. I even got a check once for twenty-one dollars. They vary.

But the film is making millions. Have you talked to the others about this? Have you talked to Tobe Hooper? How does he feel?

Tobe talks to none of us. He's a total recluse. Always has been.

Some descriptions of Chainsaw's *production indicate that things were as painful to endure in front of the camera as the finished film sometimes is for the audience. Is that true?*

Yes. Because the conditions, like I say, were like the silent film era. Nobody really knew what to do, and we were all trying to figure it out. Conditions were miserable. Goddam, it was 112 degrees in the shade. Take my scene when I had to lay down on the road after I'd been hit by the truck, with my arm tucked crazily under my head, and blood running out of my mouth. They wanted a close-up and to get it, they had to prop my head up on a rock off the road. Well, the rock and the asphalt were so hot that they literally burned my skin. What happened was that just as we were shooting, a long, thin cloud ran right in front of the sun, passing at about one foot per hour. I had to get up, but Tobe kept saying, "Wait, Ed, we have to wait till the cloud passes so we get the light for the shot." So my face fried a little bit. And, of course, the shot was ultimately cut from the film.

The joys of film acting.

Well, people don't know how rough it is. Marilyn Burns, bless her heart, suffered more than anybody. People were hot, they were pissed, they were tired, money wasn't coming in the way it should have, they promised they'd shoot your scenes and get you out in a couple of days, and then it ran into three weeks. And all this for a couple of hundred dollars, for a film that we all thought would wind up playing only at drive-ins in Round Rock, Texas. The hell with it!

One of the subtleties about Chainsaw *that struck me is that while neither you, Gunnar Hansen, nor Jim Siedow look alike, the occasional close-ups of your very similar large, white teeth indicated a family resemblance. Was that planned? Did you all have caps made?*

Well, Jim and I talked about how Gunnar ran his tongue over his teeth—he did have some fake teeth—and Jim had this great, toothy smile, so I tried to imitate both of them. It's one of those things you do as an actor to give your character something extra, knowing even as you do it that no one will probably ever notice. It's nice that you did.

Aside from the mysterious Disney episode, have any other film offers come your way? Concrete ones?

Well, as I said, I never really pursued it. But I did turn down several offers afterwards basically because they didn't want to pay me enough. And I don't mean thousands of dollars. I mean scale. I turned down *Piranha*. They wanted me for seventy-five dollars a day. No meals. No insurance. No transportation. Nothing. Thank you, Roger Corman, but *no*! Besides, the script didn't interest me at all. If you want to have some fun some time, read the script to that film. Talk about a catnap.

The finished film wasn't all that great either.

You ought to read the script! Wowie, zowie! "Hey, Dad, let's go fishing." "Okay, son, where shall we fish today?" "How about in the cove, Dad?" Good grief! This summer though, I hope to be starting a new film. You might be interested to know that it's called *Splatter*.

Good title! Tell me about it.

Well, people have been asking me to do something else. And a friend is on the verge of getting some backing now that I've committed—which made me feel real good. Right now it's in the scripting stage, and I'm trying for all I'm worth to get a lot of input beforehand so that it doesn't turn out to be a typical mad slasher thing.

Nuances of character, that sort of thing?

Yes, the stuff that made *Chainsaw* so good, that set it apart, makes it endure. When you think about some of the subtle, subtle things that went on between Franklin, the guy in the wheelchair, and his sister, Sally, the friction and antipathy between them, the sibling rivalry, etcetera, it really gave shadings to their characters. Of course, Paul and Marilyn didn't like each other much, so that helped. For example, in one scene, Marilyn grabs a flashlight away from Paul, and he just about tears her head off. It was great. It was also real, but that's beside the point.

Who's behind Splatter?

A guy who started off in U.T. film school named Ron Moore. And here's something really interesting, the tie-in between it and *Chainsaw*. Half of the things Ron knows about the film industry, he's learned from studying *Chainsaw*. He knows something far more important than what to do; he knows what not to do. He's made a long, case history study of *Chainsaw*'s distribution, and he's coming at this film with the idea that none of us are going to get screwed this time. You see, anybody can make a film. You could go out tomorrow and for fifteen thousand dollars put a movie in the can. But the real horror—you want

At the height of her ordeal, Marilyn Burns passes out. She awakens shortly thereafter in a haze, thinking her ordeal had been just a nightmarish dream. It wasn't, of course, and the terror begins all over again. (*Courtesy Edwin Neal*)

to have a horror film?—the horror comes in distribution because that's where they've got you. There're more bad people involved in distribution in the motion picture industry than Al Capone ever knew. You better believe that. I'm not just talking about Bryanston either, but everywhere.

I'm a film school graduate too. From way back in the Dark Ages, 1966. And I can attest to the fact that while you can learn all the mechanics of filmmaking in school, and swallow theory until it's coming out your ears, you never learn a thing about the practicalities involved. Like how to get your film released.

Not a film school in the world deals with it. Because none of them know. I talked to some people in L.A. about this distribution hassle, and they finally said to me: "Look, Ed, you have to understand; it's not whether you're going to stop them from ripping you off because you're not. It's a percentage game. How *much* can you stop them? That's the game." We used to get playdate sheets back from Bryanston—sheets which tell you the names of the towns where the film is playing. Well, we got a sheet from Austin one time, which listed two theaters. It was really showing in four. I called a friend of mine in St. Louis; he told me seven theaters. The sheets listed three. But the burden of proof is on you. To get an accurate accounting of the money due you, you'd have to go to every city in America to see where your film is showing. It's called monitoring the film. In the new film *Splatter,* these details will be carefully defined up front. Shooting should begin this summer. The budget should be around two hundred twenty-five thousand dollars.

Instead of crazies, do you ever think you might like to play a romantic lead sometime?

No. To tell you the truth, I don't want to be Clark Gable. I want to be Strother Martin. Or L. Q. Jones. A character actor.

Opposite page: Marilyn finally manages to escape with the help of a friendly truck driver. Making the film was an ordeal for all the actors, but especially for Marilyn Burns, who literally went through hell, Ed Neal says. This shot would seem to confirm it. (*Courtesy Edwin Neal*)

CHAPTER 10

Mainstream Splatter

It didn't take the major studios long to realize that splatter movies could mean potent box office indeed. The success of George A. Romero's miniscule-budget *Night of the Living Dead,* which has earned back its negative cost several dozen times, proved that. Imagine, producers then began asking themselves, what a full-blown Hollywood production backed by massive amounts of advertising and publicity and supported by widespread distribution might achieve? Scenes of graphic violence had been spreading by leaps and bounds throughout mainstream movies since the late sixties anyway, so why not take the plunge altogether and enter the splatter field with a vengeance? Thus Warner Bros.'s *The Exorcist* was born.

Based by screenwriter William Peter Blatty on his own very successful 1971 novel of the same name, *The Exorcist* had its roots in a news story Blatty had read while a student at Georgetown University in 1949. The story was about a fourteen-year-old boy in nearby Maryland, a suspected victim of demonic possession, who had undergone a ritual exorcism by the Roman Catholic Church in an effort to have the evil spirits driven out of him. The mythic overtones of the story—Satan's reemergence into the modern world through the vehicle of an innocent young boy—continued to haunt Blatty for almost twenty years. By that time he had become a successful screenwriter (*A Shot in the Dark,* 1964; *What Did You Do in the War, Daddy?,* 1966), but instead of developing the story for the movies, he decided to treat it in the form of a novel.

Blatty changed the fourteen-year-old boy to a virginal twelve-year-old girl, the daughter of a famous movie actress, and added two significant subplots, one dealing with a young priest, Father Karras, who is doubting his own faith, the other about an elderly priest, Father Merrin, who has performed exorcisms several times in the past. Otherwise he presented the facts of the '49 case just as he'd recorded them, occasionally mingling details with those from accounts of other cases of demonic possession and ritual exorcism he'd stumbled upon during his long period of researching the book.

Surprising as it may seem in view of how successful *The Exorcist* eventually proved to be, both as a book and as a film, the novel itself was initially rejected by every major New York publisher Blatty submitted it to. By sheer coincidence, he subsequently managed to arouse the interest of a paperback house, Bantam Books, which acquired the book, then sold the hardcover rights to Harper & Row. The rest, of course, is history. The book went on to sell millions of copies in both hard and soft covers. The film made from it went on to become one of the biggest money-makers in motion picture history. And splatter cinema, heretofore the exclusive domain of low-budget, independent, and exploitation filmmakers, finally gained the respectability it required to become a potent box-office force. It became absorbed into the Hollywood main-

Opposite page: William Friedkin's *The Exorcist* (1973) was a very posh splatter movie. (© *Warner Bros., Inc.*)

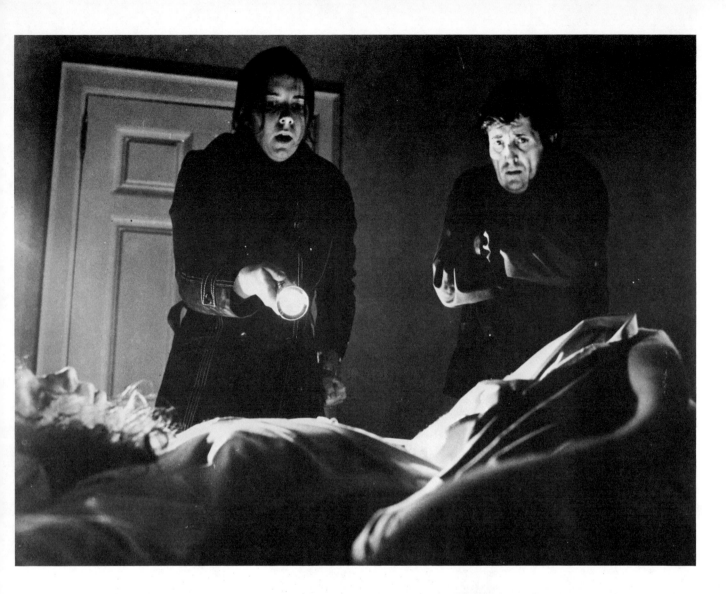

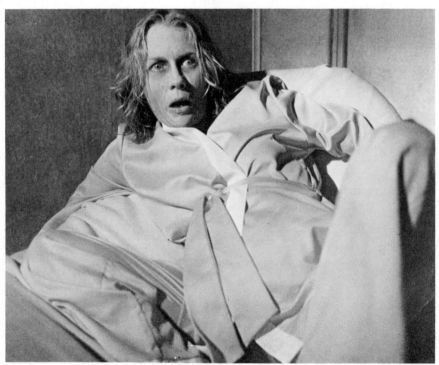

104

stream. The movies—and not just those of the horror genre—have not been the same since.

William Friedkin's *The Exorcist* is French-style *Grand Guignol* performed on an almost operatic scale, its salient themes of pain and terror hammered home to the audience with a technical brilliance no low-budget splatter movie had been able to command so far. The film even introduced a new kind of superstar to the moviegoing public, the make-up artist, a man whose impact on the art of moviemaking in the years to come would prove enormous. Dick Smith's amazing make-up and prosthetic effects for *The Exorcist* succeeded in catapulting him into a position of creative partnership with many of today's most influential filmmakers that no previous practitioner of the art of screen special effects ever enjoyed before—with the possible exceptions of Lon Chaney (who was first and foremost an actor, not an effects man) and Willis (*King Kong*) O'Brien. (More about this, however, in Chapter 12.)

Devoid of humor of any kind—even humor as perverse as that in Herschell Lewis's films—*The Exorcist* is a profoundly depressing film. Blatty and Friedkin's protestations to the contrary, it is not a film about the "mysteries of faith and goodness" at all, but a technological nightmare whose sole aim is to astonish us with the sheer power and versimilitude of its super-grisly special effects. At the end of the film, Father Karras (Jason Miller) reclaims his faith in the Christian ideal by sacrificing his own life to save that of the possessed child Regan (Linda Blair), but this single note of affirmation is literally lost in the torrent of monstrous sounds and hideous images that constitute the majority of *The Exorcist*'s two-hour-plus running time.

A great deal of pop psychologizing and speculation on the nature of good and evil and the reality of Satan's influence on the modern world did follow in the wake of the film's fabulously successful worldwide release, but still, Blatty and Friedkin are deluding themselves if they continue to believe that audiences ever really cared a damn about what *The Exorcist* meant. *"How'd they DO that?"* was the question most filmgoers had on their quivering lips as they scurried from the theater, and it's a question that has become of prime importance ever since. Audiences and film journals alike now no longer seem to care much what a film is about, *any* film; it's how that film was made, how its *effects* were achieved, that obsesses them. Some trace this all-consuming fascination with the mechanics of filmmaking to the influence of Stanley Kubrick's effects-heavy *2001: A Space Odyssey*. But this writer believes that it really began with *The Exorcist*, that truly ground-breaking work of mainstream splatter cinema, which succeeded in charting a new course for filmmakers (and critics) in the seventies and eighties by lifting splatter out of the cultural sub-basement and thrusting it into the limelight as an established and extremely vital form of filmmaking. With *The Exorcist*,

Opposite page, above: Sharon (Kitty Winn) and Father Karras (Jason Miller) look on in horror as the words "Help Me" swell up on Regan's (Linda Blair) stomach in a scene from *The Exorcist* (1973). Special make-up and prosthetic effects such as this one helped to catapult Dick Smith to well-deserved fame as a cinema magician. (© *Warner Bros., Inc.*)

Opposite page, below: Juliet Mills slobbers it up as the possessed housewife in *Beyond the Door* (1974), one of the many entries in the "let's rip off *The Exorcist*" sweepstakes that followed in the wake of the latter film's phenomenal worldwide success. (© *1974 Film Ventures Int'l*)

the medium itself became the message. Max Maurey would indeed have been proud.

As it has already been pointed out, splatter moviemakers frequently lift the plots for their films from other movies. This is done in order to get the problem of story solved as quickly as possible. The way is then free for them to concentrate on the more demanding challenge, that of creating new and more astonishing effects. *The Exorcist* spawned a host of imitations, none of them doing much to advance the cause and spectacle of mainstream splatter. One film which did take up the challenge in high style, however, was Harvey Bernhard's production of *The Omen*. Along with its two sequels, *Damien—Omen II* (1978) and *The Final Conflict* (1981), *The Omen* series makes up the first splatter trilogy. Together, these three films succeeded in introducing a new concept to the bloody arena of mainstream splatter filmmaking—the device of the "creative death."

The Omen, directed by Richard Donner, was a taut, well-crafted little splatter movie that not only left room for a sequel, but invited one. After all, how could any self-respecting producer make a film about the birth of the Antichrist and then conclude his tale when the little devil was only seven years old? A sequel was surely in the cards. After counting the box-office receipts, however, producer Bernhard got so caught up in the excitement of the moment that he decided to make not one sequel, but *three!* These would trace the life of the son of Satan from puberty on into his teens right up to the moment of his big mid-life crisis, Armageddon. Fortunately, prudence prevailed and he concluded the series with the second of these sequels, *The Final Conflict*.

Massive amounts of publicity were not heaped upon *The Omen* prior to its release; in fact, it almost sneaked its way into theaters. It turned out to be an agreeable surprise. While the film may have owed its existence to *The Exorcist*, it owed much of its style to the influence of that grand master of the occult film, Jacques Tourneur—particularly Tourneur's 1959 classic, *Curse of the Demon*. The devilish storm that blows up out of nowhere to send Father Brennan (Patrick Troughton) to his "creative death," along with the eerie, studio-shot graveyard scene, appeared to have been lifted from Tourneur's special bag of tricks, but at least director Donner had taken these ideas and run with them; he did not simply reshoot them and call them his own. *Omen II* and *The Final Conflict*, on the other hand, borrow almost exclusively from *The Omen* itself. Bernhard obviously didn't want to repeat the mistake John Boorman made with *Exorcist II—The Heretic;* that is, to give audiences a completely different film. He opted instead to give them more of the same. In fact, *Omen II* and *The Final Conflict* are not so much sequels as remakes. The only thing that separates them is the individual sense of showmanship exhibited by each film's writer and director in coming up with new and more creative ways of luring Damien's various enemies to their deaths.

At the close of *The Omen*, little Damien, who must somehow worm his way into a sphere of great political influence if he is to fulfill his villainous destiny as set forth in the Book of Revelations, winds up hand in hand with the President of the United States. They are attending the funeral of Ambassador Thorn (Gregory Peck), Damien's presumed father, who had been shot down while attempting to murder Damien in a church. *Omen II* begins as Damien is shipped off to Chicago to live with his uncle (William Holden), who has forsaken politics in order to sit at the top of a huge financial empire that has its corporate fingers into

Damien (Sam Neill) strikes a characteristically subtle pose in the last installment of *The Omen* series, *The Final Conflict* (1981). (© *1980 Twentieth Century-Fox*)

everything from museums to industry. At this point, only two people in the world on the side of Good are aware of Damien's ancestry and birthright; the rest of the do-gooders have either been shot, stabbed, decapitated, or thrown from high buildings. These last two victims are an exorcist named Buchenhagen, a holdover from the first film, and a friendly archeologist—played, but for some reason not listed in the film's credits, by Leo McKern and Ian Hendry, respectively. They are immediately killed during the film's first few minutes, the initial casualities in a growing body count that, by the conclusion of *The Final Conflict*, reaches almost absurd proportions. When Damien's grandmother (Silvia Sidney) begins to suspect the boy of being more than a little unusual, she too is killed off by a malevolent raven that encourages her to suffer a fatal heart attack.

From here the scene shifts to the military school Damien is attending with his cousin Mark, Holden's son by a previous marriage. At the school, Damien falls under the spell of a stiff-necked platoon leader, who is also a satanist, and who provides the means by which Damien finally learns of his ancestry and mission. Another of Damien's concealed benefactors is Paul Buher (Robert Foxworth), a top executive in the Thorn empire. By the end of the film, after Holden and several other obstacles have been put spectacularly out of the way, Buher sits on top, paving the way for Damien's ultimate takeover of the company and its vast resources. The time will then be ripe for Damien's bid to win the hearts and minds of the world's starving millions, so that he can thrust them into enslavement and then debacle. Foxworth's plan, you see, is for Thorn Industries to go into the famine business, to blackmail nations for food instead of oil, a scenario that has frightening possibilities. Unfortunately, the film fails to explore it in any depth.

In all three *Omen* films, unbelievably freakish "accidents" happen to just about everybody who meets Damien, let alone threatens him in any way. In *Omen II*, a doctor (who stumbles upon evidence that Damien has a body chemistry similar to that of a jackal) is forever silenced when he is split in two—the result of an elevator accident that is so spectacularly intricate, not to mention noisy, that one begins to wonder if Damien's protectors aren't trying to call attention to him rather than keep his identity a secret. Another snoop has her eyes pecked out by the same raven that gave Ms. Sidney her heart attack; she then steps out in front of an oncoming truck and gets smashed into eternity. But *Omen II*'s high point remains the elevator accident in which the doctor is cut in two. This scene is an attempt to outdo the scene in *The Omen* where David Warner gets decapitated by a flying sheet of glass. Likewise, the death of the monk in *The Final Conflict* (he slips from the catwalk above a television news set, tangles his foot in a rope, gets himself further entangled in a sheet of plastic, catches on fire, then sways back and forth across the news set until he is fried to a crisp) is an attempt to outdo the

elevator murder in *Omen II*. Every time a character in the *Omen* triology breathes an ill word about Damien, the audience knows that the breath will be his or her last. "Now how do you suppose *this one* is going to get it?" is the response that fills the theater. And that response sums up very concisely what the *Omen* trilogy is all about.

Brian De Palma pays homage to Alfred Hitchcock's *Rear Window* (1954) in this scene from *Sisters* (1973). (© *American International Pictures Corp.*)

Of all mainstream American film directors who work within the splatter genre, Brian De Palma is perhaps the most gleefully imitative. Like Alfred Hitchcock, the man whose work he parrots with such gusto, he genuinely seems to enjoy manipulating an audience to the edge of its collective seat. Unlike Hitchcock, however, he doesn't seem to know how to go about achieving this effect wholly on his own.

I recall that when I first got my hands on a movie camera (at age thirteen), the films I began turning out in my excitement all bore marked resemblances to films by Hitchcock and Hammer and everyone else whose work was having an impact on me at the time. This is a common experience among people who are bitten by the film bug at an early age— whether they eventually choose to go into a career in filmmaking or not. Later, however, when I found myself in film school (Boston University), I began making films that were, good or bad, my own. De Palma, on the other hand, did not go through this ritual period of mimicking. Like

David Cronenberg, he was not bitten by the filmmaking bug until after he'd gone to college, and the early features that helped to launch his career, *Greetings* (1968) and *Hi Mom* (1969), very clearly reflect the cinema verité approach to filmmaking so favored by East Coast colleges and film schools of the time. Prior to *Greetings*, De Palma had made one feature-length Hitchcockian thriller, the little known and rarely seen *Murder à la Mod* (1967), which served to foreshadow the direction his work would take in the seventies and eighties. But it was with the release of *Sisters* (1973) that his flirtation with the work of Alfred Hitchcock began in earnest.

In a review of *Sisters* for *Cinefantastique* magazine at the time of the film's release, I wrote that it was the most insightful and deeply felt homage to the art of Alfred Hitchcock that a devoted admirer of the master's work had yet produced, and I still feel that way. *Sisters* incorporated elements from Hitchcock films as diverse as *Psycho*, *Rear Window* (1954), and *Spellbound* (1945), but De Palma had twisted those elements to achieve his own effects—something he has ceased trying to do since.

De Palma followed the highly successful *Sisters* with the amusing, cartoonlike *Phantom of the Paradise* (1974), which flopped. Since then he has devoted himself almost exclusively to making thrillers that rely heavily on techniques and even plot devices already tested and proven by Hitchcock in order to produce their own very similar thrills.

In both *Carrie* (1976) and *Dressed to Kill* (1980), for instance, De Palma has his composer, Pino Donaggio, enhance each film's scarier moments by underscoring them with the same "screaming violins" composer Bernard Herrmann created for *Psycho*. *Dressed to Kill* goes even further, cannibalizing its entire structure from *Psycho* and lifting whole sequences not only from that film, but from *Vertigo* (1958) and *Rear Window* as well. Obviously, this goes beyond mere homage. It is, as David Cronenberg puts it, turning something around and having it appear exactly as it came in.

De Palma doesn't restrict himself to imitating Hitchcock, though. His film *Blow-Out* (1981), which deals with a movie sound-effects man (John Travolta) who unwittingly records the sounds of a murder being committed, borrows in equal measure from Francis Ford Coppola's *The Conversation* (1974), a thriller about a professional wire-tapper (Gene Hackman) who overhears a murder being planned, and from Michelangelo Antonioni's *Blow-Up* (1966), the story of a professional fashion photographer (David Hemmings) who unwittingly captures the details of a murder in progress on film. Even the title of De Palma's film recalls that of Antonioni's.

De Palma is not even above lifting ideas from his own work and replaying them. Both *Carrie* and *Dressed to Kill* begin with long, erotically charged sequences of a female (Sissy Spacek, Angie Dickinson)

Opposite page: Sissy Spacek and the unconscious William Katt are drenched in pig's blood by scheming schoolmates in Brian De Palma's *Carrie* (1976). (© *1976 United Artist Corp.*)

Below: Margot Kidder embraces a dead Bill Finley as Jennifer Salt sleeps on in *Sisters* (1973), Brian De Palma's first and best Hitchcock pastiche. (© *American International Pictures Corp.*)

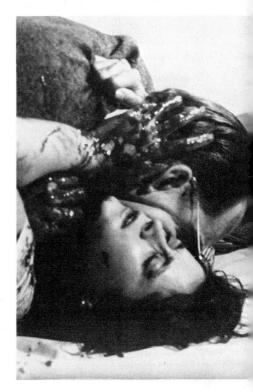

caressing her naked body while taking a shower, only to have her reverie suddenly broken by some real or imagined trauma. And both films end with the heroine (Amy Irving, Nancy Allen) sitting upright in bed and screaming as she recalls the details of a nightmare that both she and the audience had been convinced was real.

A major point in De Palma's favor, however, is that, whether he's imitating Hitchcock's work or his own, he does succeed in doing honor to his source. *Dressed to Kill* may not be *Psycho*, but it is certainly a very skillfully made and entertaining copy, as is his reuse of the shock ending of *Carrie* for the conclusion of *Dressed to Kill*. Yes, it's self-plagiarism, but it is undeniably effective nevertheless—even a second time around.

Twentieth Century-Fox's miltimillion dollar production of *Alien* (1979) remains, as of this writing, the screen's reigning splatter epic. Though not as flamboyantly grisly as *Dawn of the Dead*, its combined elements of human, alien, and robot splatter make it a unique contribution to the genre.

This film, about a single-mindedly lethal creature that is brought on board a space-age garbage scow so that it can methodically slaughter off the crew, has no pretensions to being about anything except its own grisly effects. It moves along at a breathtaking pace (once the alien shows up), derives its so-called plot from *The Thing* (1951), *It! The Terror from Beyond Space* (1958), Mario Bava's *Planet of the Vampires* (1965), and half a dozen other monster movies, and dispenses with logic as if it were the plague—which, to splatter movies, it often is. *Alien* is so derivative that it even lifts its major set piece, the infamous "chest burster" sequence, from a previous film—David Cronenberg's *They Came From Within*. It is splatter moviemaking at its most basic—imitative, empty-headed, and eye-boggling.

The significance of *The Exorcist*, *The Omen* trilogy, the films of Brian De Palma, and *Alien*—mainstream movies all—is, of course, that they served to catapult splatter into a sphere of respectability. The huge financial and popular success of these films meant that the major studios could no longer afford to look upon splatter as a purely bargain-basement form of moviemaking. One final step remained to be taken in order to draw splatter even further into the cultural mainstream. Low-budget splatter itself had to be made respectable. Paramount took that step when it picked up—for a song—Sean Cunningham's low-budget, independently made *Friday the 13th* and promoted it into a worldwide box-office winner.

When *Friday the 13th* mushroomed into such a huge financial success for Paramount, that studio, along with many of the other majors, began scouting for other low-budget, independently made splatter quickies to pick up and turn into an instant goldmine. Paramount's *My Bloody Valentine* (1981), Twentieth's *Terror Train* (1981), and Columbia's *Happy*

Opposite page, above: In *Dressed to Kill* (1980), De Palma has his composer, Pino Donaggio, underscore the film's scarier moments with the same "screaming violins" composer Bernard Herrmann created for Hitchcock's *Psycho* (1960). (© *Filmways Pictures, Inc.*)

Opposite page, below: John Travolta, a movie sound effects man who records the sounds of murder by chance, lies unconscious against the steering wheel of his car in Brian De Palma's Antonioni pastiche, *Blow Out* (1981). (© *1981 Filmways Pictures, Inc.*)

Above: Low-budget splatter finally enters the cultural mainstream in *Friday the 13th* (1980). (© *1980 Georgetown Productions*)

Right: Sigourney Weaver, Yaphet Kotto, and Harry Dean Stanton search for the deadly creature that has infiltrated their spacecraft in *Alien* (1979). (© *1979 Twentieth Century-Fox*)

Birthday to Me (1981) followed in fairly rapid succession, but none of them topped *Friday* at the box office.

What developed then was the decision on the part of some major studio executives to enter the schlock film arena themselves, to start from scratch and pump millions of dollars into the making of their own *big*-budgeted exploitation films. These films would contain all the elements that had made their low-budget brethren so popular, but be treated on a much grander scale. As of this writing, we have only seen the tip of the iceberg insofar as these megabuck exploitation films are concerned, but of the ones that have been released so far, John Landis's *An American Werewolf in London* (1981) stands out as a premiere example of this new trend in filmmaking: *the sleaze epic*.

Produced on location in England for an estimated $10 million—much of which went into the creation of some elaborate and very striking werewolf transformation effects by make-up wiz Rick Baker, *An American Werewolf* is an exploitation film to the core, replete with R-rated language, steamy sex scenes, lowbrow humor, gobs of graphic splatter, mindless car crashes, and blaring rock and roll music. Landis even stages one of his low camp humor-cum-splatter set pieces in a porno film house in Piccadilly Circus so that he could interject an atmosphere of even greater sleaziness into the scene than it might have had otherwise.

In its overpowering combination of polish and trashiness, *An American Werewolf in London* reminds one of what might have been the result if David Lean had directed *Blood Feast*. Here's a film that really makes one take the closing words of John Waters's autobiography to heart: "At least I've never done anything really decadent. The budgets of my films could hardly feed the starving children of India."

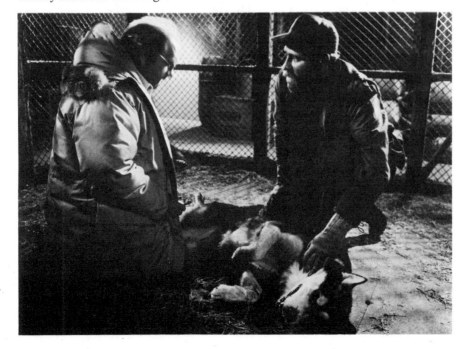

A. Wilford Brimley (left) and Richard Masur examine a dog that has been taken over by an alien life form in John Carpenter's big-budget, splattery remake of *The Thing* (1982). (© *1982 Universal*)

CHAPTER 11

Splatter 'Round the World: The Rise of the Exploitation Film

In a sense, all motion pictures exploit the subjects they deal with simply by dealing with them in the first place. But for the purposes of our discussion here, let's define the purely exploitative film as that kind of film that capitalizes chiefly on an audience's curiosity. When Herschell Lewis made *Blood Feast,* for example, he didn't *know* that an audience of gorehounds existed out there to lap his film up, but he did know intuitively that if he made a film that aroused people's curiosity, enough of them would go see that film to make it profitable. Explicit gore, which audiences were unaccustomed to seeing before in films, was what he chose to exploit in order to arouse this curiosity. As we all know, he succeeded in spades.

The first movies, the nickelodeons, were by their very nature exploitation films because they too traded chiefly on audience curiosity, namely the curiosity to see something that had never been seen before: pictures that moved. Action was the item being exploited: fires, speeding trains, dancing girls, and so on. When the narrative cinema was born, audiences became more sophisticated and demanding. They wanted a story; later, they wanted stars. And so the motion picture industry was born. Major studios grew to the point where they had a stranglehold on motion picture production and distribution. By opening their own chains of theaters across the country, they managed to sew up motion picture exhibition as well, making it all but impossible for anyone working outside the major Hollywood studio system to get his films shown. Thus the exploitation film as we know it today came into being.

In order to arouse exhibitor interest and audience curiosity in their films, the early exploitation film pioneers determined to make films about subjects no major studio could or would touch: drugs, nymphomania, murder, madness, and so on. But they had it tough for a number of reasons. First, the major studios' monopolistic hold over exhibition denied them access to most theaters. And second, they had the strict Motion Picture Production Code to contend with. Until the late forties, when the major studios were forced by law to divest themselves of their theaters, the first obstacle remained virtually insurmountable. Exploitation filmmakers were forced to play their films in specialty theaters such as burlesque houses, but at least they could get them shown. The second obstacle proved more frustrating, however, because of the severe restrictions the Code put on motion picture content and subject matter. To get over this hurdle, the early exploitation filmmakers had to demonstrate genius. One of them who did was Dwain Esper.

Esper, who died in 1982 at the age of eighty-three, remained in the exploitation film business practically until his death. One of his last coups was to pick up the rights to Tod Browning's *Freaks* (1932), which was made at MGM but quickly shelved by studio head Louis B. Mayer because of its "unsavory" subject matter, and rerelease it independently, making himself a small fortune. But he began making his own exploita-

Opposite page: Film noir melds with splatter and science-fiction in director Ridley Scott's eclectic follow-up to Alien, Blade Runner *(1982). (© 1982 The Ladd Company)*

116

tion films in the early thirties. He and his wife, Hildegarde, called their outfit the Hollywood Producers & Distributors–Roadshow Attractions Company. Some of their films include *Modern Motherhood* (1936), *Marihuana, Weed with Roots in Hell* (1936), *How to Undress in Front of Your Husband* (1937), and *Maniac* (1934), a forerunner of the modern, mad slasher-type horror film, which eschews graphic bloodshed (except for one scene in which the title character plucks out a cat's eye and eats it) but wallows in other kinds of grotesqueries such as rape (again, not graphically).

Ironically, Esper managed to get his films past the Code by seeming to be its chief upholder. In *Maniac*, for example, he attached a prologue to the film stating that the film was educational in nature, that its chief goal was to explore the sickness of mental illness for the purpose of helping people. Subsequently he even issued a proclamation on "the making and showing of motion pictures" that contained many of the Code's own by-laws. He called it "Dwain Esper's Platform," and in it, he maintained that filmmakers everywhere should continually strive to keep stars who are favorites with children in wholesome pictures, eliminate scenes depicting the technique of committing crime, eliminate the glorification of promiscuity, and so on. His own films, of course, ran counter to these ideals, but were always carefully disguised to seem in perfect keeping with them. As a result, his films passed the censors unnoticed and went on to make money for both Esper and his exhibitors. Thirty years later, when the exploitation film came into full bloom, Dwain Esper's tactics would serve as a manifesto for exploitation filmmakers everywhere to follow, making him truly the father of the exploitation film.

Even after the major studios were compelled to release their stranglehold on motion picture exhibition, exploitation filmmakers continued to have it tough. Censorship still existed, but even more importantly, they had the staple Hollywood B picture to compete with. Many of these B pictures, while not exploitation films exactly, offered exploitative ingredients in their plots. The dark, brooding genre now known as *film noir* (which flourished throughout the forties) grew out of the B picture, and then spread to the As. A reflection of America's postwar disillusionment, *film noir*'s themes have much in common with themes found in many of the exploitation films that followed later as the censors became more permissive. Greed, corruption, violence, sordid sexuality, pain, disillusionment: these were the central themes of *film noir*, whose salient image is that of the dark, mean street down which the world-weary hero or heroine cannot pass without suffering either some loss of personal integrity or outright loss of life—or both. Some years later, exploitation films in general and splatter movies in particular would treat explicitly the very same themes these *films noir* could only hint at back in the forties.

The exploitation film did not come into its own until the B picture was finally put to death by the advent of television. At this time, moviegoing ceased to be a weekly habit for many millions of Americans, who now preferred to sit home in front of their tubes. The major studios were forced to cut their production schedules drastically, leaving many theater owners, particularly those in the hinterlands, hungry for product. Exploitation filmmakers like H. G. Lewis quickly stepped in to fill the gap. Today, exploitation filmmakers have a better shot at securing major national and international distribution for their films than ever before. And as discussed in the previous chapter, many of the major studios have now started making purely exploitative pictures of their own in order to compete with them. How the tables have turned!

Film noir is a distinctly American film genre with roots in the American pulp magazines, hard-boiled detective novels, and films of the twenties and thirties. Splatter cinema, on the other hand, has no particular cultural identification. It was born and raised in the United States, but it has its roots in French *Grand Guignol* theater and British Gothic literature. As a result, it is a genre that is peculiarly adaptable to the filmmaking styles and traditions of most countries. A western, for example, can be made in Italy with American actors, but it still retains the look and feel of a spaghetti western. Italian splatter movies, on the other hand, are virtually interchangeable with those made in America, England, Spain, or wherever. Only the language is different. Perhaps this is why splatter movies are now being made in practically every country in the world. They are a truly international phenomenon, and their appeal is global. Here's a brief overview:

Spaghetti Splatter

After establishing himself as one of Italy's most accomplished lighting cameramen, Mario Bava turned to directing in 1960 with *Black Sunday*, a Hammer Films–inspired Gothic occult fantasy, which has since become a cult favorite with many horror film buffs. Marred by atrocious dubbing, mediocre acting, and a so-so plot about a resurrected witch (Barbara Steele) who swears revenge against the descendants of those who originally put her to the stake, *Black Sunday* is nevertheless a gorgeous-looking film, sumptuously dressed, and atmospherically photographed by Bava himself.

Bava preferred to shoot his films almost entirely in the studio because of the greater control it gave him. While many of his films lack dramatic impact, they are almost always visually striking, particularly the early ones like *Black Sunday, Hercules in the Haunted World* (1961), and *Black Sabbath* (1964), in which he was able to exercise his preference for in-studio shooting to the fullest. Later, as audience tastes changed and his budgets fell, he was forced to move away from the expensive, Gothic-style horror film that had made his name, and begin making more

Above: Black Sunday (1961) was a gorgeous-looking film, sumptuously dressed and atmospherically photographed by director Mario Bava himself. His best films share these characteristics. (© *1961 American International Picture*)

Right: When audience tastes began to change and his budgets fell, Bava was forced to move away from expensive, period horror films and turn to splatter with films like *Twitch of the Death Nerve* (1973). (*Courtesy Barry Kaufman*)

overtly realistic horror films with lots of graphic violence, such as *Blood and Black Lace* (1964), *Twitch of the Death Nerve* (1973), *Hatchet for a Honeymoon* (1976), and *Beyond the Door II* (1979). He died in 1982.

Frequently called "the poor man's Mario Bava," Italy's second most famous splatter filmmaker, Dario Argento, actually seems less influenced by Bava than by Hitchcock, Roger Corman, and, particularly, Michelangelo Antonioni, whose 1966 film *Blow-Up* seems to hold a special fascination for him, stylistically anyway. His cult favorite, *Deep Red* (1976), even stars David Hemmings, the alienated hero of Antonioni's film. In *Deep Red*, Hemmings again witnesses a murder and determines to get to the bottom of it. And, again, as in *Blow-Up*, he carries out his detective work as if totally uninvolved. Argento even goes so far as to include such Antonioniesque images of alienation as having Hemmings walk through the brightly lit streets of the big city where the film takes place, alone and lost in thought about the perplexities of the mystery, the streets deserted by all but him.

A former film critic, Argento made his directorial debut in 1969 with *The Bird with the Crystal Plumage*, a violent but stylish psychodrama about an American writer (Tony Musante) living in Rome who witnesses a murder and thereafter becomes a target for murder himself. *Cat O' Nine Tails* (1971) and *Four Flies on Grey Velvet* (1971), two other graphically violent murder mysteries, with strong overtones of Hitchcock's *Psycho*, followed in quick succession before Argento finally hit the horror big time with *Deep Red*. This film and *Suspiria* (1977), a film about occult murders at a German dance academy, remain his two most

The Bird with the Crystal Plumage (1969), a violent, but stylish psychodrama, marked the splatter moviemaking debut of former film critic turned director, Dario Argento. (*Courtesy Cinemabilia*)

popular splatter movies to date. His most recent film, *Inferno* (1980), received only spotty release in the United States.

Argento also professes a fondness for the work of George A. Romero. Argento and his Italian backers helped to finance Romero's watershed splatter movie *Dawn of the Dead* and Argento also provided the Romero film with its score. Look in the credits and you'll see "Music by Dario Argento and The Goblins."

Another master of spaghetti splatter who professes great admiration for Romero's work is Italy's reigning King of Splatter, Lucio Fulci. Fulci, along with fellow Italian Luigi Cozzi (who frequently signs his films "Lewis Coates"), follows the precepts of splatter filmmaking to the letter. His films are boldly imitative (usually of Romero's), totally empty-headed, and filled with eye-popping scenes of graphic gore. His most successful film as of this writing is *Zombie* (1980), a rip-off of Romero's *Dawn of the Dead* in which a mad doctor (Richard Johnson) sets up shop on a remote tropical island in order to conduct a series of bizarre experiments in secret. To preserve this secrecy, he has his island hideaway guarded by an army of killer zombies. In Italy, Fulci's film was released as *Zombie II* in order to capitalize on the success of the Romero film, which was released under the title *Zombie*. Fulci's most recent film is *Twilight of the Dead* (1983), a further rip-off of the Romero film.

Unlike Fulci, Luigi Cozzi tends to imitate whatever successful film

Above: With *Deep Red* (1976), his first major box office success, Argento finally hit the splatter big time . . . right on the head. (*Courtesy Barry Kaufman*)

Opposite page, above: Lucio Fulci's *Zombie* (1980) was a blatant attempt to out-gross (as well as gross out) George A. Romero's *Dawn of the Dead* (1979). (© *1980 the Jerry Gross Organization*)

Opposite page, below: Suspiria (1977) was a film about occult murders at a German dance academy. Nothing too occult-looking about this splattery demise, however. (*Courtesy Hollywood Book & Poster*)

comes along. His *Starcrash* (1979), for example, was made to cash in on the success of *Star Wars*. But his splatter masterpiece has got to be *Alien Contamination* (1980), a sort of unofficial sequel to *Alien* in which some strange eggs are brought back to earth by a team of astronauts. When the eggs hatch, the gore begins, all to the accompaniment of a pounding rock score by The Goblins.

Andy Milligan and Pete Walker

Next to H. G. Lewis, there's probably no other splatter moviemaker in the history of the genre who has managed to turn out more films for less money than Staten Island's Andy Milligan. By Milligan's own admission, the budgets for his films have never risen above $20,000 and were frequently as low as $7,500. By comparison, the average $40,000 to $60,000 budget for a Lewis production seems astronomical.

Milligan moved from the garment business to the exploitation film business in the early sixties. His first films were shot on an Auricon 16mm single-system optical sound camera, the same kind of camera used by most television news departments at the time for shooting stand-ups. Shooting single system, where the live soundtrack is optically printed on the film as footage is being shot, inhibits any kind of sophisticated editing afterward, particularly of dialogue sequences. As a result, early Milligan efforts such as *The Naked Witch* (1964), *The Degenerates* (1967), and *The Ghastly Ones* (1968) seem primitive indeed, especially when blown up to 35mm for theatrical distribution.

Above: Fulci followed up *Zombie* with *Twilight of the Dead* (aka *Gates of Hell*) in 1983. Even the film's ads tried to ape Romero's *Dawn of the Dead* this time around.

Right: When the eggs hatch, the gore begins in Luigi Cozzi's *Alien Contamination* (1980), a sort of unofficial sequel to . . . you guessed it! . . . *Alien* (1979). (*Courtesy Barry Kaufman*)

Despite his crippling low budgets, Milligan has always preferred setting his gore epics in period, usually Europe of the late nineteenth century (or earlier). The reason for this, he says, is that it prevents his films from appearing dated when they are retitled and rereleased for another round at the drive-ins and New York City grind houses. *Blood-thirsty Butchers* (1969), the story of Sweeney Todd, was the first of his costumed splatter movies to actually be shot on location in England. Milligan remained there to shoot his next four period bloodbaths as well: *The Body Beneath* (1970), *Torture Dungeon* (1970), *Guru, the Mad Monk* (1971), and *The Rats Are Coming, The Werewolves Are Here!* (1972). As a result, many people mistakenly assume Milligan to be a British director. Alas, no—his roots are in New York City, where he remains to this day, operating a legitimate Off-Broadway theater, and, perhaps, planning his next period-gore film. His last was *Blood!*, shot in 1974 in both British and Staten Island locales.

The only bonafide British director to achieve a solid reputation among splatter movie fans so far is Pete Walker, whose work demonstrates a significant technical polish over that of most of his colleagues in the low-budget splatter filmmaking field. Most of Walker's splatter

British director Pete Walker prefers to call his gore extravaganzas "terror films," but they look like splatter movies to me. From *Frightmare* (1977). (© *1975 Ellman Films Entertainment, Inc.*)

Walker could move into mainstream moviemaking if he wanted to, for his films are generally well crafted and eschew that low-budget look. From *The Comeback* (1979). (*Courtesy Barry Kaufman*)

movies (he prefers to call them "terror films") are of the mad slasher variety. *Die, Beautiful Maryanne* (1969), *The Flesh and Blood Show* (1973), *Schizo* (1976), *The Confessional* (a.k.a. *House of Mortal Sin*, 1977), *Frightmare* (1977), and *The Comeback* (1979) all fall into this category. But his most well known and widely distributed splatter movie is *House of Whipcord*, a 1974 exploitation film about a women's prison scripted by frequent Walker collaborator David McGillivray, a British film critic and author of *The History of British Sex Movies 1957-1981*.

Walker began making his outrageously gore-filled "terror films" set in modern-day England as a reaction to the Gothic-style traditions of British horror filmmaking established by Hammer Films. Like Hammer, however, he has always managed to get good British actors and actresses with many years of stage and screen experience behind them to appear in his films—people like Susan George, Stephanie Beacham, John Fraser, Anthony Sharp, Ray Brooks, and others, whose performances have done much to elevate Walker's work above the level one expects from exploitation films. Clearly, Walker could move into mainstream moviemaking if he wanted to, for his films are not only generally well acted, but well scripted and photographed too. His most recent film, *House of the Long Shadows* (1983), is, perhaps, an attempt to do just that. Ironically, this bigger-budgeted production is a Gothic-style horror film in the Hammer mold, marking a return to the very traditions he had originally resisted. Its stars: Peter Cushing and Christopher Lee.

Paul Naschy's character Waldemar Daninsky, a Polish nobleman and werewolf, turns good guy for the moment to do battle with a villainous vampire countess in *The Werewolf Vs. The Vampire Woman* (1972). (© *1972 Western International*)

Paul Naschy

Spain's Paul Naschy is a good example of the actor as *auteur*. Since 1968, he has starred in over thirty horror/splatter movies, many of which he also wrote under his given name, Jacinto Molina. Naschy's films are big business in Spain, France, Germany, and Mexico, but get little distribution in the United States except for an occasional play on the late, late, late show—usually in versions that are poorly dubbed and severely cut. But in those countries where his films do get widespread release, Naschy's name is as revered by horror fans as those of Boris Karloff, Christopher Lee, Peter Cushing, and Vincent Price.

Like those four gentlemen, Naschy too has played all manner of movie monsters throughout his career, ranging from The Mummy and Count Dracula to Jack the Ripper and a villainous hunchback. But Naschy also plays heroes, occasionally combining both the hero and the monster into one part, such as in his most famous screen role, El Hombre Lobo—The Wolfman.

A former architect, Naschy made his debut as a lead in 1971's *Mark of the Wolfman*, the film that also marked the debut of his continuing character, Waldemar Daninsky, a Polish nobleman who is bitten by a werewolf and thus condemned to become a werewolf himself. While this film and many of his others clearly demonstrate the influence of Hammer Films, they also reflect a fondness for the Universal horror thrillers of the thirties and forties. Naschy's Daninsky is not unlike Lon Chaney, Jr.'s Larry Talbot in *The Wolfman* (1941) in that he is essentially a sympathetic character who seeks to find a cure for his affliction from film to film. Naschy played the Daninsky role in six more films, the most well known

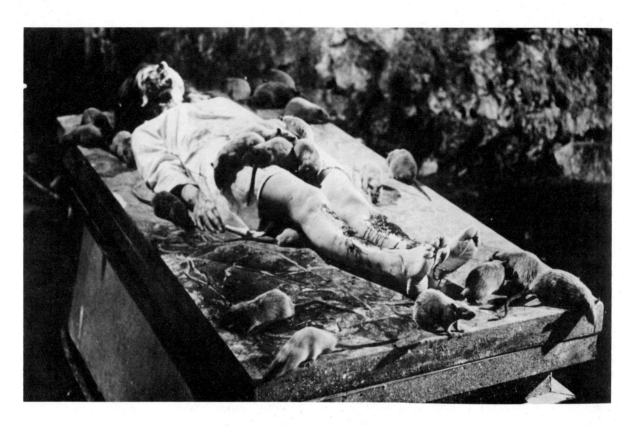

Naschy has played all manner of monsters throughout his career. In *Hunchback of the Morgue* (1975), he plays a misshapen creature who supplies bodies for a mad scientist's bizarre experiments. Here's one of his latest deliveries. (*Courtesy Barry Kaufman*)

of which, stateside, is probably *The Werewolf Vs. the Vampire Woman* (1972), in which his monster/hero assists two female medical students in destroying a vampire countess patterned after Elizabeth Bathory, the legendary countess who murdered over six hundred young girls and drank and bathed in their blood.

Spain's relaxed censorship laws regarding screen violence have allowed Naschy and his directors to give free reign to their splattery sensibilities. Films such as *Horror Rises from the Tomb* (1976) and *Dracula's Great Love* (1979), therefore, contain large doses of exploitative gore. But *Dracula's Great Love,* one of Naschy's favorites, also contains a fair amount of eroticism as well, which was quite a breakthrough not only for Naschy but for the Spanish film industry as well.

Snuff

Snuff is the kind of exploitation film that not only makes people a little curious, but also a little worried. That, of course, is its goal, because these two elements combined add up to big box-office success.

Released in 1975, its advertising traded on a persistent rumor that its on-screen mayhem was not simulated, but, in fact, bloodily real. Also, its title traded on an equally persistent rumor that there was a new form of pornography then beginning to spring up in underground film circles across the land: snuff films, super low-budget movies in which performers were actually being murdered on screen in order to provide a new and sick kind of "entertainment" for jaded audiences. These

128

audiences were thought to include isolated pockets of America's jet set located in Los Angeles and New York City. According to no less an authority than Joseph Wambaugh, however, snuff films are a hoax, for no sample of one has ever been found either by the LAPD or any other police department in the country.

The film *Snuff*, too, is a hoax. It began as a low-budget, 1971 Argentinian zombie movie called *Slaughter*, which was picked up for U.S. distribution and retitled *Snuff* in order to capitalize on the American public's growing curiosity about this bizarre new form of underground filmmaking. Some added scenes of a young girl being hacked up by the film's cast and crew were then staged and shot in the New York area by independent splatter and porno filmmaker Michael Findlay, and later sandwiched into the release print in order to spice up the film's otherwise dull plot. *Snuff* was then released by Alan Shackleton's Monarch Pictures with the slogan: "Made in South America—Where Life Is Cheap!" Implying, of course, that the film's blood and gore were real. The film also excluded any mention of cast or other technical credits in order to perpetuate the myths surrounding its purportedly illegal manufacture.

Snuff really became notorious, however, when certain feminist groups began lobbying against it. Ironically, it was the film's distributor who brought *Snuff* to the attention of these groups in the first place. People began flocking to the film not just to see the gore, which was rather unconvincing and already old hat in films by that time anyway, but to see what all the hullabaloo was about. This was just what the distributor was hoping for, and the film became a big hit.

Today this Cardiff Giant of splatter-exploitation films is successfully being marketed on videocassette in almost the exact same manner. Its slogan: "Too real to be simulated!" Proving after all that in the arena of exploitation film, P. T. Barnum continues to be right.

Snuff (1975) remains the Cardiff Giant of splatter-exploitation films because it purported to show real murders on screen, not just staged ones. Alas, it was all a gimmick designed to lure the curious away from their TV sets and into the theaters. But it worked. Ah, the power of advertising!

Another zestful scene of Spanish splatter from Naschy's *House of Psychotic Women* (1974), directed by frequent Naschy collaborator Carlos Aured. (*Courtesy Barry Kaufman*)

CHAPTER 12

Splatter's Make-Up Master: Tom Savini

"Lon Chaney, my idol, was incredibly versatile; he acted, did his own make-up and stunts. Hopefully, people will eventually come away thinking that way about me."

Tom Savini (in a conversation with the author)

Film is a collaborative art, but the nature of that collaboration has seldom remained constant over the years. During the silent era, the director and the cameraman were predominantly responsible for a film's look, tone, and even content. A powerful actor or actress like Douglas Fairbanks or Mary Pickford frequently shaped the films they appeared in as well, but, in the main, the silent film director and his cameraman held sway over the most memorable films of their day. D. W. Giffith and Billy Bitzer, F. W. Murnau and Charles Rosher, Rex Ingram and John B. Seitz, Clarence Brown and William Daniels, Maurice Tourneur and John van der Broek—these were teams to remember, for they were undeniably the chief architects of their films.

With the advent of the talkies, however, the writer began to assert himself, demanding—because of the very nature of the talkies—a more active role in the collaborative process. For a while, the writer even usurped the cameraman's position as the director's right-hand man, as in the pairings of Frank Capra and Robert Riskin, or John Ford and Dudley Nichols.

In the forties, the cameraman's star rose once again. Sound had been tamed and the camera no longer had to be held in chains. Audiences had again gotten used to movies that actually *moved* and had developed a particular fondness for the gritty, atmospheric form of filmmaking critics have since dubbed *film noir*. The cameraman again became so important to the collaboration that the director often favored him over the writer as a teammate. Nowhere is this more evident than in the classic *Citizen Kane* (1941), at the end of which director Orson Welles chose to share his final credit not with his co-writer, Herman Manckiewicz, but with his cameraman, Gregg Toland.

The widespread acceptance among critics and industryites of the *auteur* theory during the late fifties and sixties catapulted the director alone into a pre-eminent position as the guiding light of the film. The names Hitchcock, Fellini, Bergman, and Truffaut reverberated everywhere. All but Hitchcock wrote their own screenplays and even Hitchcock did not collaborate with any single writer for any great length of time. Certainly he never teamed with anyone. Writer John Michael Hayes came the closest, and even he only wrote four of the sixteen films Hitchcock made during the fifties and sixties—*Rear Window, To Catch a Thief* (1955), *The Trouble with Harry* (1956), and *The Man Who Knew Too Much* (1956).

All four of these directorial giants did team up consistently with a special cameraman. Alfred Hitchcock with Robert Burks; Federico Fellini with Giuseppe Rotunno; Ingmar Bergman with Sven Nykvist; François Truffaut with Nestor Almendros. But in the eyes of everyone, the director, not the director-cameraman team, still remained the dominant creative force in film during the *auteur* period.

The nature of the collaboration shifted dramatically in the seventies

Effects wizard Tom Savini in make-up as Morgan, the Black Knight, in George A. Romero's *Knightriders* (1981). (© *1981 United Film Distribution Co.—United Artists Corporation*)

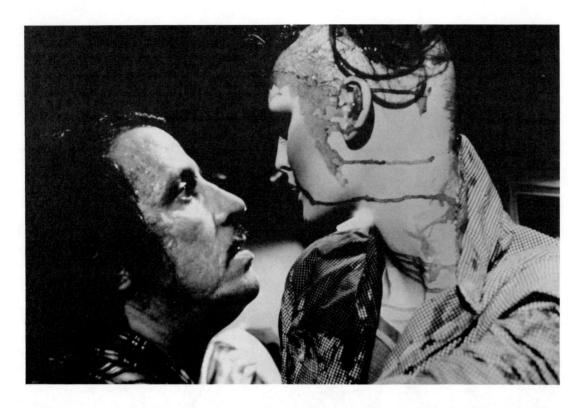

Fans liked the effects in *Maniac* (1981), but the film itself was just sleaze. Savini would have preferred a better showcase. (© *Analysis Film Releasing Corp.*)

when a new player was added to the frontline creative team: the special effects man. Prior to the seventies, special effects men had served a vital technical function in the making of movies. They had created earthquakes. They had burned Atlanta. They had taken us to the enchanting Land of Oz. But very few of them had ever risen above the status of "technician" to become a full creative partner along with the director, writer, and cameraman in shaping the films they made. (Willis O'Brien and, later, Ray Harryhausen, were two of the very few.)

Today, however, the special effects man, in tandem with the director, has assumed a considerable role in the filmmaking process, one that extends far beyond his bringing off that amazing trick or two. As so many of today's films—splatter movies in particular—are increasingly effects-oriented, the one-time technician has advanced to the position of unofficial co-director. The cameraman, the writer, and even the star actor or actress have all slipped significantly into less powerful roles in the collaborative process.

The first sign of this change occurred in 1968 when Stanley Kubrick's technically astounding *2001: A Space Odyssey* boosted special effects chief Douglas Trumbull into a position of creative eminence. Three years later, Trumbull was directing and designing the effects for his own film, *Silent Running* (1971). The release of *The Exorcist* then caused a different kind of technician's stock to soar: the make-up man. Dick Smith's breathtaking orchestration of *The Exorcist*'s myriad of hideously powerful—and baffling—make-up and prosthetic effects

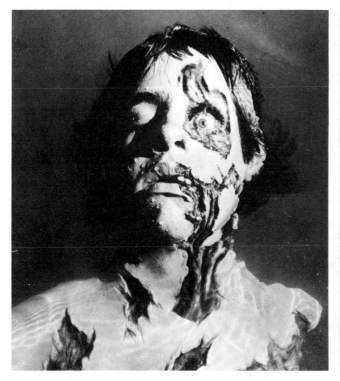 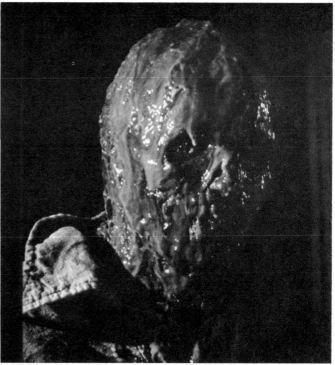

turned him into a star almost overnight, even though he had been doing make-up for over twenty years.

Smith's profound impact on film in the seventies encouraged a number of younger make-up enthusiasts like Rick Baker, Rob Bottin, and Tom Savini to pursue similar careers as screen make-up masters. When they too achieved fame and subsequent creative clout for their ingenious work on films as diverse as the remake of *King Kong* (Baker, 1979), *Piranha* (Bottin, 1979), and *Dawn of the Dead* (Savini, 1979), another wave of young make-up men were prompted to enter the field, including Dick Smith's own son Dave, Chris Walas, and Carl Fullerton, to name but a few.

The relaxation of censorship rules pertaining to scenes of explicit gore and violence and other taboo subjects on the screen had much to do with the professional rise in stature of the special make-up effects technician during the seventies and, now, eighties. When the call for "More realism!" went out at the close of the sixties, someone had to emerge to meet that growing demand. Dick Smith and his colleagues were—luckily for them—in just the right place at just the right time. When *The Exorcist* was released with only an R rating, the walls of film censorship crumbled completely. All systems were suddenly go. And they have remained so ever since.

Splatter movies ultimately emerged because, in a variety of forms, they had been steadily chipping away at censorship restraints over the years. When those restraints were finally lifted, the special make-up

Left: Splattery effects from *Piranha* (1979) created by Rob Bottin, one of the busiest of today's movie make-up masters. (© *New World Pictures*)

Right: The title character of *The Incredible Melting Man* (1978) in mid-melt—an example of Rick Baker's make-up wizardry. (© *1977 American International Pictures*)

133

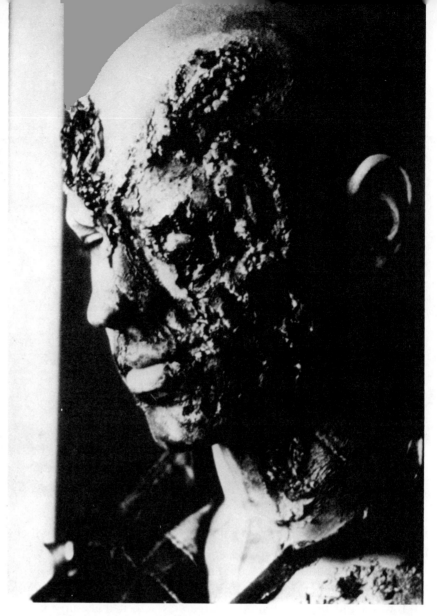

One of Savini's zombie make-ups for Romero's splatter spectacular, *Dawn of the Dead* (1979). (© *Dawn Associates, 1978/K. Kolbert*)

effects technician was on hand to give splatter its final boost to maturity. And with that boost, the effects man himself suddenly became the cinema's hottest new *auteur*.

Dick Smith, Rick Baker, Rob Bottin, and Tom Savini are currently the most well known and busiest of today's movie make-up masters. In addition to *The Exorcist*, Smith's incredible versatility as a special make-up effects technician can be seen in such films as *Godfathers I* and *II* (1972, 1975), *Taxi Driver* (1976), *Altered States* (1980), and David Cronenberg's *Scanners* (1981). Recently, Smith has made it known that he wants to steer away from projects that are overtly splatter-oriented if he can—as has Smith's protégé, Rick Baker, who began his career working alongside Smith on *The Exorcist*, then went on to solo with such splatter movies as AIP's *Squirm* (1976), and *The Incredible Melting Man* (1977). At twenty-three, Rob Bottin (Rick Baker's own protégé), is the youngest of the quartet, though even at this tender age he has firmly established himself as a veteran in his field. His remarkable effects for films like *Piranha, Humanoids from the Deep* (1980), *The Fog*, (1980), and, especially, *The Thing* (1982) have earned him a reputation as a modern make-up master.

134

Of the four, however, the equally youthful Tom Savini is the one who is most closely identified with the splatter film form, a fact due in large part to his close association with splatter movie kingpin George A. Romero on such projects as *Martin* and *Dawn of the Dead*. Other Savini splatter movies include *Deathdream* (1972), *Deranged* (1973), *Maniac* (1981), *Friday the 13th*, *The Burning* (1981), *Eyes of a Stranger* (1981), and the first George A. Romero/Stephen King collaboration, *Creepshow* (1982).

Contributing also to Savini's being typecast as the reigning make-up king of splatter is the fact that he is the only one of the four to have been singled out (and vilified) by *Chicago Tribune* and syndicated television movie critic Gene Siskel in his campaign to have splatter movies (which Siskel often refers to as "anti-independent women movies,") driven from the nation's movie screens. (More about that controversy, however, in the next chapter.)

Completely self-taught in the art of theatrical and screen make-up, Tom Savini first got hooked on the idea of becoming a movie make-up master (as well as an actor and stuntman) when he saw James Cagney in *The Man of a Thousand Faces* (1956), the biography of silent film superstar Lon Chaney. "It was as if a bell had suddenly gone off," Savini told me. "Right then and there, I knew that this was what I wanted to do with my life." Chaney, who was not only a consummate make-up artist but a fine actor who performed many of his own stunts as well, has served as Savini's guiding inspiration ever since. Savini even named his son Lon in honor of the late star.

Savini's big break came, of course, when George A. Romero signed him to create the virtual flood of astonishing, splatter-filled special effects for his *Dawn of the Dead*. There has been no looking back since. Today, he is in constant demand, much to Gene Siskel's chagrin, to lend his considerable skills as a special make-up effects technician to one new splatter movie after another.

To find out how Tom Savini feels about his sudden fame and prestige in the movie industry, about his feelings toward splatter movies in general, and his own notoriety as the form's grand master in particular, I decided to go straight to the source.

Tom Savini's idol: Lon Chaney, the Man of a Thousand Faces. Here, Chaney prepares for his role as a hunchback in *The Octave of Claudius*, later retitled *A Blind Bargain* (1922). (*Museum of Modern Art/Films Stills Archive*)

A Conversation with Tom Savini

You were a combat photographer in Vietnam. What effect, if any, do you think that experience has had on your work?

Well, I certainly saw a lot of the same things I create for movies. Only I saw them for real. I almost stepped on an arm once—a Viet Cong was shot by a buddy of mine and when he fell, a grenade he'd had primed under his armpit went off and just blew him to smithereens. I have a picture of him afterwards. But oddly enough, there is this distancing effect about being behind a camera. I felt safe—illogical as that may sound—because I was behind a camera and everything in front of the camera seemed like it was part of a movie. I saw a lot of grisly stuff all right, and my stuff in films has been pretty grisly. If I've got anything of a reputation at all, I'm probably notorious for how real my stuff looks . . . well, most of the time. I would say in that respect, the realism of my stuff, the grisliness, the *anatomical* correctness of it probably does come from that experience.

When you're creating some super-splattery effect—for a film like Maniac, *for instance, do you ever flash back on your Vietnam experience?*

Well, I can't say that when I'm doling out the blood that it doesn't cross my mind. But I don't want to give the impression that I do this work because of my war experience. Not at all. It would be easy to say, "Well, Savini just paints three-dimensional pictures of what he saw." But I don't. It's all in the script. Somebody writes this stuff. Only when it's a George Romero project do I ever get to go . . . foot loose and fancy free.

Does the extent of your participation in the making of a film differ in any way from Rob Bottin's, for example, or Dick Smith's? As to when you're first brought in for consultation, I mean.

It's in my contract that I get to direct the sequences that my effects appear in because, well, they *are* illusions after all, and they depend on certain surrounding shots to make the magic of the whole effect come through. I understand that on *The Howling*, Bottin was able to do his own lighting as well as set ups for his effects shots. Dick Smith, I'm sure, suggests surrounding shots to make his illusions work. For example, in *Altered States*, I'm sure there was only one way to shoot that transforming arm so that you wouldn't see the tubes and stuff. Obviously, for that effect, there was only one way to shoot it—Smith's way. However, in the bathroom scene where William Hurt looks in the mirror and his forehead swells, you don't get to see that happen as well. Dick Smith says he might just as well have put a solid appliance on Hurt—you know, already swollen out—because Hurt moved so quickly that you didn't get to see the effect. And for that reason, I try to get as many things in my contract as possible, like directing those sequences that my effects are in.

What else is in your contract?

I insist on having a single credit—"Special Make-Up Effects by Tom Savini"—at the beginning of the film so that my name doesn't get lost in the shuffle of credits at the end. And I get a videotaped copy of the finished film. What I've been doing on my last couple of films too is videotaping my effects so that I can see them right away. In *Friday the*

13th, for instance, there was one effect we had to do over again, call the actress back—it was the axe murder scene—because the tubing was showing. I was counting on the cameraman to make sure that everything was copascetic as far as the tubing was concerned because I was down below the girl pumping up blood and couldn't see a damn thing. And the tubing showed up. Now I videotape beforehand to avoid that sort of thing.

Are you ever called on to modify or do an alternate version of your effects in view of a potential television sale?

Yes. We sometimes shoot a non-bloody—or not so bloody—version for television. But often there's no way to do that. No way to break the shot up or modify it. You either show it or you don't.

What directors do you enjoy working with most?

Well, George Romero, I'd have to say first of all. He says I think like a director and so he lets me go when I want to do something. He lets me improvise; he lets me try something on my own, maybe even take over a scene. He asked me to look for a project of my own, and I've been reading a couple of titles that George owns. I can't say what they are because he doesn't want anybody to know, but one's an airplane-disaster thing and another is kind of a zombie thing, but actually, I think that one is being done already by somebody else. Also Sean Cunningham is a guy that I would love to work for anytime. He's totally organized. He does his homework. He comes on the set and he knows exactly what he wants to do and that saves a lot of time as well as pressure.

How did you first meet George Romero?

I was in high school here in Pittsburgh and George was out looking for young talent for a movie to be called *Whine of the Fawn*, and I was one of two people who got called in for a screen test, but the movie never got made. Then years later when he was making *Night of the Living Dead*, I was in college, a journalism major at Carnegie-Mellon in downtown Pittsburgh, where his studio was. Anyway, I heard about the film, and I went over to see him. When the elevator opened on the floor where his office was, *bang*, he was standing there. To my surprise, he not only remembered me from that previous time—about six years earlier—but he remembered my name too. I told him I was doing make-up now and he said he'd like to see my stuff, maybe I could work with him on *Living Dead*. Well, I had enlisted in the army on the hold program and all of a sudden they called me and off I went, so I didn't get to work on the movie. About six years later, I was back in Pittsburgh again and I heard George was doing a film called *Martin*, a vampire film, so I went down to audition for the vampire, which turned out to be already cast. George was very busy, but I kept following him around with my portfolio from office to office, flipping through pages, and finally he hired me to do make-up. I also wound up doing the stunts as well and even playing a small part. Then, a little later, I was doing a play in North Carolina, and I got a telegram from George saying: "I've got another gig, call me." And that was *Dawn of the Dead*, and he told me to start thinking of ways to kill people. The rest, as they say, is history.

Was the basic tone of that film—the flamboyantly grisly approach— established by Romero beforehand, or did a lot of it come out in improvisation during the shooting?

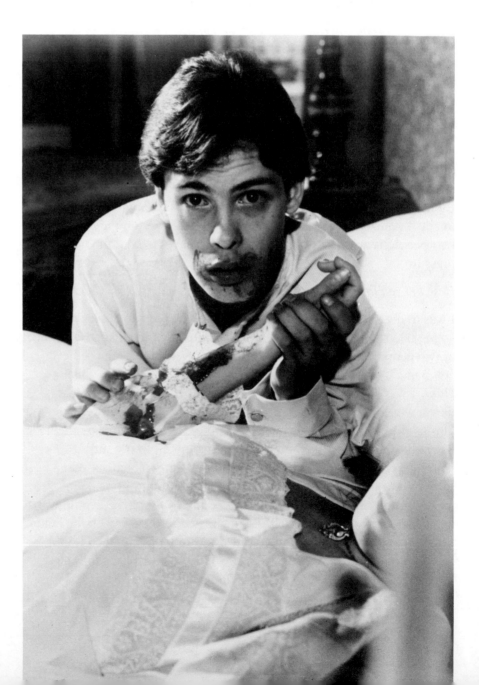

The vampire (John Amplas) dines in courtesy of master chef Tom Savini. From *Martin* (1978). (© *1977 Braddock Associates*)

George is terrifically organized. He put all the scenes in *Dawn of the Dead* down on index cards, so that when you spread them out, you had the whole movie spread out before you. And those scenes all overlapped, so that if you removed one, part of the puzzle was missing. That's by way of saying, yes, *Dawn of the Dead's* grisliness was definitely in the script. We did improvise some of the stuff, but well over fifty percent of it was in George's script beforehand.

Do you feel that the emphasis being placed on effects in today's movies— splatter movies and otherwise—as well as the passion people are developing to learn how they were done is serving to drown out any interest or concern with content?

Yes, I think the effects people are becoming the stars of the films. What the critics say about films like *Friday the 13th*, they don't have much plot or characterization, that they're an exercise in one death after another, is absolutely true. They're right. The special effects are the stars of those movies. I get tons of letters from people asking how these things are done—kids who want to get into screen make-up and effects and so on. And the fan magazines have certainly done their utmost to publicize the effects and the people who bring them off.

Of course there's a double-edged sword to all of this. It's good for your career, but at the same time, people are no longer discussing what a film's about anymore. And consequently, many of them are not about anything. Does this bother you?

I can't honestly say that it bothers me, no. But I will say that there was a magic alive in a lot of the older movies—the horror films, the swashbucklers, whatever—that we don't see today. Those films didn't have a lot of elaborate, graphic effects, and yet they were fabulous! You're going to find this hard to believe, but I personally feel that it's a lot smarter to leave things to a person's imagination, let him fill things in for himself. When your own mind completes something, it's much more valuable to you, I think.

Does it bother you that you're being typed as a wizard of gore?

Well, it's great to be famous for something. But seriously, it would bother me if I hadn't done anything else. But I have. I've acted—I've got a starring role in *Knightriders*—and I've done stunt work. Lon Chaney, my idol, was incredibly versatile; he acted, did his own make-up and stunts. Hopefully, people will eventually come away thinking that way about me.

Tell me a bit about your theater background—both at school and professionally.

Well, I'll tell you when I lost my stage fright. I was in sixth grade, and they were having this bake sale, and they wanted me to go from classroom to classroom dressed as a girl, to advertise this bake sale and do this little skit. Now this was at the height of my insecurity as a child. In fifth grade, somebody told me that I had a big nose, and from that day on I was called things like "eagle-beak" and "banana-puss," stuff like that. All this harassment about my looks gave me a horrible inferiority complex, and it led me to not even dating in high school because I was so embarrassed about myself. Anyway, back in sixth grade, I pleaded with my teacher not to make me dress up for this bake sale, but she convinced me, and it turned out to be the greatest experience. I just got so lost in this little part. It was so much fun. From that day on, I had the bug. After I got back from Vietnam, I was stationed in North Carolina. I decided to stay there after I got out of the army because there were three theaters in the area and I became the make-up director for each of them. I wound up doing a show every two months for six years. I also played a lot of parts. I was Little Chap in *Stop the World*, Ben Franklin in *1776*, Happy in *Death of a Salesman*, King Arthur in *Camelot*, Thoreau in *The Night Thoreau Spent in Jail*. I was playing romantic leads in *Cactus Flower*, Mortimer in *The Fantastiks*, Prince Philip in *The Lion in Winter*—a lot of fabulous parts. And, of course, I was also doing make-up—which, by the way, I designed for the mirror and not for the stage. Ben Franklin took me three hours a night to make-up, just to get the effect right even up close in the mirror. I was training myself for the movies even without knowing it because I was trying to get very realistic stuff.

But you had gotten your feet wet before this with Bob Clark's Deathdream *and* Deranged. *How did you come to do those two films?*

In between shows in North Carolina, I painted signs. One day I was delivering some signs to this bar, and there was this guy standing outside the bar apparently waiting for someone. He had a beard, a very interesting-looking guy. And he turned out to be the art director for *Children Shouldn't Play with Dead Things*, which director Bob Clark was doing with writer Alan Ormsby. The guy said his name was Forrest Carpenter. He also told me he was gearing up to do another film with Clark to be called *The Night Andy Came Home*, which later went through a lot of titles before it finally became *Deathdream*. I happened to have my portfolio with me in my car, so I showed it to him and about a week or a month later, I was called, and that was my first movie. We shot *Deathdream* in Brooksville, Florida, near Tampa. And about a month after we finished *Deathdream*, I got a call from the same company to come and do a film called *Deranged*.

Deranged *is based on the story of Ed Gein, the Wisconsin cannibal-killer whose exploits also provided the basis for* Psycho *as well as* The Texas Chainsaw Massacre.

The horribly disfigured killer Cropsy (Lou David) as created by Savini for *The Burning* (1981). (© *Filmways Pictures Corp.*)

Yes, that's right. We shot *Deranged* in Canada, and while we were shooting it, I found out that Gein was alive and had become a trustee in the penitentiary where he was imprisoned. I don't know if he's still alive, or if he saw the film, but he was when we shot it. And he was a trustee!

Did you ever attempt any effects such as those you do in movies on the stage—a la French Grand Guignol?

Oh, yeah. I did a play by Robert Marasco called *Child's Play*. I played Paul Reese, a gym instructor in this school where some sort of mind possession is going on. Kids are hurting other kids and so on. At one point, I slice my hand open with a broken piece of glass that I've just pulled out of a wastebasket and the blood gushed right out on stage. I loved it because I could feel the audience rising up out of its seat to see how I did it.

How did you do it?

I did it right before their eyes, standing right out in the middle of the stage. What I did was, I put a baby's ear syringe filled with stage blood and a pre-cut piece of glass into the wastebasket. Then, during the scene, I threw a bottle into the wastebasket, then reached in and, palming the syringe, took the pre-cut piece of glass, which was supposed to be a part of the broken bottle, lifted it up so that the stage lights gleamed off it and began slicing my hand, all the while pumping the syringe. Blood gushed all over the place, and the audience was just blown away. For *Macbeth*, I did a fairly realistic beheading, but on the whole, I haven't done an awful lot of gory effects on stage, no.

Of the films you've worked on so far, which satisfies you the most?

Well, *Dawn of the Dead*. How can I describe it? A constant flow of effects and stunts. I was all over the place. I liked *Friday the 13th* too for the same reason.

Least favorite?

Probably *Maniac* because it's, well, it's just *sleaze*. I was on a talk show in New York talking about the spirit and soul behind *Knightriders*, and a guy called up and asked me, "Where's the spirit and soul behind *Maniac?*" People aren't too fond of *Maniac*. They like the effects, but I would have preferred them to have been in a better showcase.

Do you think it's possible to determine a make-up artist's signature in his work?

Sometimes, yes. In *Marathon Man* there was a scene where Olivier cuts this guy's throat, and I knew right away it was Dick Smith's work even though I hadn't known he'd been connected with the film.

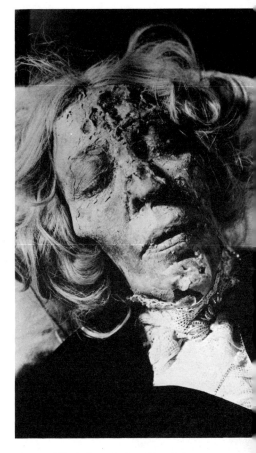

Some of Savini's early handiwork in *Deranged* (1974), the story of mass murderer Ed Gein, whose exploits were also the basis for Hitchcock's *Psycho* (1960) and Tobe Hooper's *The Texas Chainsaw Massacre* (1975). (© 1974 American International Pictures/Courtesy Hollywood Book & Poster)

"If I've got anything of a reputation at all, I'm probably notorious for how real my stuff looks," says Savini. Here a shot fired through a car windshield successfully blows off the head of the driver. From *Maniac* (1981). (© *Analysis Film Releasing Corp.*)

How did you know?

Well, it's like the difference between fencing with a foil and fencing with a saber. You just have to see the moves over and over again before you know that a blow coming to your head is actually coming to your shoulder. In seeing that particular effect, the way the blood bubbled up out of the artery, then came around, the cleanness of the appliance itself, I knew it had to be him. Dick Smith's the best. He's a scientist.

Smith has intimated in print that some of the effects he's been called upon to do in films like Taxi Driver *and* The Sentinel *have bothered him a lot—to the extent that he now tries to avoid the gorier assignments if he can.*

Yes, Rick Baker has said the same thing. He doesn't like to do the gore stuff anymore. Well, he doesn't need to. He's gone on to do some beautiful stuff—*King Kong* and Sidney the ape in *The Incredible Shrinking Woman*. Dick Smith doesn't need to do it anymore either. Of course, he did have a hand in the ending of *Scanners*—a great hand—but that was probably because he just wanted to try out some new techniques of his. So, who's left? Me. Bottin, Chris Walas. Carl Fullerton. Now we've got most of the work. But I'd like to get out of it myself actually. Do more acting.

What do you think the basic appeal of splatter movies is?

Well, Bill Lustig, the director of *Maniac*, described that film as a kind of rollercoaster ride. You have the climb up to the peak, and you *know* you have to go down. If you didn't, you'd be disappointed. That's the appeal, and it's also the danger. Now, when you don't show something, there's a percentage of the audience that's disappointed. The way an effect is done sometimes also creates an appeal. Take George Romero, for example. When he's going to show you some splatter, he often

142

includes a little comic moment before or after it, so that the way the sequence is handled is not what you expected. You might be given a severed head, but it'll have a bag over it that reads "Shop at K-Mart." Little things like that are what George is into, and he's very much aware of it.

Do you see the splatter trend continuing or do you see the wrath of the censors coming down on them? Gene Siskel's crusade comes to mind.

Well, I think the censors are going to have an effect, but I really think splatter will just naturally dwindle down. How many ways can you go on killing people? They'll probably stay alive until somebody spoofs them. Like you knew that the Frankenstein and werewolf movies were no longer scaring anybody and that the genre was dying when they started making comedies out of them with Abbott and Costello. So, now I hear they're planning a spoof called *Thursday the 12th*, and, who knows, if it's done well, that may be the death knell right there.

William Friedkin offered you a shot at directing a film for him. What happened to that? How did it come about?

Well, I was doing *The Burning*, and I got a call from William Friedkin, and I was beside myself with glee. He came on the phone and said he wanted to fly me out to the Coast as soon as I could make it to talk about a long-term proposition between him, myself, and Warner Brothers. Naturally, my heart fell down to my shoes. I had another commitment, a film called *Graduation* right away, so that was that for awhile. He called me while I was on that film and told me to remember that as soon as it was over, I was committed to having this meeting with him in California. But when I was finished with *Graduation*, he was in Japan doing some lecturing. Anyway, we finally had our meeting— here, not on the Coast, and he gave me a copy of a script he had in mind, to which I made some changes, all of which he liked. Then his attorney sent me a contract. We were about to finalize the deal, but then Friedkin decided he couldn't wait until September for me to finish *Creepshow*, and that was that.

Is someone else set to direct it now?

I don't think so. Not yet. Haven't read anything about it anyway. I can't mention the title because it's a property of Friedkin's and he really doesn't want anyone to know about it. It's a murder mystery, kind of a genre thing as far as the effects and stuff, but it's also a lot more. Something really different.

How did you meet Stephen King?

I met Stephen King during *Knightriders*. There's a character in that film named Steve, a lawyer, and one day we were on the set and George said

Above and opposite page: A gallery of
Savini ghouls designed for George A.
Romero's *Creepshow* (1982). (© *Warner
Bros., Inc.*)

to me, "Come on over, I want you to meet Steve." And this guy said, "Oh, I just got back from Cannes, and I saw *Maniac*, and I loved it. I love all your work. I've followed all of it. I've seen *Friday the 13th* and *Dawn of the Dead*, etcetera, etcetera." And I shook his hand and thanked him and sat down and George came over and said, "You know who that was?" And I said, "Yeah, that's the guy playing Steve." And he said, "No, that's Stephen King!" And I just groaned. But I had a lot of meetings with him and George afterwards, talking about all the effects in *Creepshow*. He's just a big kid. Like me. And like George.

If you could put your dream film together right now—with you taking part as actor, director, make-up artist, and stuntman—what sort of film would that be? Splatter?

No. To tell the truth, what I'd really like to do is make the most spectacular version of *The Mark of Zorro* that people have ever seen.

145

CHAPTER 13

The Splatter Controversy

Horror movies have always been somewhat controversial due to the overtly grisly nature of their subject matter as well as their frequent reveling in morbid and even taboo themes. Inevitably, splatter cinema, that modern stepchild of the horror film, would renew this controversy because of its graphic approach to dealing with many of these same themes.

In the vanguard of today's renewed discussion of the perils and pitfalls of showing graphic violence on the screen is *Chicago Tribune* film critic and co-star of the syndicated television series "At the Movies," Gene Siskel. Together with his "At the Movies" compatriot, *Chicago Sun-Times* and Pulitzer Prize-winning film critic Roger Ebert, Siskel mounted an all-out campaign on the pair's previous movie review program, "Sneak Previews," to run splatter movies out of town.

What triggered the controversy was Paramount Pictures' acquisition of Sean Cunningham's low-budget shocker *Friday the 13th*, which Paramount then proceeded to ballyhoo into a major box-office success. Both critics found the film to be purely exploitative in its mayhem and, worse still, extremely vicious in its attitude toward women. They were appalled that a major studio such as Paramount would lower itself to releasing such a film. When *Friday* was followed in quick succession by a series of similar films—*He Knows You're Alone* (1980), *Silent Scream* (1980), *The Boogey Man* (1980), *I Spit on Your Grave* (1980), *Fade to Black* (1981)—Siskel felt compelled to publicly raise a red flag.

In an open letter to Paramount's top executives, Siskel attacked the studio for having gotten behind such a blatantly violent and exploitative film as *Friday the 13th*. Paramount's execs didn't exactly take Siskel's message to heart: within a year, the studio released two more low-budget splatter movies, a Canadian acquisition called *My Bloody Valentine* (1981), as well as the sequel to its controversial hit film of the summer before, *Friday the 13th—Part II* (1981). Siskel's protestations had fallen on deaf ears.

Piqued, the critic urged *Tribune* readers who were sympathetic to his cause to boycott all Paramount releases, regardless of their content, as a gesture of unified protest. By this time, Roger Ebert had also joined in the angry fight.

The big push came when both critics devoted a special edition of their nationally syndicated PBS "Sneak Previews" program to a vitriolic assault on what they termed "a disturbing new trend in today's movies." Subsequently, the pair has appeared on NBC's "Today," Metromedia's syndicated "Phil Donahue Show," and a host of other television and radio programs in an effort to get their views across. As a result, they themselves have become media stars and the controversy they helped to spark has developed into a minor *cause célèbre*.

Siskel and Ebert's anger with splatter cinema is directed not just at the form's basic blood and gore content, but, more significantly, at its

Right: Halloween (1978), a splatter movie that contains every element anti-splatter crusaders Gene Siskel and Roger Ebert seem to despise. And yet they remain staunch supporters of the film. (© *Compass International Pictures Corp.*)

virulent attitude (in their view) toward independent women. Splatter movies, they say, aim most of their violence at female characters who are sexually liberated and who act independently of men. Those female characters who are chaste and rather more dependent on the male of the species, they say, come through these films relatively unscathed. There's an underlying message here, they conclude, and it's not a very healthy one.

What the pair also finds offensive and sick about these films is the fact that when these independent women are finally dealt their hack-and-slash "comeuppance," the camera very often assumes the point of view of the killer, his heavy breathing filling the soundtrack, as he bears down on his helpless birds of prey, transforming them into cringing, screaming victims.

Gene Siskel, Roger Ebert, and other critics who agree with them have built a strong case against splatter movies, because on the surface, everything they say about them is true. On the other hand, while I don't want to appear as an apologist for splatter movies (indeed, many of them *are* junk!), I must confess to a certain unease with the evidence the pair has accumulated. It's entirely too superficial and a bit too specious as well. Not only that, the pair's attitudes are not always consistent from film to film.

Below: Karen MacDonald is about to be decapitated by a helmeted mad slasher in *Night School* (1980). Characteristic splatter movie sequences like this one in which women are shown as helpless, screaming victims at the mercy of their male assailants have led to speculation that splatter movies may be guilty of harboring virulent, anti-feminist attitudes. (© *1980 Fiducial Resource International, Inc.*)

A liberal dose of the absurd, not just the degree of bloodshed, is what separates one kind of splatter movie from another. Demonstrating the two approaches are: above, the light-hearted and absurd *Piranha* (1979)—just get a load of those newspaper headlines!—and below, *Maniac* (1981), a relentlessly depressing audience turn-off. (*Piranha* © New World Pictures; *Maniac* © Analysis Film Releasing Corp.)

For example, one of the pair's favorite shockers of the past few years, John Carpenter's *Halloween*, is a splatter movie that contains every element the pair seems to despise. In that film, a group of teenage girls is stalked by a knife-wielding phantom who has escaped from an insane asylum. During the course of the film, all the girls who might be described as sexually liberated are murdered. At the conclusion, only the virgin among the group (Jamie Lee Curtis) survives. Also, the film is loaded with sequences shot from the killer's point of view, most notably the film's long opening sequence, which details the psycho's murder of his nude older sister.

What sets this film apart, in Siskel and Ebert's view, from a film like *Friday the 13th*, a much gorier film admittedly, but one in which boys and girls alike are done in by the film's machete-wielding maniac, not just the independent females? And to further add to the confusion, there is this to consider: *Friday*'s killer, unlike *Halloween*'s, is a woman.

Siskel and Ebert say that what raises *Halloween* above its sleazier competition are its occasional stylistic flourishes, such as cinematog-

rapher Dean Cundey's lighting techniques, and director John Carpenter's sure hand at creating suspense. However, is this truly a meaningful difference? All that it really implies is that it is artistically valid to hack up independent female characters on screen, as long as you do so with suspense and flair.

The major fault I find with Siskel and Ebert's analysis of the splatter movie phenomenon, however, is that they just haven't looked deeply enough into it. They view splatter as "a disturbing new trend." And yet the reader of this book surely realizes by now that the splatter genre is not new at all. It has been struggling to reach maturity a good many years, a process that began in the mid-fifties with the release of Hammer's *Curse of Frankenstein*. And splatter's roots in theater as well as in film extend even further back than that.

If, in fact, the freedom of the screen had not been restricted for almost forty years, the art of film, like the art of painting and literature before it, would in all likelihood already have had its flirtation with "realism" some time ago. Censorship only served to delay the inevitable appearance of splatter movies. All of which means that if Siskel and Ebert really want to run splatter movies out of town, all they need do is bite their tongues, sit back, and wait a bit, for splatter cinema will eventually run its course and fade away. Even its chief practitioners, like Tom Savini, admit that splatter must naturally dwindle. Or at least change its shape.

Siskel and Ebert's other conclusions about the splatter movie phenomenon are no less superficial. Their idea that certain splatter movies are guilty of harboring a virulent and unconcealed anti-feminist viewpoint is a good case in point. Yes, it's a provocative idea, and, yes, on the

Above: Now this is what you call getting it in the neck! From Ulli Lommell's *The Boogey Man* (1980), one of the many splatter movies that followed in the wake of *Friday the 13th*'s unexpected box office success. (© *The Jerry Gross Organization*)

Right: Another mad slasher goes on the stalk in *Prom Night* (1980). (© *Embassy Pictures*)

150

MBV-C-5055

surface it seems reasonable enough. But Siskel and Ebert are really giving many of these films much more credit for having a brain in their head—albeit a warped one—than they actually deserve. A film like *Friday the 13th,* for example, is not guilty of expressing an anti-feminist viewpoint, for it has no viewpoint at all. It's not *about* anything. *Friday* exists mainly as a showcase for its grisly and astonishing special effects. And that it contains so many varied effects is precisely why splatter fans were drawn to it in such large numbers.

The fact that so many of the female characters who get stalked and killed in these movies are independent women has less to do with any dark and sinister underlying message than it does with society's changing attitudes toward women as a whole. One must remember, splatter movies by their very nature are eclectic. Often there isn't a new idea or plot device in them, for creativity is usually reserved for the special effects alone. The plot device of the "damsel in distress" is as old as the storytelling arts themselves. It has never been out of fashion. Splatter

Above: Paramount's execs obviously took Siskel's message to heart; within a year the company released another low-budget, mad slasher splatter movie in the *Friday the 13th* mold, *My Bloody Valentine* (1981). (© 1981 Paramount)

151

movies have merely taken this tired old theatrical and literary device and updated it with an eye to current attitudes. Surely if the movie heroine of today continued to behave like the movie heroine of yesteryear—Fay Wray, for example—she'd be laughed off the screen. I might also add that those occasional splatter movies which do evidence some intelligence and a viewpoint on something—Bob Clark's *Deathdream*, for instance, or the work of George A. Romero and David Cronenberg—either relegate the damsel in distress device to a distinctly subordinate role in the plot or dispense with it altogether.

While it is certainly not impossible for a specific writer or director to be a closet misogynist as well, or for a specific splatter movie to be guilty of expressing a puritanical and repressive attitude toward the libidinous behavior of its characters, the idea that there is a conspiracy afoot to promote sexism and sexual loathing throughout the genre seems quite ridiculous, the result of a complete misreading of one of the major clichés endemic to the horror film form. Why do so many boys and girls in today's splatter movies get knocked off during or shortly after engaging in sex? Precisely because that's when they're most alone, most vulnerable. Yesterday's movie heroes and heroines used to get knocked off by the monster while they were petting inside their parked cars on some lonely stretch of Lover's Lane. What's changed over the years is censorship. Nowadays, these same characters can simply go straight to bed. And as a result, today's movie monsters, in order to slake their thirst for blood, head straight for the bedroom.

Many critics who continue to point out the so-called "anti-feminist elements" in splatter cinema also choose to ignore the substantial number of splatter movies that have been made over the years—and continue to be made in increasing numbers—that reverse the genre's female-in-jeopardy clichés, or that employ the same clichés, but are directed by women. Israeli director Meir Zarchi's *I Spit on Your Grave* falls into the first category while Amy Jones's *Slumber Party Massacre* (1982) falls into the second.

Zarchi's raw and unpleasant splatter cheapie (which was originally titled *Day of the Woman*) starts off like a remake of *Last House on the Left*. A young girl (Camille Keaton) is repeatedly raped in the Connecticut woods by a quartet of thugs who eventually get what they deserve by being castrated, hanged, or axed to death. Zarchi's film sharply departs from *Last House*, however, by having this grisly revenge meted out not by the victims' parents, but by the victim herself, who has managed to survive her ordeal. In addition to this and its overall better acting and slicker technique, *I Spit* also departs from *Last House* by deriving its central plot thrust not from Bergman's *The Virgin Spring*, but from John Boorman's *Deliverance* (1972) and Sam Peckinpah's *Straw Dogs* (1971).

Visually, *I Spit* makes its debt to *Deliverance* quite clear. The treatment of the rape scenes in the woods, particularly the second rape in which the girl is sodomized over a rock, as well as the boating sequences shot on an isolated stretch of the Connecticut River, seem virtually lifted from *Deliverance*. Thematically, however, the film is more closely allied to Peckinpah's.

Keaton, like Dustin Hoffman in *Straw Dogs*, flees from the big city to find quiet in a small town where she plans to write a book. Her summer idyll is broken, however, when she is assaulted by four locals, who treat her not only as an outsider, but as a plaything. Like Hoffman, she then proceeds to exact her retribution in a calculating manner. After she has killed them all, she speeds away from the carnage in a motor boat, her face an inscrutable blank. This recalls the ending of *Straw Dogs*, when Dustin Hoffman drives away in his car after dispatching his last victim and smiles with inscrutable bemusement: both characters have discovered the "sleep of reason" (in C. P. Snow's phrase) within themselves and for the moment are morally lost. Grotesquely unpleasant and sleazy though it may be, *I Spit on Your Grave* does manage to separate itself from other films of its type if only by virtue of the more serious-minded films it tends to borrow from.

Taking a different but no less demonstrative approach to portraying women either as James Bond–like superheroes or as sexual sadists capable of dishing out violence with the best of their male counterparts are such splattery gems as these: *The Doll Squad* (1973); any of the films starring Cheri Caffaro as a buxom secret agent named Ginger (1972's *The Abductors* is a good example); *Ms. 45* (1981); *Foxy Brown* (1974); *The Female Butchers* (1972); *Ilsa, She Wolf of the SS* (1974) and its sequel, *Ilsa, Harem Keeper of the Oil Sheiks* (1976), among many others.

Camille Keaton goes on the rampage against the men who brutally raped her in *I Spit on Your Grave* (1980), also known as *Day of the Woman*. (© 1980 The Jerry Gross Organization)

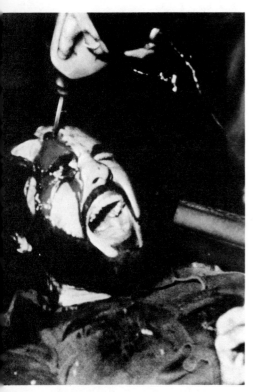

Above: Abel Ferrara's *Driller Killer* (1979) seems to prefer victims of both sexes. In Ferrara's follow-up film, *Ms. 45* (1981), the heroine is a disturbed young woman who sets out to become an avenging angel against a sexist society. (© *1982 Wizard Video*)

Slumber Party Massacre, on the other hand, is a typical mad slasher-style splatter movie that contains all the ingredients critics like Siskel and Ebert have denounced as being "anti-feminist." And yet the film's director, Amy Jones, is a woman, and its writer, Rita Mae Brown, is a lesbian and feminist author *(Rubyfruit Jungle, Southern Discomfort).* In it, an escaped psycho takes to murdering comely coeds at a San Francisco high school with a power drill—shades of Abel Ferrara's *The Driller Killer* (1979). *Slumber* is filled with stereotypically violent images of young women being stalked and killed by the drill-wielding maniac. And, as often as not, the more promiscuous of these coeds are the first to be splattered. Barbara Peeters's *Humanoids from the Deep* and *Bury Me an Angel* (1975) are likewise filled with the same genre expectations and pay-offs as those splatter movies directed by her male (and presumably sexist) colleagues.

Siskel and Ebert are not entirely wrong, however, when they conclude that not all splatter movies are alike. They have merely chosen the wrong pair with which to make a comparison. *Friday the 13th* is certainly more demonstrative in its splatter than *Halloween,* but otherwise there's scarcely a dime's worth of difference between the two films. Both are blatantly eclectic, full of implausibilities, wholly dependent on technique to keep the audience's attention, and, most importantly of all, firmly cast in the same lighthearted, EC horror comics mold that George A. Romero first introduced to the screen with his *Night of the Living Dead.* Despite their emphasis on realistic effects, both *Friday the 13th* and *Halloween* are patently illogical and absurd, and it is their absurdity that takes the psychological sting out of them.

Films like *Last House on the Left* and the more recent *Maniac,* on the other hand, turn audiences off for precisely the opposite reason. They aren't absurd enough. *House* director Wes Craven himself admits that his film was a downer because it was simply *too* grim, as was William Lustig's *Maniac.* It's not the film's splatter that turns most audiences off, but its mixture of splatter with an oppressive mood of unrelenting grimness—*sleaze,* Tom Savini calls it. *Friday the 13th* and *Halloween* bring a comic book approach to the grisly events they portray. *Last House on the Left* and *Maniac* do not.

Ironically, on an earlier edition of "Sneak Previews" dealing with bad movies that the show's two co-hosts happen to enjoy (even if no one else does), Roger Ebert confessed to having a special fondness for the profoundly depressing *Last House on the Left.* Gene Siskel is at least a little more consistent in his tastes. He tends to dislike most splatter movies indiscriminately.

The chief fear most critics harbor about splatter movies is that they might eventually seduce audiences into craving the real thing on the screen: actual murders, not staged ones. Snuff films. This fear, however, is based on a false supposition: that the people who go to see these films do so purely because of the violence in them. They don't. The main reason they go is to marvel at the grisly and astonishing special effects—to see if the effects in this *new* splatter movie will outdo the effects in the last one they saw. Fans of a film like *Friday the 13th* perceive the splatter in it as an element of the special effects and enjoy it mostly on that level.

I do not for a moment suggest that there aren't crazies in the world who go to splatter movies because they genuinely do get a kick out of seeing blood, gore, and suffering on the screen, even if they are only illusions. Nor do I deny that the action and violence in splatter movies sometimes provide a catharsis for some who are actively seeking a vicarious release for their pent-up hostilities. A visit to any 42nd Street grind house will reveal the truth of that. But I do have my doubts that the splatter movie phenomenon is indicative of a growing appetite for violence spreading throughout society as a whole. If anything, the graphic, overdrawn, and frequently absurdist images of fictitious carnage in splatter movies are serving to desensitize audiences to the threat of *real* violence, to the fear that this violence—rape, murder, terrorism, the possibility of nuclear war—may someday reach out and claim them as victims also. One would have thought, for example, that the mass death and destruction that followed the dropping of the atomic bomb on Hiroshima and Nagasaki in 1945 would have driven away forever any desire on the part of the Japanese people, young and old alike, to see similar carnage portrayed on the screen. And yet the opposite happened. Within a decade or so after the bombs were exploded, films like *Godzilla* (1956) and *Rodan* (1957) began to proliferate and strike box-office gold in Japan—films that portrayed the mass destruction of Tokyo and other Japanese cities by grotesque, nuclear-spawned monsters. The kung-fu craze that followed shortly thereafter has still not abated, and as has already been noted, companies like Hammer Films began adding extra scenes of gore to their films exclusively for the Japanese market in order to satisfy a specific demand for them. Could it be that these gore- and destruction-filled movies were being used in the wake of Hiroshima and Nagasaki to transform remembered images of real violence and destruction into images of pure fantasy—thus taking the sting out of them? Possibly. And just as possibly, the audiences of today are using splatter movies for much the same kind of purpose. For thanks, notably, to the nightly newscasts, which bring images of real and escalating world violence into our homes every evening, the specter of violence, the threat to one's personal safety, has never loomed greater for most people than it does today.

Another reason why splatter movies are so popular may also be due to the cinema's growing "democratization" over the years. Given the easy accessibility to 16mm, Super-8, and now portable home video equipment, anyone who wants to can now go out and make a movie. At one time, only a select few movie buffs knew what a matte shot was. Now even the manner in which such a shot is executed is practically common knowledge. Exhaustive, methodology-oriented articles regularly appearing in such popular film magazines as *American Cinematographer, Cinemagic, Fangoria,* and *Cinefantastique* continue to outline for aspiring filmmakers, as well as for those people who have no desire to pick up a camera, all the mechanics of filmmaking—photography, editing, special effects, make-up, and so on. The mystique surrounding the filmmaking process gone, audiences are now able to feel more like insiders when they watch a film. Thus, even when a film is poorly made—as so many splatter movies are—audiences respond to it; in fact, they may even embrace it more fully because it allows them to say, "Hey, even I could do better than that!" The growing appeal among today's moviegoers of schlock movies in general—not just those belonging to the splatter genre—would seem to confirm this.

The real danger of splatter movies, I'm convinced, is not that they are seducing viewers into craving more violence on the screen, but that their appealing superficiality will eventually foster a generation of filmgoers that demands little else from movies except gaudier, more contrived melodramatics, and increasingly more mind-boggling special effects. And if a film doesn't deliver these surface goods, that film will be deemed a failure.

Signs of this developing "splatter mentality" are already in evidence; witness the hostile reception accorded Stanley Kubrick's *The Shining* (1980) by so many horror film fans in this country. When it was announced that director Kubrick was going to bring superstar novelist Stephen King's bulky, EC horror comics–influenced ghost story-cum-splatter best-seller to the world's movie screens, horror fans everywhere began gearing up for the event with an almost breathless sense of anticipation. And what exactly was it that was being awaited so breathlessly? Well, it was thought, if Stanley *"2001"* Kubrick were making the film, *The Shining* would just have to be the *ultimate horror movie!*

As it turned out, audiences who went to Kubrick's *The Shining* expecting to see a faithful translation of Stephen King's novel (or even another *Carrie*) were gravely disappointed, for Kubrick's film, in style and substance, owes less to King than to Henry James, Oliver Onions, and many other Victorian-era practitioners of the novel of ghostly fear. Ironically, this was precisely the kind of switch we should have expected from this expatriate American filmmaker who has given us the screen's only stately science fiction film to date. Set to the music of Richard Strauss, *2001: A Space Odyssey* went against everything audiences had previously held dear about sci-fi flicks, specifically their free-wheeling pulpiness. *The Shining* is a film of fear cut from the same mold.

Jack Nicholson stars as Jack Torrance, a former schoolteacher who hires on as winter caretaker of a remote Colorado mountain hotel, the Overlook, in order to gain the solitude he needs to write his Great

American Novel. Torrance is a dreamer, a loser, and an alcoholic to boot. There is much hostility and self-hatred in this man who just can't seem to get out of his own way long enough to make a success of his life. Even before we learn that he dislocated his son's shoulder in a fit of drunken rage (though that's not how *he* explains the incident), we can see this inner hostility lurking in the caustically edged smiles and wry comments he dishes out to his future employer, Mr. Ullman (Barry Nelson), during his initial interview. Torrance, like the sexually repressed Miss Giddens in Henry James's novella *Turn of the Screw* and the bottled-up writer in Oliver Onions's *The Beckoning Fair One*, is a character whose flaws are primed for the right set of circumstances in which to turn fatal. Solitude is the last thing the brooding Torrance needs. But he is accustomed to doing what's bad for him, then blaming the outcome on someone else—usually his wife Wendy (Shelley Duvall) or his son Danny (Danny Lloyd). So they go off together to the Overlook, a hotel with a history of unsavory happenings—the last caretaker, Ullman tells Torrance, murdered his family with an axe and then killed himself—and the classic ghost story situation is established: the doomed comes home at last. ("You were always the caretaker here," an Overlook apparition tells Torrance. How true.)

Complicating the plot is the fact that Torrance's son has "the shining," an insight into the past and the future. As soon as Danny enters the Overlook, he is confronted by images of the previous caretaker's two murdered daughters. Immediately he knows that death ("red rum") is in the hotel, ready to be summoned by he who thirsts for it most: his father.

As in *2001*, *Paths of Glory* (1958), *Lolita* (1962), and *A Clockwork Orange* (1972) particularly among Kubrick's past work, we are here given a potentially volatile triangle in order to see how well its members work together. The answer is, usually, not very well. In *2001*, the triangle consisted of astronauts Poole and Bowman and a computer named HAL. Frictions surface among them while they travel on the spaceship *Discovery:* Poole is killed, HAL "goes mad" and must be dismantled; the journey goes awry due to human error. In *Paths of Glory*, three frontline soldiers accused of cowardice, two corrupt general staff members, and a lawyer-colonel (Kirk Douglas) with a passion for justice lock horns within the confines of a World War I military court. The soldiers lose their lives, the generals their honor, and Douglas his case. In *Lolita*, there is the romantically obsessed Humbert Humbert (James Mason), the nymphet-object of his erotically charged affections (Sue Lyon), and the spoiler (Peter Sellers), each of whom comes to a bad end. And in *A Clockwork Orange*, a sterile society victimized by violent youth gangs, a government eager to restore order and keep power even if it has to alter the concept of free will to do so, and a conscienceless punk named Alex (Malcolm McDowell) all strive for their own unmerited survival in a claustrophobic nightmare world of the future. Success, for all, is mixed.

Above: Jack Nicholson as the tormented Jack Torrance in Stanley Kubrick's *The Shining* (1980), a film that most horror fans hated because it denied them the splattery effects and big scares they have come to demand. (© *Warner Bros., Inc.*)

In *The Shining,* Kubrick's triangle is the archetypal family group, and it's ripe for destruction. Unlike the novel, which unfolded chiefly through Danny's eyes, Kubrick's film switches points of view, beginning with Danny's, moving on to Torrance's, and concluding with Wendy's. Wendy is the last to open her eyes to the truth about the situation: she can no longer pretend that her marriage to Jack has storybook potential (at one point, she is seen watching *Summer of '42* on television). The hotel elevators are metaphorically awash with blood, Torrance has an axe and is out to kill those who he is convinced are trying to destroy him (his family), and the rotting corpses of the hotel's previous inhabitants—who were similarly unlucky in life and love—are finally revealed for her to see and learn from. She decides that she and the boy must depart, leaving the self-destructive Torrance to consume himself.

Kubrick has discarded much of King's novel in order to concentrate on that aspect of it which interested him most: the story of the self-immolation of a human mind. As in the works of Henry James and Oliver Onions, the ghosts in Kubrick's story could be real, but more likely they have been *made real,* called into familiar shapes by Torrance himself in an effort to aid him in achieving what he desires most: his own

destruction. This is precisely what happens in *Turn of the Screw* and *The Beckoning Fair One*, where the protagonists conjure up elements from their own troubled psyches and externalize them because they need these ghostly visitations to help spur their growing madness. When Torrance unburdens himself to Lloyd the bartender (Joe Turkel) in the Overlook's ornate restaurant and Lloyd provides all the right reassurances ("Whatever you say, Mr. Torrance"), Torrance is really reassuring himself. But he needs Lloyd because, as with everything else in his life, he needs to place responsibility elsewhere—even the responsibility for his own thoughts.

Later, when Torrance enters the Overlook's mysterious Room 237, he finds a manifestation of his own subconscious attitude toward his marriage: an image that combines desire and eroticism with revulsion and fear. The manifestation pulls the attitude from his subconscious and releases it for real. His hostility zooms out of control. But again, in his own mind, he is not the one responsible for its final vindictive release. Interestingly, in the novel, it is through Danny's eyes that we witness this manifestation, which just serves to illustrate how vastly different Kubrick's approach to the material is from Stephen King's. Having Danny

Above: Director Stanley Kubrick, creator of the screen's only stately science fiction film so far, *2001: A Space Odyssey* (1968). His *The Shining* (1980) was, alas, no splatter movie, but a film of fear cut from the same mold. (© *Warner Bros., Inc.*)

witness and be attacked by the manifestation provides the reader with a pleasurable but momentary *frisson*. Kubrick aims instead for a subtler, but more thematically consistent, turn of the screw.

No small part of the success of Kubrick's film is due to Jack Nicholson's detailed performance as the self-destructive Torrance. One moment subdued, the next raving, Nicholson is the incarnation of madness. When he chops down a door to get to Duvall and shouts "Here's Johnny!" prior to bursting in for the kill, he reveals the face of lunancy itself—total disorientation masked by an unnameable glee.

With *The Shining*, director Kubrick—aided considerably by his co-scenarist, the novelist Diane Johnson, his photographer, John Alcott, and his choice of Bela Bartok music—has served up the classiest screen ghost story since Roman Polanski's similarly themed but more Kafka-esque *The Tenant* (1976). The fact that so many horror film fans were profoundly disappointed by it and continue to remain openly hostile to it is unfortunate. But that reaction has less to do with what Stanley Kubrick set out to accomplish and, in fact, achieved—a genuinely Jamesian scare show decked out in modern dress—than it does with his having left out the required bold and baffling special effects and big scares that the growing "splatter mentality" of today's fans increasingly demands.

Perhaps, Gene Siskel, Roger Ebert, and other participants in the great splatter controversy should be more concerned about that.

CHAPTER 14

New Directions in Splatter

What of splatter's future? Will it dwindle naturally, as Tom Savini suggests? Will a renewed effort on the part of the censors among us to toughen screen restrictions on graphic violence and sex result in splatter's scurrying underground once more? Or will splatter cinema simply alter its shape by absorbing additional genres into its collective cinematic bloodstream in order to continue regenerating itself? My guess is the latter.

Walter Hill's *The Long Riders* (1980), for example, is a western, but it is also very much a splatter movie. It borrows its plot—the Great Northfield Minnesota Raid of Jesse James and his boys—from at least a hundred other westerns and lifts technique from directors as varied as Sam Peckinpah, John Ford, and Robert Altman so that it can dispense with these elements as quickly as possible and get down to the real business at hand: *effects.*

Effects in *The Long Riders* range from endless stretches of graphic violence, which are so stylized that they eventually take on an aura of unreality (a characteristic also of Hill's *The Warriors* (1979), to which *The Long Riders* owes an additional debt) to gimmicks in casting. Hill has David, Keith, and Robert Carradine, Stacy and James Keach, and Randy and Dennis Quaid play the real life Younger, James, and Miller brothers, members of the historic James gang, as a unique audience come-on.

Hill followed up *The Long Riders* with *Southern Comfort* (1981), a revenge melodrama about redneck National Guardsmen who raise the ire of the local Cajuns while on maneuvers in the Louisiana bayou, and are picked off one by one as they try to make their way out of the swamp. Once again, Hill dispensed with plot as quickly as possible by lifting it almost wholly from other films—namely, *Deliverance* and, most notably, from John Ford's *The Lost Patrol* (1934).

Like George Romero's *The Crazies, Southern Comfort* is also designed to serve as a metaphor for America's Vietnam experience, but Hill's reliance on action, splatter, and stick-figure characters (who behave like buffoons much of the time) to propel the plot along drains the film of any real seriousness and turns it instead into a parody of that experience.

The Long Riders and *Southern Comfort,* therefore, are not so much westerns or war films as they are live-action comic book versions of the western and the war film, all viewed from an adolescent perspective. In this respect, they're a lot like George Romero's horror films and Steven Spielberg's equally eclectic and effects-oriented live-action comic book, *Raiders of the Lost Ark* (1981). They are *splatter movies* pure and simple.

Monty Python and the Holy Grail (1975) can be viewed as an outright splatter comedy for many of the same reasons. And Alan Parker's *Pink Floyd the Wall* (1982), with its emphasis on blood and pop culture, adolescent angst, and a visual style that is drawn straight from the films

Above and opposite page: With its emphasis on blood, pop culture, adolescent angst, and liberal doses of absurdity, Alan Parker's *Pink Floyd the Wall* (1982) breaks new ground by spiriting the genre in a new direction—the splatter musical. (© *1982 MGM/UA Entertainment Co.*)

of Ken Russell (specifically *Tommy*, 1975), breaks the horror film stranglehold on splatter cinema altogether by taking splatter into the realm of the movie musical.

Splatter cinema may very well be passing through the September of its years as a sub-genre of the horror film (though even this is doubtful), but there are plenty of other genres out there on the cinematic horizon to which splatter can lend its demented qualities. Splatter cinema, it seems clear, is spreading. As long as audiences continue to seek an astonishment fix at the movies, the form will prosper. And that means that splatter movies will be with us for a long, long time to come.

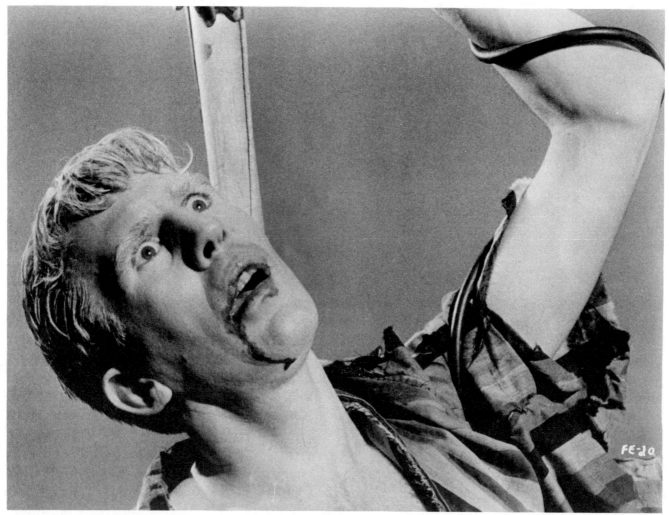

The Flesh Eaters, 1964 (*courtesy Barry Kaufman*)

A Splatter Movie Gore-Nucopia

What follows is a checklist of over 500 splatter movies that have been produced and have earned some kind of distribution, however limited, somewhere in the world during the past two decades. The films of many countries are represented. Still, I make no pretense that this list is a definitive one; some titles have inevitably fallen through the cracks of my research. I apologize, therefore, for any omissions or errors.

Gore alone does not a splatter movie make, and therefore each title was carefully selected on the basis of having at least two additional qualities characteristic of the splatter genre (as outlined previously in Chapter 1).

Films that I have deemed notable because of their historic contribution to the development of splatter, or because they offer something extra in the way of aesthetic interest or merit, I have denoted with an asterisk (*). The name which follows each title is that of the director of record. Titles are listed alphabetically by year.

The symbol (†) denotes those titles which are available for home viewing on videocassette in the United States and Canada and/or overseas. Readers should consult their local home video store for the names of the companies which distribute them.

1963

†*Blood Feast* (Herschell Gordon Lewis)

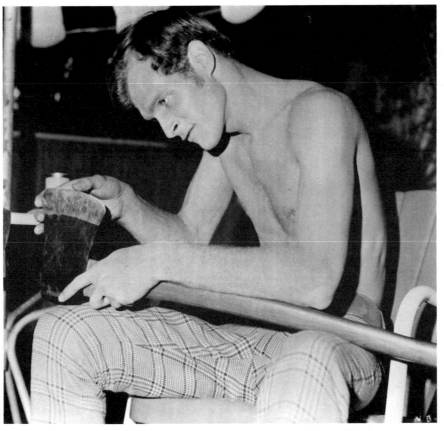

1964

Blood and Black Lace (Mario Bava)
†*Color Me Blood Red* (Herschell Gordon
  Lewis)
The Flesh Eaters (Jack Curtis)
The Naked Witch (Andy Milligan)
†*2000 Maniacs* (Herschell Gordon
  Lewis)
*The Wrestling Women Vs. the Aztec
  Mummy* (Rene Cardona)

Horror of the Blood Monsters, 1970 (© 1970 Independent-International Pictures Corp.)

Night of Bloody Horror, 1970 (© 1969 Taste of Blood Corp.)

1965

Bloodthirst (Newton Arnold)
Horror Castle (Antonio Margheriti)
Monster-A-Go-Go (Herschell Gordon Lewis, Bill Rebane)
Moonshine Mountain (Herschell Gordon Lewis)
†*Motor Psycho!* (Russ Meyer)

1966

Blood Bath (Jack Hill)
The Blood Drinkers (Gerardo De Leon)
†**Faster, Pussycat! Kill! Kill!* (Russ Meyer)
†*The Gruesome Twosome* (Herschell Gordon Lewis)
†*Something Weird* (Herschell Gordon Lewis)

1967

Berserk! (Jim O'Connelly)
†*Blood of Dracula's Castle* (Al Adamson)
The Degenerates (Andy Milligan)
A Taste of Blood (Herschell Gordon Lewis)
The Undertaker and His Pals (David C. Graham)

1968

Any Body . . . Any Way (Charles Romine)
The Ghastly Ones (Andy Milligan)
Kiss Me Monster (Jesus Franco)
†*The Murder Clinic* (Elio Scardmaglia)
†**Night of the Living Dead* (George A. Romero)
**She-Devils on Wheels* (Herschell Gordon Lewis)

1969

†*The Bird with the Crystal Plummage* (Dario Argento)
†**Bloodthirsty Butchers* (Andy Milligan)
†*Cherry, Harry and Raquel* (Russ Meyer)
†*Die, Beautiful Maryanne* (Pete Walker)
Horror and Sex (Rene Cardona)
Mondo Trasho (John Waters)
Pigpen (Pier Paolo Pasolini)
†*Psycho Lover* (Robert Vincent O'Neill)
Satan's Sadists (Al Adamson)
Scream, Baby, Scream (Joseph Adler)

1970

†**Beyond the Valley of the Dolls* (Russ Meyer)
The Body Beneath (Andy Milligan)
Cycle Savages (Bill Brame)
†*Female Bunch* (Jim Kilroy)

I Drink Your Blood, 1971 (© The Jerry Gross Organization)

Invasion of the Blood Farmers, 1971 (© 1971 NMD Film Distributing Co., Inc.)

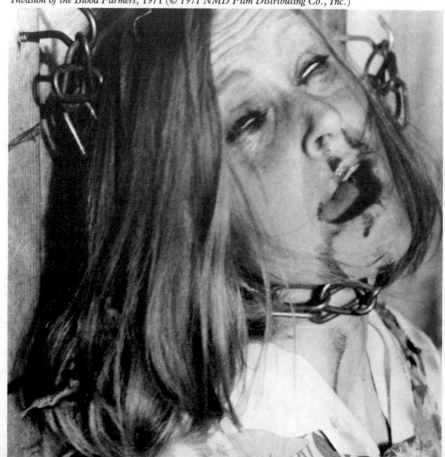

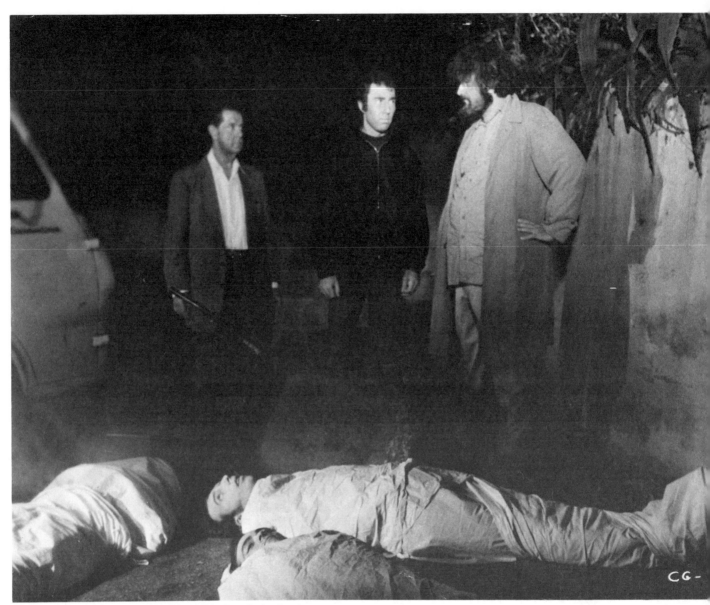

The Corpse Grinders, 1971 (© 1971 Gemeni Film Distribution Corp.)

The Twilight People, 1972 (© 1972 Dimension Pictures, Inc.)

Twins of Evil, 1972 (© Hammer Films)

Flesh Feast (B.F. Grinter)
Horror of the Blood Monsters (Al Adamson)
House of Dark Shadows (Dan Curtis)
†*The Losers* (Jack Starrett)
**Mark of the Devil* (Michael Armstrong)
Multiple Maniacs (John Waters)
†*Night of Bloody Horror* (Joy N. Houk)
†*Something Is Creeping in the Dark* (Mario Colucci)
†*Torture Dungeon* (Andy Milligan)
**The Vampire Lovers* (Roy Ward Baker)
†*The Wizard of Gore* (Herschell Gordon Lewis)

1971

†*The Abominable Dr. Phibes* (Robert Fuest)
Beast of the Yellow Night (Eddie Romero)
Blood (Mario Caiano)
Blood and Lace (Philip Gilbert)
Blood of Ghastly Horror (Al Adamson)
The Blood Seekers (Al Adamson)
Brain of Blood (Al Adamson)
†*Carnival of Blood* (Leonard Kirtman)
The Cat O'Nine Tails (Dario Argento)
The Corpse Grinders (Ted V. Mikels)
Crucible of Terror (Ted Hooker)

Daughters of Darkness (Harry Kumel)
Death Smiles on a Murderer (Aristide Massaccesi)
El Topo (Alexandro Jodorowsky)
Four Flies on Gray Velvet (Dario Argento)
The Gore Gore Girls (Herschell Gordon Lewis)
Guru, the Mad Monk (Andy Milligan)
The House That Dripped Blood (Peter Dufell)
The House That Screamed (Narcisco Ibanez)
The Hunting Party (Don Medford)
†*I Drink Your Blood* (David Durston)
†*I Eat Your Skin* (Del Tenney)
†*Invasion of the Blood Farmers* (Ed Adlum)
Jack the Ripper (Jacinto Molina)
†*Legacy of Blood* (Carl Monson)
†**The Mark of the Wolfman* (Enrique L. Eguilus)
Next! (Luciano Martino)
Night of Dark Shadows (Dan Curtis)
†*The Scars of Dracula* (Roy Ward Baker)
Schizoid (Lucio Fulci)
This Stuff'll Kill Ya! (Herschell Gordon Lewis)
†*Werewolves on Wheels* (Michael Levesque)

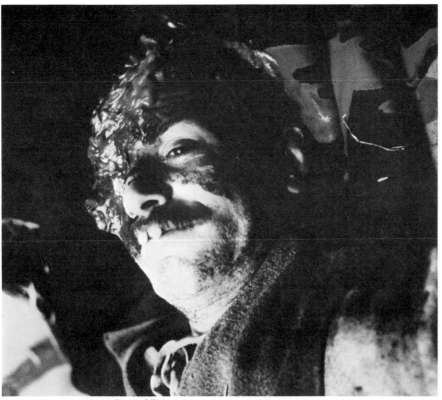

Jonathan, 1972 *(courtesy Cinemabilia)*

Devil's Nightmare, 1972 (© *1972 Hemisphere Pictures Inc.*)

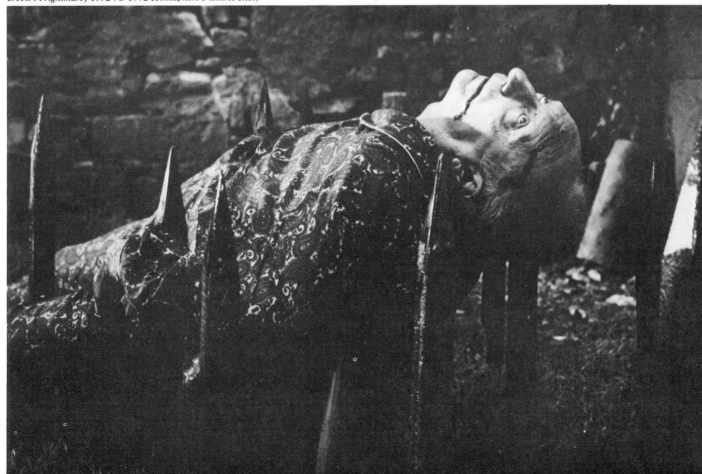

Raw Meat, 1973 (© 1973 American-International Pictures)

1972

The Abductors (Ralph T. Desiderio)
†*Asylum* (Roy Ward Baker)
Baron Blood (Mario Bava)
Beware the Brethren (Robert Hartford-Davies)
Black Angels (Laurence Merrick)
The Black Belly of the Tarantula (Paolo Cavara)
Blacula (William Crain)
Bracula—the Terror of the Living Dead (Jose Luis Merino)
Caged Virgins (Jean Rollin)
†*Children Shouldn't Play with Dead Things* (Bob Clark)
Countess Dracula (Peter Sasdy)
†*The Creeping Flesh* (Freddie Francis)
†*Dear Dead Delilah* (John Farris)
The Demons (Jesus Franco)
†*Devil's Nightmare* (Jean Brismee)
Disciple of Death (Tom Parkinson)
Dr. Phibes Rises Again (Robert Fuest)
Dracula Saga (Leon Klimovsky)
Dracula Vs. Frankenstein (Jesus Franco)
The Female Butcher (Jorge Grau)
Folks at the Red Wolf Inn (Bud Townsend)
†*Fright* (Peter Collinson)
*Hands of the Ripper (Peter Sasdy)
Invasion of the Dead (Rene Cardona)
*Jonathan (Hans V. Geissendorfer)
*Last House on the Left (Wes Craven)
Lips of Blood (Ken Ruder)
The Mad Butcher (Guido Zurli)
The Man with Two Heads (Andy Milligan)
The Night of the Cobra Woman (Andrew Meyer)
The Nightcomers (Michael Winner)
Please Don't Eat My Mother (Carl Monson)
The Possession of Joel Delaney (Warris Hussein)
†*The Rats Are Coming, the Werewolves Are Here* (Andy Milligan)
Scream Bloody Murder (Robert J. Emery)
Sweet Kill (Curtis Hansen)
Sweet Sugar (Michael Levesque)
*Tales from the Crypt (Freddie Francis)
The Thing with Two Heads (Lee Frost)
†*The Twilight People* (Eddie Romero)
Twins of Evil (John Hough)
Vampire Circus (Robert Young)
Virgin Witch (Ray Austin)
Vuelven Los Campeones Justicieros (Frederico Curiel)
The Weekend Murders (Michele Lupo)

†*The Werewolf Vs. the Vampire Woman* (Leon Klimovsky)
The Womanhunt (Eddie Romero)

1973

†*And Now the Screaming Starts* (Roy Ward Baker)
†*The Baby* (Ted Post)
The Bell of Hell (Claudio Guerin Hill)
†*Blackenstein* (William A. Levey)
The Blind Dead (Amando De Ossorio)
Blood Orgy of the She-Devils (Ted V. Mikels)
Cannibal Girls (Ivan Reitman)
*The Crazies (George A. Romero)
Crypt of the Living Dead (Ray Danton)
†*The Devil's Wedding Night* (Paul Solvay)
Doctor Death, Seeker of Souls (Eddie Saeta)
The Doll Squad (Ted V. Mikels)
†*Don't Look in the Basement* (S.F. Brownrigg)
†**The Exorcist* (William Friedkin)
†**The Flesh and Blood Show* (Pete Walker)
†*Frankenstein's Castle of Freaks* (Robert H. Oliver)
Happy Mother's Day . . . Love George (Darren McGavin)
Hex (Leo Garen)
†*Invasion of the Bee Girls* (Denis Sanders)
†*The Killing Kind* (Curtis Harrington)
†*Magnum Force* (Ted Post)
†*Night of the Strangler* (Joy N. Houk)
Nightmare Hotel (Eugenio Martin)
*Raw Meat (Gary Sherman)

Torso, 1973 (courtesy Barry Kaufman)

Andy Warhol's Frankenstein, 1974 (© 1974 Bryanston Pictures)

Scream Blacula, Scream (Bob Kelljan)
Seeds of Evil (Jim Kay)
†*The Severed Arm* (Thomas S. Alderman)
†*Silent Night, Bloody Night* (Theodore Gershuny)
†**Sisters* (Brian DePalma)
Slaughter Hotel (Fernando DiLeo)
Sssssss! (Bernard L. Kowalski)
Tales That Witness Madness (Freddie Francis)
**Theatre of Blood* (Douglas Hickox)
Tomb of the Blind Dead (Amando De Ossorio)
†*Torso* (Sergio Martino)
Twitch of the Death Nerve (Mario Bava)
†*Vault of Horror* (Roy Ward Baker)
Wicked Wicked (Richard L. Bare)
Witch Who Came From the Sea (Alex Ramieltanne)

1974
†*Abby* (William Girdler)

†*Alice Sweet Alice* (Alfred Sole)
†**Andy Warhol's Frankenstein* (Paul Morrissey)
Apartment on the 13th Floor (Eloy de la Iglesia)
Barbed-Wire Dolls (Don Ramcock)
The Bat People (Jerry Jameson)
†*Beyond the Door* (Oliver Hellman)
Black Six (Matt Cimber)
Blood! (Andy Milligan)
†**Blood for Dracula* (Paul Morrissey)
The Blood Splattered Bride (Vincent Aranda)
†**The Cars That Ate Paris* (Peter Weir)
†*The Curse of the Headless Horseman* (John Kirkland)
**Deathdream* (Bob Clark)
Deranged (Jeff Gillen)
†*Devil Times Five* (Sean McGregor)
Dr. Jekyll and the Wolfman (Leon Klimovsky)
Exorcismo (Juan Bosch Palau)

Silent Night, Bloody Night, 1973 (*courtesy Cinemabilia*)

Scum of the Earth, 1974 (© *1974 Dimension Pictures*)

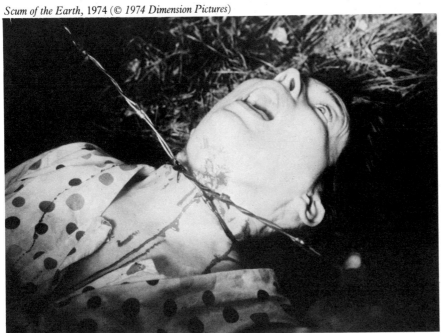

Female Trouble, 1975 (© *1975 New Line Cinema*)

Exorcism's Daughter (Rafael M. Alba)
Foxy Brown (Jack Hill)
Frankenstein and the Monster from Hell
  (Terence Fisher)
†*Horror High* (Larry Stouffer)
House of Psychotic Women (Carlos Aured)
†**House of Whipcord* (Pete Walker)
†*I Dismember Mama* (Paul Leder)
I Hate My Body (Leon Klimovsky)
It's Alive (Larry Cohen)
*La Grand Bouffe (Marco Ferreri)
†*The Legend of Spider Forest* (Peter Sykes)
Lightning Swords of Death (Kenji Misumi)
Mark of the Devil, Part II (Adrian Hovan)
The Mutations (Jack Cardiff)
Night of 1000 Cats (Rene Cardona)
**Phantom of the Paradise* (Brian DePalma)
†*Pink Flamingos (John Waters)
Psychopath (Larry Brown)
Scum of the Earth (Nick Zoed)
*Seizure (Oliver Stone)
The Seven Brothers Meet Dracula (Roy
  Ward Baker)
Seven Women for Satan (Michel Lemoine)
Shriek of the Mutilated (Michael Findlay)
Tenderness of the Wolves (Ulli Lommel)
†*The Thirsty Dead* (Terry Becker)
Those Cruel and Bloody Vampires (J.P.
  Tabernero)
The Vampire's Night Orgy (Leon
  Klimovsky)
†*Warlock Moon* (William Herbert)
†*Welcome to Arrow Beach* (Laurence
  Harvey)

The Thirsty Dead, 1974 (*courtesy Barry Kaufman*)

PF-1

175

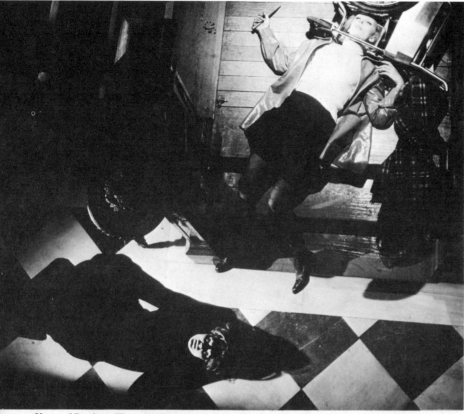

House of Psychotic Women, 1974 (courtesy Barry Kaufman)

1975

Alucarda (Juan Lopez Moctezuma)
Andy Warhol's Bad (Jed Johnson)
Asylum of Satan (William Girdler)
The Bare Breasted Countess (Jesus Franco)
Barn of the Naked Dead (Alan Rudolph)
Black Gestapo (Lee Frost)
Breakfast at the Manchester Morgue (Jorge Grau)
†*Bury Me an Angel* (Barbara Peeters)
The Corruption of Chris Miller (Juan A. Bardem)
†*Death Race 2000* (Paul Bartel)
†*The Devil's Rain* (Robert Fuest)
El Inquisidor (Bernardo Arias)
Female Trouble (John Waters)
Friday Foster (Arthur Marks)
From Beyond the Grave (Kevin Connor)
Hunchback of the Morgue (Javier Aguirre)
†*Jaws* (Steven Spielberg)
Knife for the Ladies (Larry Spangler)
Kiss Me Kill Me (Carole Pierre Suere)

Knife for the Ladies, 1975 (© 1973 Bryanston Pictures)

Vampyres, 1975 (*courtesy Barry Kaufman*)

Don't Open the Window, 1976 (*courtesy Barry Kaufman*)

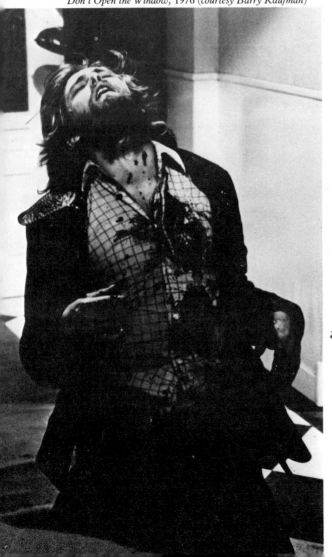

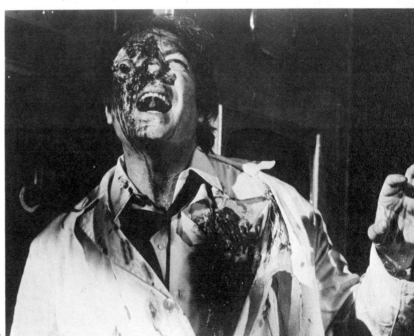

Hunchback of the Morgue, 1975 (*courtesy Barry Kaufman*)

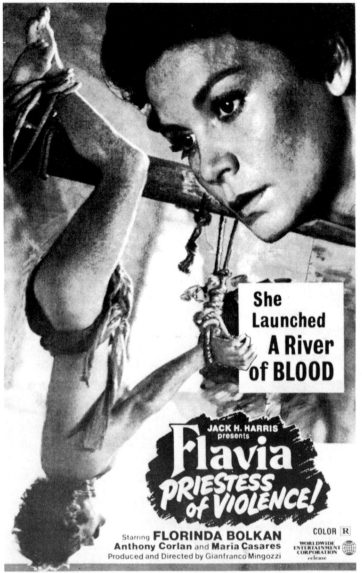

Flavia—Priestess of Violence, 1976 (*courtesy Barry Kaufman*)

Love Me Deadly (Jacques La Certe)
Mary, Mary, Bloody Mary (Juan Lopez Moctezuma)
†*Monty Python and the Holy Grail* (Terry Jones, Terry Gilliam)
†*P*E*T*S* (John Rally)
Race with the Devil (Jack Starrett)
†*Rollerball* (Norman Jewison)
Shockwaves (Ken Wiederhorn)
†*Snuff* (Michael Findlay)
†*The Supervixens* (Russ Meyer)
†*The Texas Chainsaw Massacre* (Tobe Hooper)
Vampyres (Joseph Larraz)
Vengeance of the Zombies (Leon Klimovsky)
Would You Kill a Child? (Narciso Ibanez Serrador)

1976
†*Assault on Precinct 13* (John Carpenter)
Blood Bath (Joel M. Reed)
Bloodlust (Marijan Vajda)
†*Bloodsucking Freaks* (Joel M. Reed)
Burnt Offerings (Dan Curtis)
†*Carrie* (Brian DePalma)
The Crimes of the Black Cat (Sergio Pastore)
Curse of the Devil (Carlos Aured Alonso)
Death Machines (Paul Kyriazi)
†*Deep Red* (Dario Argento)
†*The Demon Lover* (Donald G. Jackson, Jerry Younlins)
The Demon (Larry Cohen)
The Devil Within Her (Peter Sasdy)
Dr. Black and Mr. Hyde (William Crain)
†*Dr. Tarr's Torture Garden* (Juan Lopez Moctezuma)
Don't Open the Window (Jorge Grau)
†*Drive-In Massacre* (Stuart Segall)
Eaten Alive (Tobe Hooper)
†*Flavia—Priestess of Violence* (Gianfranco Mingozzi)
†*Food of the Gods* (Bert I. Gordon)
†*Gator Bait* (F. and B. Sebastian)
†*Grizzly* (William Girdler)
Hatchet for a Honeymoon (Mario Bava)
Horror of the Zombies (Amando De Ossorio)
†*Horror Rises from the Tomb* (Carlos Aured)
†*The House of Exorcism* (Mario Bava)
Ilsa, Harem Keeper of the Oil Sheiks (Don Edmonds)
Ilsa, She Wolf of the SS (Don Edmonds)
The Killer Snakes (Keiui Chi-Hung)
Kiss of the Tarantula (Chris Munger)

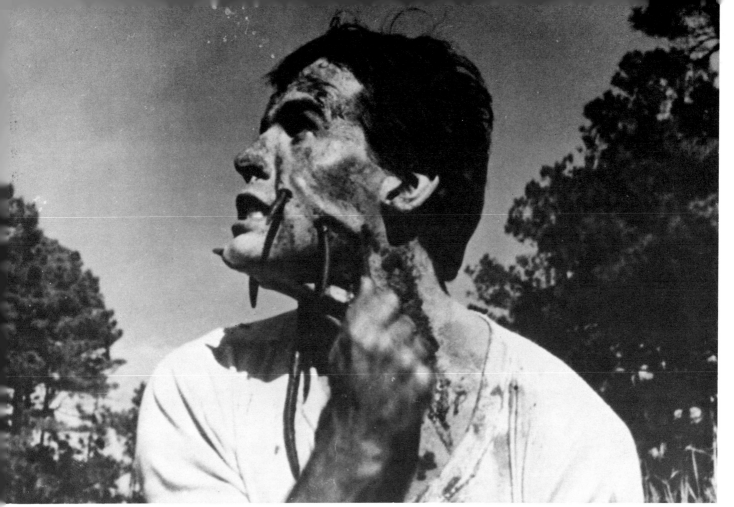

Squirm, 1976 (© 1976 American-International Pictures)

Horror of the Zombies, 1976 (courtesy Barry Kaufman)

Frightmare, 1977 (© 1975 Ellman Films Enterprises, Inc.)

Desperate Living, 1977 (© New Line Cinema)

Halloween, 1978 (© *Compass International Pictures*)

Lady Cocoa (Matt Cimber)
†*Land of the Minotaur* (Costas Carayiannis)
Legacy of Satan (Gerard Damiano)
†*The Legend of the Wolf Woman* (Rino Di Silvestro)
†*Mansion of the Doomed* (Michael Pataki)
The Night of the Sorcerers (Amando De Ossorio)
†*The Omen (Richard Donner)
Rattlers (John McCauley)
Schizo (Pete Walker)
Shoot (Harvey Hart)
†*Squirm* (Jeff Lieberman)
Spasmo (Umberto Lenzi)
†**They Came From Within* (David Cronenberg)
They're Coming to Get You (Sergio Martino)
†*To the Devil . . . a Daughter* (Peter Sykes)

1977

†*Bloodrage* (Jeff A. Martinez)
Blood-Relations (Wim Lindner)
†*The Child* (Robert Voskanian)

Claws (Robert Bansbach)
†*The Confessional* (Pete Walker)
†*Crash!* (Charles Band)
†*Day of the Animals* (William Girdler)
*Desperate Living (John Waters)
†*Eraserhead* (David Lynch)
Fight for Your Life (Robert A. Endelson)
†*Frightmare* (Pete Walker)
†**The Hills Have Eyes* (Wes Craven)
†*The Hollywood Meatcleaver Massacre* (Evan Lee)
†*The House by the Lake* (William Fruet)
†*Island of Dr. Moreau* (Don Taylor)
It's Alive II (Larry Cohen)
†*Jabberwocky* (Terry Gilliam)
†*Kingdom of the Spiders* (John "Bud" Cardos)
Night of the Howling Beast (M.I. Bonns)
†*Orca* (Michael Anderson)
†*Rabid* (David Cronenberg)
†*Ruby* (Curtis Harrington)
Salo, the 120 Days of Sodom (Pier Paolo Pasolini)
The Sentinel (Michael Winner)
*Suspiria (Dario Argento)

The Legacy, 1979 (© 1979 Universal)

Piranha, 1979 (© New World Pictures)

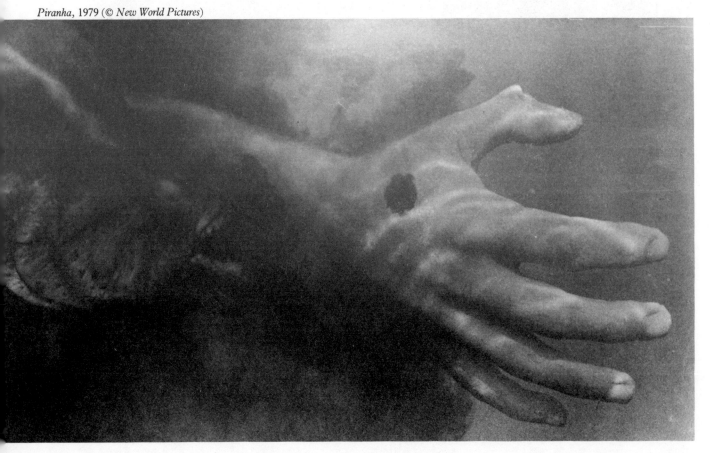

The Incredible Melting Man, 1978 (© 1977 American-International Pictures)   *Tourist Trap*, 1979 (*courtesy Hollywood Book & Poster*)

†*Tentacles* (Oliver Hellman)
†*Tintorera* (Rene Cardona)
†*The Toolbox Murders* (Dennis Donnelly)

1978

The Alpha Incident (Bill Rebane)
Autopsy (Armando Crispini)
Barracuda (Harry Kerwin)
†*The Bees* (Alfredo Zacharias)
†*Cannibal Massacre* (Ruggero Deodato)
The Chosen (Alberto De Martino)
†*Damien—Omen II* (Don Taylor)
†*Death Sport* (Henry Suso, Allan Arkush)
†*The Eerie Midnight Horror Show* (Mario Gariazzo)
†*The Eyes of Laura Mars* (Irvin Kershner)
†*The Fury* (Brian DePalma)
†*Halloween* (John Carpenter)
The Incredible Melting Man (William Sachs)
†*Invasion of the Body Snatchers* (Phil Kaufman)
Island of the Damned (Narciso Ibanez)
Jack the Ripper (Jesus Franco)
†*Jaws II* (Jeannot Szwarc)
Killer's Moon (Alan Birkinshaw)
†*Laserblast* (Michael Rae)
Legacy of Blood (Andy Milligan)
†*Magic* (Richard Attenborough)

†*The Manitou* (William Girdler)
†*Martin* (George A. Romero)
New House on the Left (Evans Isle)
†*The Redeemer* (Constantine S. Gochis)
†*Savage Weekend* (David Paulsen)
The Tempter (Alberto De Martino)
Warlords of Atlantis (Kevin Connor)
†*Wolfman* (Worth Keeter III)

1979

†*Alien* (Ridley Scott)
†*The Alien Factor* (Don Dohler)
†*Beyond the Door II* (Mario Bava)
The Brood (David Cronenberg)
†*The Comeback* (Pete Walker)
†*The Dark* (John "Bud" Cardos)
†*Dawn of the Dead* (George A. Romero)
†*Dracula* (John Badham)
†*Dracula's Great Love* (Javier Aguirre)
†*The Driller Killer* (Abel Ferrara)
Effects (Dusty Nelson)
†*The Evictors* (Charles Pierce)
†*Killer Fish* (Antonio Margheriti)
The Legacy (Richard Marquand)
†*Love Butcher* (Ron Ellison)
†*Mad Max* (George Miller)
Maggots (Bill Rebane)
Meat (Rainer Erler)
†*Microwave Massacre* (Thomas Singer)

Friday the 13th, Part III (in 3-D), 1982 (© 1982 Paramount)

The Awakening, 1980 (© Warner Bros., Inc.)

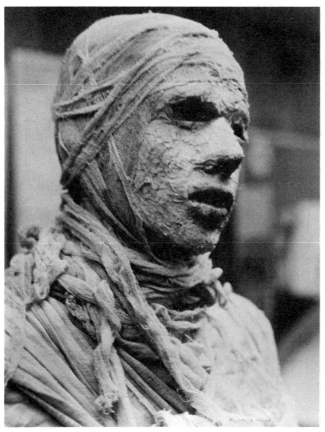

Fade to Black, 1980 (© *Compass International Pictures*)

When a Stranger Calls, 1979 (© *1979 Columbia Pictures*)

Halloween II, 1981 (© *1981 Universal*)

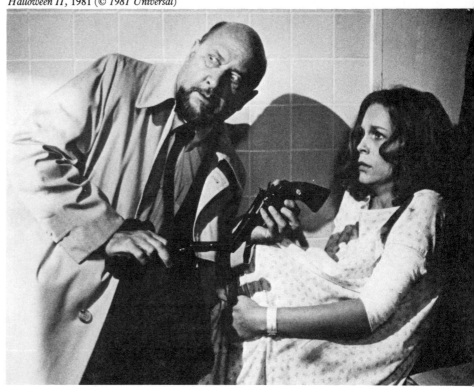

The Orphan (John Ballard)
†*Phantasm* (Don A. Coscarelli)
†*Piranha* (Joe Dante)
†*Prophecy* (John Frankenheimer)
†*The Psychic* (Lucio Fulci)
Screams of a Winter Night (James L. Wilson)
†*Tourist Trap* (David Schomoeller)
†*When a Stranger Calls* (Fred Walton)

1980
†*Alien Contamination* (Luigi Cozzi)
†*The Alien Dead* (Fred Olen Ray)
Alien Encounters (James T. Flocker)
Anatomy of a Horror (Mario Azzopardi)
Aquella Casa en las Afueras (Eugenio Martin)
†*The Awakening* (Mike Newell)
†*Battle Beyond the Stars* (Jimmy T. Murakami)
Beyond Terror (Tomas Aznar)
Bloodeaters (Chuck McCrann)
Bloody Birthday (Ed Hunt)
†*The Boogey Man* (Ulli Lommcl)
†*Cathy's Curse* (Eddie Matalon)
The Children (Max Kalmanowicz)

Q, 1982 (© *United Film Distribution Co.*)

Fear No Evil, 1981 (© *1980 LaLoggia Productions*)

†*Deadly Games* (Scott Mansfield)
Death Ship (Alvin Rakoff)
†*Don't Answer the Phone!* (Robert Hammer)
†*Don't Go in the House* (Joseph Ellison)
†*Dressed to Kill* (Brian DePalma)
†*The Exterminator* (James Glickenhaus)
†*Fade to Black* (Vernon Zimmerman)
†*The Fog* (John Carpenter)
Forced Entry (Jim Sotos)
†*Friday the 13th* (Sean Cunningham)
†*Funeral Home* (William Fruet)
†*He Knows You're Alone* (Aarmand Mastroianni)
†*Human Experiments* (J. Gregory Goddell)
†*Humanoids from the Deep* (Barbara Peeters)
†*I Spit on Your Grave* (Meir Zarchi)
Inferno (Dario Argento)
†*The Island* (Michael Ritchie)
†*Keep My Grave Open* (S. F. Brownrigg)
†*The Long Riders* (Walter Hill)
†*Massacre at Central High* (Renee Daalder)
Midnight (John Russo)
Motel Hell (Kevin Connor)
The Nesting (Armand Weston)

186

The Sender, 1982 (© 1982 Paramount)

Venom, 1982 (© 1982 Paramount)

Xtro, 1983 (© 1983 New Line Cinema)

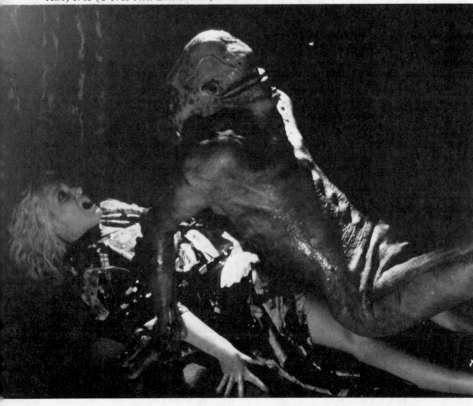

†*New Year's Evil* (Emmett Alston)
†*The People Who Own the Dark* (Leon
　Klimovsky)
†*Prom Night* (Paul Lynch)
†*Saturn III* (Stanley Donen)
†*Schizoid* (David Paulsen)
†*Silent Scream* (Denny Harris)
Terror Train (Roger Spottiswoode)
We're Going to Eat You (Tsui Hark)
When the Screaming Stops (Amando De
　Ossorio)
Without Warning (Greydon Clark)
†*Zombie* (Lucio Fulci)

1981

†*Alligator* (Lewis Teague)
†**An American Werewolf in London* (John
　Landis)
The Beyond (Lucio Fulci)
†*Blood Beach* (Jeffrey Bloom)
†*Blow Out* (Brian DePalma)
The Boogens (James L. Conway)
†*The Burning* (Tony Maylam)
Caligula (Tinto Brass)
†*Dawn of the Mummy* (Armand Weston)
†*Dead and Buried* (Gary Sherman)
†*Deadly Blessing* (Wes Craven)
†*Dr. Butcher, M.D.* (Frank Martin)
†*Dr. Jekyll's Dungeon of Death* (James
　Wood)
†*Escape from New York* (John Carpenter)
†*Evilspeak* (Eric Weston)
†*Eyes of a Stranger* (Ken Wiederhorn)
†*The Fan* (Edward Bianchi)
†*Fear No Evil* (Frank La Loggia)
†*The Final Conflict* (Graham Baker)
†*Friday the 13th Part II* (Steve Miner)
†*The Funhouse* (Tobe Hooper)
Galaxy of Terror (Bruce Clark)
†*Ghost Story* (John Irvin)
†*Graduation Day* (Herb Reed)
Grim Reaper (Joe D'Amato)
†*Halloween II* (Rick Rosenthal)
†*The Hand* (Oliver Stone)
†*Happy Birthday to Me* (J. Lee
　Thompson)
†*Hell Night* (Tom DeSimone)
†*The Howling* (Joe Dante)
Inseminoid (Norman J. Warren)
†*Kill and Kill Again* (Ivan Hall)
Kill to Love (Tam Kau Ming)
†**Last House on Dead End Street* (Victor
　Juno)
†*Madman* (Joe Giannone)
†*Maniac* (William Lustig)
†**Ms. 45* (Abel Ferrara)
†*Mother's Day* (Charles Kaufman)
†*Nightmare* (Romano Scavolini)

Night School (Ken Hughes)
†*Outland* (Peter Hyams)
†*The Prowler* (Joseph Zito)
†**Raiders of the Lost Ark* (Steven
  Spielberg)
†*Scanners (David Cronenberg)
Scared to Death (William Malone)
Screamers (Dan T. Miller)
†*Sharkey's Machine* (Burt Reynolds)
Shogun Assassin (Kenji Misumi)
†*Southern Comfort* (Walter Hill)
†*Strange Behavior* (Michael Loughlin)
†*Swamp Thing* (Wes Craven)
†*The Sword and the Sorcerer* (Albert Pyun)
†*Tattoo* (Bob Brooks)

The Entity, 1983 (© 1981 Pelleport Investors, Inc.)

Alone in the Dark, 1982 (© 1982 New Line Cinema)

189

Threshold (Richard Pearce)
Time Slip (Kosei Saito)
†*The Unseen* (Peter Foleg)
†*Wolfen* (Michael Wadleigh)
X-Ray (Boaz Davidson)

1982

†*Alone in the Dark* (Jack Sholder)
†*Basket Case (Frank Henenlotter)
Battletruck (Henry Cokliss)
†*The Beastmaster* (Don Coscarelli)
†*The Beast Within* (Philippe Mora)
†*Blade Runner* (Ridley Scott)
Blood Shack (Wolfgang Schmidt)
Bloody Moon (Jesus Franco)
†*Butcher, Baker, Nightmare Maker* (William Asher)
†*Cat People* (Paul Schrader)
†*The Challenge* (John Frankenheimer)
†*Class of 1984* (Mark Lester)
†*Conan the Barbarian* (John Milius)
†*Creepshow (George A. Romero)
†*Death Valley* (Dick Richards)
†*Death Wish II* (Michael Winner)

Demonoid (Alfredo Zacharias)
†*Forbidden World* (Alan Holzman)
†*48 Hours* (Walter Hill)
†*Endangered Species* (Alan Rudolph)
†*Friday the 13th Part III* (Steve Miner)
†*Great White* (Mark Princi)
†*Halloween III: Season of the Witch* (Tommy Wallace)
†*The House Where Evil Dwells* (Kevin Connor)
†*Humongous* (Paul Lynch)
†*Megaforce* (Hal Needham)
†*Parasite* (Charles Band)
†*Pink Floyd the Wall* (Alan Parker)
†*Poltergeist (Tobe Hooper)
Possession (Andrzej Zulawski)
†*Q* (Larry Cohen)
†*Road Games* (Richard Franklin)
†*The Road Warrior* (George Miller)
†*The Seduction* (David Schmoeller)
†*The Sender* (Roger Christian)
**Slumber Party Massacre* (Amy Jones)
†*The Soldier* (James Glickenhaus)

†*The Thing (John Carpenter)
†*Venom* (Piers Haggard)
†*Vice Squad* (Gary Sherman)
†*Visiting Hours* (Jean Claude Lord)

1983

†*Boogey Man II* (Ulli Lommel)
†*Curtains* (Jonathan Stryker)
†*Cujo (Lewis Teague)
†*The Deadly Spawn* (Douglas McKeown)
†*The Entity* (Sidney J. Furie)
*The Evil Dead (Sam Raimi)
†*House on Sorority Row* (Mark Rosman)
†*The Hunger* (Tony Scott)
†*Incubus* (John Hough)
†*Jaws 3-D* (Joe Alves)
†*Mausoleum* (Michael Dugan)
†*Monty Python's Meaning of Life* (Terry Jones)
†*Psycho II* (Richard Franklin)
†*Twilight of the Dead* (Lucio Fulci)
†*Videodrome (David Cronenberg)
†*Vigilante* (William Lustig)
†*Xtro* (Harry Bromley Davenport)

Mausoleum, 1983 (© 1983 MPM, Inc.)

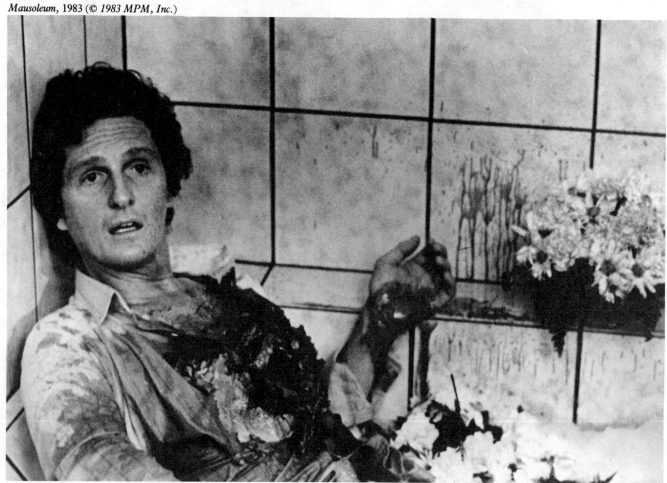

The first movie John McCarty recalls seeing was a 1949 thriller called *The Window,* the story of a little boy who witnesses a murder, but because he is so prone to spinning fanciful stories, no one will believe him—except the killer. "I was five," John says. "And that movie scared the pants off me. I could really identify with that kid." The experience marked the beginning of John's lifelong fascination with films of suspense, terror, the supernatural, and horror. *Splatter Movies,* John's probing analysis of what he calls "a bonafide sub-genre of the horror film," is a result of that fascination.

A graduate of Boston University's film school, John has written articles and reviews on films of horror and other genres for publications as diverse as *Cinefantastique, Filmmaker's Newsletter, Classic Images,* and *Take One.* He lives in upstate New York.

Bill DeMichele

John McCarty

Index